architecture

PRINCETON FIELD GUIDES TO ART

Francesca Prina

architecture

elements, materials, form

PRINCETON UNIVERSITY PRESS
PRINCETON AND OXFORD

Page 2
Albrechtsburg, Meissen,
begun 1471,
detail of the stairs

Published by Princeton University Press, 41 William Street, Princeton, New Jersey 08540
In the United Kingdom: Princeton University Press, 6 Oxford Street, Woodstock, Oxfordshire OX20 1TW

Library of Congress Cataloging-in-Publication Data

Prina, Francesca.
  [Saper vedere l'architettura. English]
  Architecture : elements, materials, form / Francesca Prina.
      p. cm. -- (Princeton field guides to art)
  Includes bibliographical references and indexes.
  ISBN 978-0-691-14150-3 (pbk.)
  1. Architecture. I. Title.
  NA2520.P7513 2009
  720--dc22
                            2008040842

British Library Cataloging-in-Publication Data is available
press.princeton.edu
Printed in Spain
10 9 8 7 6 5 4 3 2 1

Contents

Introduction

"The work of art is a private matter for the artist. The house is not." This declaration from Adolf Loos, the Austrian architect credited with giving birth to rationalism in architecture, can be taken as a summary of the idea of an architectural work. All too frequently considered only in terms of its historical and stylistic aspects, and overlooking its semantic aspects, architecture speaks to the viewer—who may in reality also be the inhabitant, user, passerby, or even destroyer—and does so with a highly precise grammatical language based on structural elements, materials, and techniques that are fitted together to make up the syntax of the building.

It is this highly particular aspect of architecture that this book illustrates, analyzing the elements of architecture and the symbolic meanings within it. Each section in the book calls out the principal structural components of buildings, by identifying their fundamental characteristics—from the column to the capital, from the wall to the dome—as well as the elements of an architectural organism: façade, doors, windows, stairs, and so on. While the primary purpose of architecture is to meet basic needs for shelter and protection, it accomplishes this goal through the use of the materials that nature makes available, and it is thus forced to observe closely the natural laws inherent in those materials. This material dependence on natural laws and limitations confers a certain necessary character on architecture. These elements are not simply accessories within the construction of an architectural work; they are indissolubly linked to the historical context, to the level of technological evolution, and to the personality of the architect. They become bearers themselves of the symbolic language of architectural images.

The book opens with a brief analysis of the preliminary phase of design, then discusses the translation of an imagined architectural program in terms of space and volume with the tools available to the architect, from the design to the actual project to the most modern systems of three-dimensional digital projection. This interrelationship between initial idea and eventual building solutions represents the truly creative activity through which an architectural work comes into being. Architecture is made by architects. Thus the characteristics of a certain physical and material world, along with its social dynamics, can be translated into architecture only through the mediation of the architect, who, as a complex social being, bears within him- or herself a unique key to interpreting the world.

As for the choice of buildings illustrated, a certain preference has been given to works of European architecture. This has not, however, ruled out the inclusion of buildings from the Americas, Africa, and the Far East. The logic behind the organization of the entries varies as needed to fit the subject: the images illustrate the various themes being discussed and examine the evolution of forms, from the simplest to the most complex, without following a strict chronological order. At times the sequence coincides with chronology and at times it does not. However, an effort is always made to end with some non-Western examples. In some cases it was useful to contrast images from widely different periods in order to emphasize—over the centuries and across different cultures—the persistence of forms.

The book ends with a chapter dedicated to those buildings considered archetypes of architectural history, beginning with classical Greece, the cradle of Western culture, and ending with examples drawn from the Middle East and extending all the way to Japan. The goal is to assemble the fragmented language of architecture into a single coherent discourse, to fashion those many disparate ideas into a single guiding principle—which is nothing but the architectural organism itself. This is a matter not of traditional stylistic notions (although they inevitably do appear) but rather of the different ways of composing the architectural alphabet—creating a language that changes, a language that speaks of the geography of locales, the availability of funds, the patrons, the goals to be served, and the creative personalities involved.

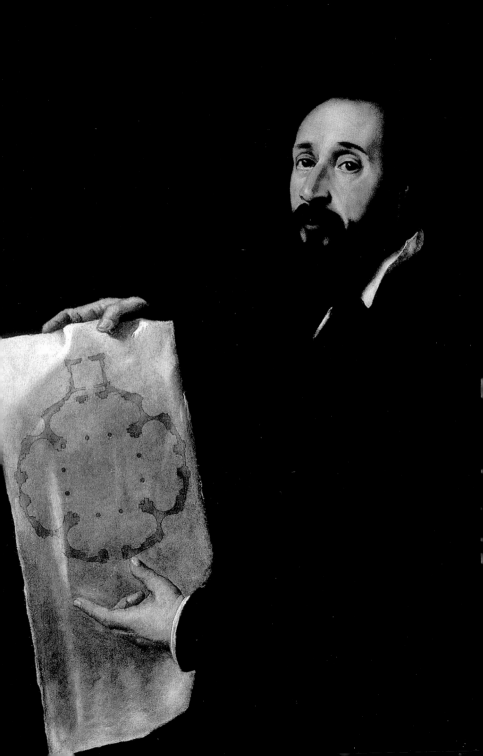

The Tools of the Architect

The Figure of the Architect / Descriptive Geometry / Plan and Planimetry / Elevation and Section / Architectural Drawing / Project / Model / Rendering / Architecture and Engineering / Architectural Theory

The Figure of the Architect

The architect is the person who designs works of architecture and then provides plans for their construction. In the ancient world the architect was a figure of enormous professional dignity, and the names of many of the first architects have survived. There is Imhotep, director of Djoser's pyramid complex at Saqqara (2649–2575 BCE), as well as Ictinus and Callicrates, creators of the Parthenon. Outstanding figures from the Roman age include Apollodorus of Damascus and Rabirius, but the most exalted from that period is Vitruvius, whose fame stems more from a treatise—*De architectura* (31–15 BCE)—than from any actual constructions.

Throughout most of the Middle Ages the practice of architecture was relegated to the field of the mechanical arts, but by the early twelfth century names associated with specific works begin to appear once more: Lanfranco and the cathedral of Modena, Buscheto and the cathedral of Pisa, William of Sens and the cathedral of Canterbury.

On the worksites of the great Gothic cathedrals architects began developing a broad geometrical-mathematical understanding of their work, and the School of Chartres began to define God as the *elegans architectus*, the supreme architect, creator of the cosmos following a rational and geometric order. As the Renaissance drew near, this metaphor inspired architects to claim status as intellectuals because of the breadth of learning required for their practice. No longer a mere craft, architecture required the study of arithmetic, geometry, and history, as made clear by the Vitruvian tradition and the reality of ancient monuments. The architect thus explicitly became both planner and maker.

The rise of academies during the second half of the sixteenth century helped fashion a new identity for the architect that was deeply related to the profession and its symbols, the square and the compass—a view that was in a sense undone two centuries later with the appearance of forceful, strikingly individualistic professionals. The Industrial Revolution brought a marked change in the professional stature of the architect, while modern architects have become true designers of space. Today the architect's sphere of action is vast, and the profession requires enormous cultural and professional preparation. The architect stands at the center of an extensive network of economic, social, and political relationships.

Origins of the Term
The word first appears in Plautus (c. 254–184 BCE) in the form *architékton*; in the Latin and medieval worlds the term had become *architectus* and was applied to the person directing the activities at a worksite.

Related Entries
Architectural Drawing; Project; Architectural Theory

God as the Architect of the Universe, miniature from a *bible moralisée*, 1220. Österreichische Nationalbibliothek, Vienna

Bust of Peter Parler in
the Saint Vitus Cathedral,
Prague, fourteenth
century

During the Middle Ages, the term *parler* was used for the professional figure who, in the absence of the master builder, had the role of translating the design into stone.

During the fourteenth century, *parler* became a family name, applied to one of the most important architectural dynasties: that of the Parlers, responsible for many advances in architecture in central-eastern Europe.

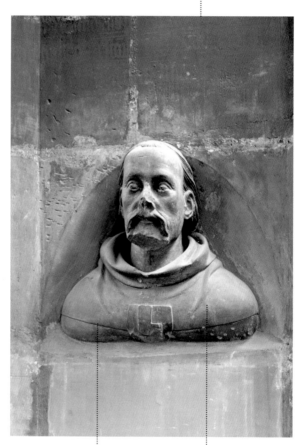

The presence of a portrait bust of Peter Parler inside the work considered to be his masterpiece, the Saint Vitus Cathedral at Prague, testifies to the increasing importance attributed to the figure of the architect over the course of the fourteenth century. No longer merely a master mason, the architect was considered an intellectual: the designer of the plan and also the director of its execution—an explicit recognition of the independence of the creator.

The most renowned member of the Parler family, Peter Parler (1333–99) was a leading figure in the late Gothic style in Europe. He distinguished himself by the great originality of his designs, the sources for which ranged from contemporary English works to those of northern Germany. He thus broke with the themes of French Rayonnant architecture.

Carlo Fontana, "The Obelisk Being Lowered," from *The Vatican Temple and Its Origins*, Rome, 1694, book 3, chap. 9, 142

The letter A at the top of the machine identifies the wooden armature to which the pulleys and cords supporting the obelisk were attached; C indicates the cables that stabilized the wooden frame constructed to support the obelisk; D identifies the beams that supported the inclined obelisk; H labels the winches operated by men and horses.

From earliest times the organization of construction worksites reflected a strict separation of functions, with specialized workers led by master architects who oversaw the progress of the labor in each phase. The Renaissance saw the birth of the worksite as understood in the modern sense, in which various masters were absorbed into the single figure of the architect, while the workers, although still specialized, were transformed into executors of the plan. The organization of the worksite came to demonstrate a sharp separation between intellectual activity and the performance of the actual work.

This print illustrates both a worksite practice and a feat of engineering: the wooden frame built especially to lower the obelisk to transport it to Saint Peter's Square in the Vatican, part of Pope Sixtus V's plans for urban renewal.

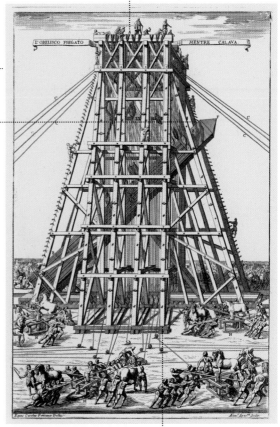

Special constructions were required to move or position such heavy monolithic elements as obelisks. These apparatuses were designed to combine safety with optimal working conditions. The wooden structure depicted here was designed by Domenico Fonatana.

Descriptive Geometry

Descriptive geometry involves the representation of two- and three-dimensional figures in one or more planes. It is a tool of fundamental importance in architectural design and rendering, a practical discipline designed to meet the needs of engineers, architects, and cartographers. The principal methods of depiction are central projection, or perspective rendering, and axonometry.

Perspective makes possible the depiction of three-dimensional bodies in a plane, as well as the depiction of distance through the use of a fixed viewpoint to produce the illusion of relief and depth. There are two fundamental types of perspective: linear, which is created through the ideal convergence of the lines of the depicted bodies toward a fixed vanishing point, and aerial, or atmospheric, which achieves the depiction of distance by means of the gradual shading of light and color. In the seventeenth century perspective went from a matter of art to the object of mathematical study, and it was translated into the forms of descriptive geometry and projective geometry. Various treatises offered practical rules for perspective foreshortening. Perspective was put to special use in architecture by Andrea dal Pozzo, who used *quadratura*

perspective (in which the lines of focus begin at the corners and converge at a central vanishing point) for the depiction of architecture on walls and ceilings, and by Ferdinando Galli da Bibiena, who used perspective in the field of theatrical design.

Axonometry makes possible the reconstruction of a three-dimensional figure through the orthogonal projection of the important points of the figure on Cartesian planes. It is widely used in architectural drawing for representing the volume and forms of a building with clarity and efficiency.

Origin of the Term
The origins of descriptive geometry date to Renaissance studies of perspective renderings. Its modern theory is based on the work of Gaspard Monge, who at the end of the eighteenth century formulated the basic rules for representing three-dimensional objects in a projected plane.

Related Entries
Rendering

Ferdinando Galli da Bibiena, geometric method for the establishment of proportions, from *Direzioni della Prospettiva Teorica Corrispondenti a Quelle dell'Architettura*, Bologna, 1732, plate 41

Albrecht Dürer,
"Draftsman Drawing a
Recumbent Woman,"
from *Underweysung der
Messung* (Instruction
in measurement), 4,
Nuremberg, 1538

Linear perspective is a system of rules that make possible the reproduction of three-dimensional forms on a flat surface. The most important elements in a perspective rendering are the visual pyramid, the vanishing point, orthogonal lines, and the horizon line.

In his *De pictura* (1436) Leon Battista Alberti introduced the fundamental principle of perspective painting, presenting it as an intersection between part of the visual pyramid and the surface on which a painting was to be made. This is the first rule of perspective.

In this engraving Dürer presents the so-called veil of Alberti (or grid) being used to create a foreshortened rendering of a female figure. The veil corresponds to the "painting," meaning the intersection of the pictorial plane with the visual pyramid that has its top in the eye of the observer and its base in the object to be depicted.

For the depiction of small figures and objects Alberti recommended the use of a transparent gridwork veil positioned between the eye of the artist and the object to be depicted. Working with a sheet of paper with an identical grid, the artist could accurately reproduce the features of the object. Aside from its eminently practical applications, the veil is a concrete embodiment of the geometric concept of intersection.

Anonymous artist,
Ideal City, c. 1475.
Galleria Nazionale delle
Marche, Urbino

The system of geometric perspective is perhaps the clearest expression of the Renaissance concept of man as located at the center of the cosmos. Perspective provides a rational ordering of space, a symmetrical division of the several parts of a composition, and a clear vision of objects in the foreground. In this ideal city the central point of view and the perspective vanishing point converge exactly at the door of the round temple, creating a perfect spatial dimension, suspended in time and history.

Perspective construction establishes a direct and definitive relationship with the spectator; the architectural space is projected on the basis of strict proportional modules that follow the vision of the observer and that reflect a unitary concept of buildings.

So powerfully persuasive were Renaissance theories that many centuries passed before anyone cast doubt on them by pointing out that perspective constructions do not, in fact, exactly correspond to true vision.

The abstract mathematics of the
town square, the many references
to classical structures, and the
perfect geometry of the temple
hark back directly to Alberti's
theories and also to the crystal-clear
geometrics of the pictorial world
of Piero della Francesca.

Throughout antiquity no distinction was
drawn between optics and perspective.
It was only during the Renaissance, as
part of the rational measurement of
space and its depiction to scale, that
the rules of correct perspective
representation originally invented by
Brunelleschi—with orthogonal lines
converging at a single vanishing point
(or at two, in the case of bifocal perspective)—were codified by Alberti.

Donato Bramante, false choir in the church of Santa Maria presso San Satiro, Milan, 1479–82

This church represents the first instance of the expression of perspective illusionism in a building. Bramante used pictorial means to achieve a sort of equivalence between actual space and illusory space—to invent through the use of perspective space that does not actually exist.

Since the available space did not permit creation of a choir sufficiently deep to give symmetry to the internal spaces, Bramante created a "perspective" choir in painted stucco, the illusory depth of which provides the dome with the visual support it needs on the fourth arm of a hypothetical Latin cross.

The choir possesses a certain structural logic: Bramante exploited the thickness of the wall as far as possible to give three-dimensionality to the perspective view, employing the same materials, colors, and ornamental motifs present in the actual building.

The architecture has immediately perceptible proportions analogous to those of an actual work of architecture: in a real depth of 120 centimeters (1 cm = 0.39 inches), Bramante created a wing that apparently extends about 11 meters (1 m = 39.37 inches), marked off by three bays resting on piers. In doing so he adopted a somewhat high horizon line to emphasize the importance of the sacred image and the altar.

In this choir Bramante harmoniously fused the actual structures and those suggested by the illusionist possibilities of perspective. Perspective ceased to be merely a pictorial effect applied to architecture and became instead a work of architecture itself.

Giovanni Santini,
Saint John Nepomuk,
Z'dar, Czech Republic,
1719–22

The dynamic design of the interior is made apparent on the exterior by the cornice of the dome. The number five recurs several times in the structure, with the presence of five entrances, five chapels, and five altars: in the moment of the saint's death, five stars were said to have appeared around his head.

The elongated tongue-like shape of the windows is a symbolic reference to the martyrdom of Saint John of Nepomuk: King Wenceslas IV had him killed when he refused to reveal what the king's wife, Sofia, had said in confession.

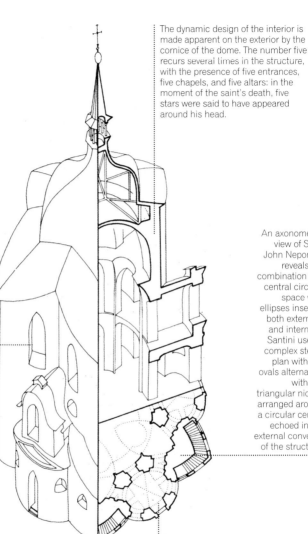

An axonometric view of Saint John Nepomuk reveals the combination of a central circular space with ellipses inserted both externally and internally. Santini used a complex stellar plan with five ovals alternating with five triangular niches arranged around a circular center, echoed in the external convexity of the structure.

Unique in the Late European Baroque era, the Church of Saint John Nepomuk is a Gothic-style church with a strongly nostalgic and irrational character. In fact Santini designed a splendid system of interwoven ribs that are purely decorative, serving no structural function.

The use of a central plan without an indication of the centripetal or centrifugal forces that inform it, the juxtaposition of the volumes, and the continuous walls all make the spaces appear closed.

That Santini drew on a broad cultural repertoire is clear in the internal surfaces, decorated in stuccowork and in pale plasterwork and connected to a system of Gothic ribs; his skillful arrangement of the windows provides abundant illumination.

Plan and Planimetry

A plan is a section in a horizontal plane, in reduced scale, of a building, part of a building, or an architectural element. Presented from a certain height, it becomes a depiction in orthographic projection of the position and size of the internal spaces and the elements that compose them, such as doors, windows, stairs, and support structures. Although abstract and unrelated to concrete visual experience, the plan is of great importance in design work and is an effective tool for interpreting an architectural work.

The most common kinds of plans are the central plan, in which the structures are arranged symmetrically around a central point; the axial or basilican plan, in which the structures are arranged symmetrically and longitudinally along a median axis; and the cruciform plan, closely related to Christian architecture, with its clear evocation of the symbolic shape of the cross, which has variants in the Greek cross (with arms of equal size), the Latin cross (with the longitudinal arm, corresponding to the nave, longer than the transverse arm, corresponding to the transept), and the St. Anthony cross or tau (shaped like a T). There are also elliptical plans, composed of a concatenation of ellipses, and open or free plans, unrelated to any particular volumetric forms and not bound by symmetrical schemes or relationships. In modern and contemporary architecture the plan responds exclusively to the rational and functional needs of the building or to the architect's personal interpretation of spatial reality.

Planimetry is the creation of a flat topographical projection that gives no indications of relief. It is used in urban planning to establish how a given piece of land will be used, including the design of any structures.

Origin of the Term
The term *plan* was introduced to the language of architecture in the sixteenth century to replace the more learned *iconografia*, taken from Vitruvius and meaning the drawing of forms on a plane.

Related Entries
Elevation and Section;
Architectural Drawing;
Project

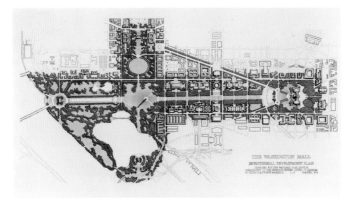

Skidmore, Owings & Merrill, *The Washington Mall*, 1974, planimetric development plan

In central-plan buildings, all the parts are symmetrically arranged around a center: their shape is based on a regular geometric shape—a circle, ellipse, square, octagon, and so on, sometimes interconnected—and the connected spaces are subordinate to the central space, also in terms of their roofing type.

The development of ancient central-plan structures reached its zenith in the Pantheon in Rome; it was not until the early Christian and Byzantine architecture of baptisteries and *martyria* that more architecturally differentiated forms appeared.

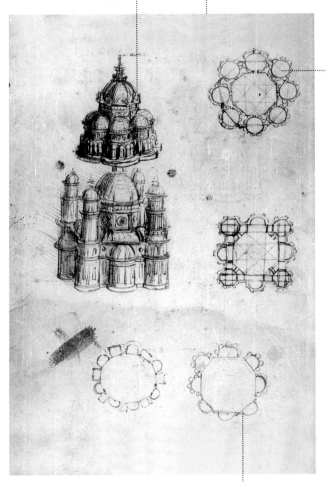

All the art of the Italian Renaissance follows a speculative investigation of the ideal form of the central-plan religious building; based on the balanced integration of geometric shapes and the simple solids of the sphere and cube, this form represented the apex of the search for spatial synthesis and the clearest translation into rational forms of the celestial vault and the worlds revolving around the earth—and thus of man as the ideal hinge of the universe.

Leonardo da Vinci, studies of central-plan churches, from Codice B, c. 1490, Institut de France, Paris

This drawing illustrates an idea for a church with a central plan based on a precise symmetrical arrangement: four equal axes intersecting at the center.

This leads to the creation of the circular radiating chapels, attached to the central parallelepiped; the design is also repeated in the hierarchy between the main dome and the secondary coverings.

Alexandre-Jean-Baptiste Le Blond, plan of the abbey of Saint-Denis (France) with the Valois Chapel, from M. Félibien, *Histoire de l'Abbaye Royale de Saint Denys en France*, Paris, 1706

In the longitudinal or basilican plan, all the structures of a building are arranged along a median axis. The plan has been widely used for religious buildings in part because it can be seen as emblematic of the spiritual route followed by mankind.

The choir has a double ambulatory, an idealized continuation of the side aisles, and radiating chapels; large windows pierce its walls. The plan gives a sense of the thin columnar support elements but not the elegant ribbed vaults.

The Valois Chapel, designed by Primaticcio, presents a central plan articulated radially around a complex of walls that incorporate the shape of the trefoil chapels. The plan indicates how the late Renaissance chapel, conceived as an autonomous unit, was grafted onto the longitudinal medieval structure.

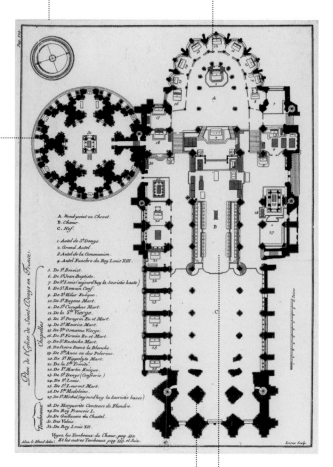

In the plan of the church of Saint-Denis, the longitudinal space is measured off by a series of columns that form a route leading from the entrance to the altar. Clearly visible are the nave and side aisles, the nave being twice the size of the aisles; the transept, which hardly projects; and the row of side chapels.

The church's use as an abbey is made clear in the division between the area reserved for the faithful and that reserved for the monks.

Carlo Fontana, plan of Saint Peter's, from *The Vatican Temple and Its Origins*, Rome, 1694, book 5, chap. 8

The plan illustrates how the longitudinal shape of the Latin cross was applied to the original central plan designed for Saint Peter's by Bramante; different tonalities are used to identify various phases in the construction of the building.

The darker areas identify parts built from the pontificate of Julius II (r. 1503–13) up to and excluding that of Paul V (r. 1605–21); the paler areas are those built under Paul V, when the Greek-cross plan was abandoned with the extension of the eastern wing.

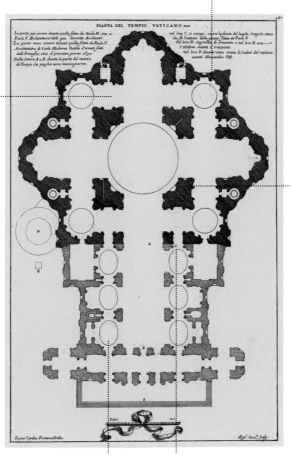

Bramante's original layout was based on a Greek-cross plan with a hemispherical dome positioned over the inter-section of the wings, four smaller domes located at the four corners, and a series of apses with corner towers included within the external walls, with only the main apses extending beyond those walls.

Four enormous piers, still existing, support the arches on which the dome, roughly 40 meters in diameter, rests.

The longitudinal body adds a nave with aisles and side chapels; the aisles are covered by ellipsoid domes. The façade is preceded by a portico.

Fontana makes clear the imperfect juxtaposition of the two plans along the median axis, indicating with the letters A and B the slight northward shift of the nave. The letter C identifies the attachment of a column with an acute angle instead of a right angle, caused by this shift.

Guarino Guarini, plan
of the church of Santa
Maria della Divina
Provvidenza, Lisbon,
1656–59, from
Architettura Civile, Turin,
1737, plate 17

The plan appears to be arranged in
a conventional manner, based on a
basilican layout with a transept and
apses. But the longitudinal axis is
defined by a series of elliptical vaults
in such a way that the constructive
unities of the nave and transept
are developed at the same time,
generating a continuous movement.

Guarini composes the space from
cells organized following the
principles of pulsating juxtaposition,
creating an undulating movement
along the nave that makes the
columns seem to vibrate. In fact, the
complex shape of the columns, with
their mixtilinear outlines flanked by
smaller individual columns, is
structured in accordance with the
same scheme, which shapes even
the small oval chapels themselves.

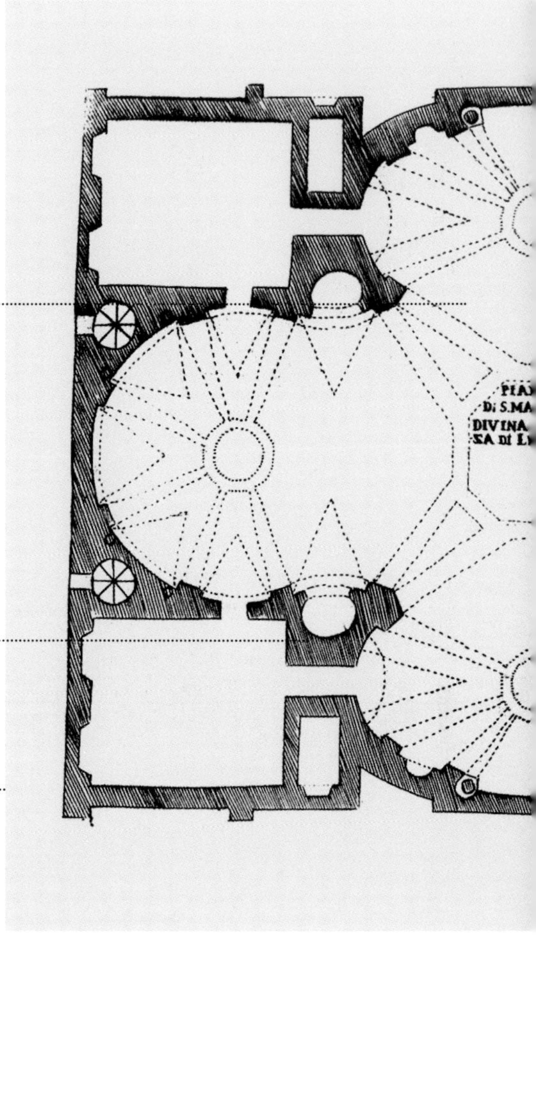

Both scientist and architect,
Guarini here applied geometric
rules in a maniacal manner that is
nevertheless based on precise
symbolic correspondences.

Typical of the Baroque age, the plan is based on the linking, in a series, of the geometric figure of the ellipse, by means of which the unity of the structure is broken into an aggregation of independent spatial cells.

This approach, called *ars combinatoria*, results in an ongoing effect of surprise and disorientation based on the absence of any straight-line axes.

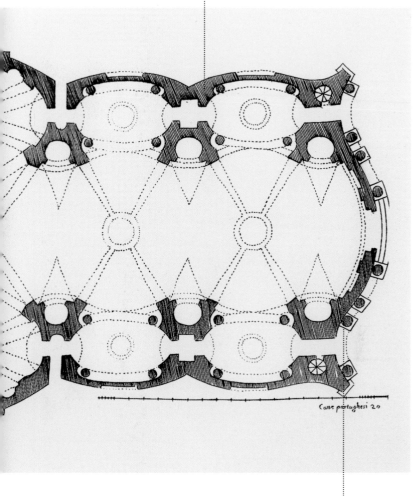

Cane portughesi 20

The church is constructed using curving lines, beginning with the concave-convex façade and continuing along the undulating walls and vaults, which eliminate any dividing lines.

Richard Meier,
conceptual drawing of
the Neugebauer House,
Naples, Florida, 1995–98

Contemporary architecture relies heavily on the so-called open plan: one not bound to any symmetrical scheme or composition but responding exclusively to rational and functional needs or to the architect's personal interpretation of spatial reality.

Richard Meier, an architect known for his extreme rationality, here designs a building based on straight lines arranged orthogonally, with a linear series of rooms that are more or less identical in size.

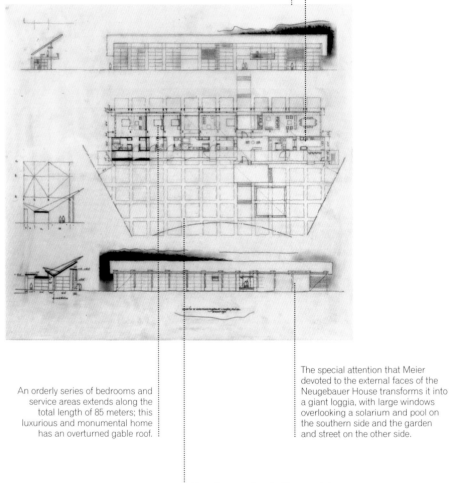

An orderly series of bedrooms and service areas extends along the total length of 85 meters; this luxurious and monumental home has an overturned gable roof.

The special attention that Meier devoted to the external faces of the Neugebauer House transforms it into a giant loggia, with large windows overlooking a solarium and pool on the southern side and the garden and street on the other side.

Given the overall perfectly geometric layout, the slightly off-center arrangement of the two entrances is surprising, although in fact they appear aligned. Meier also designed the garden; it too is organized along a precise geometric grid.

Carlo Maciachini, general planimetric view of the Monumental Cemetery of Milan, 1863. Archivio Storico Civico, Milan

The drawing depicts the arrangement of Milan's cemetery and its relationship to the land destined to house it; intended specifically as a tool for urban planning, it does not include relief lines.

The planimetric view illustrates the arrangement of the buildings and the memorial chapel around the garden, destined to house the funerary chapels of the city's leading families.

The drawing includes a metric scale and a legend along with an elevation, a section, and a perspective view of the memorial chapel, all of which demonstrate the use of decorative elements drawn from the repertoire of thirteenth- and fourteenth-century Lombard architecture.

The perspective drawing of the central building reveals two porticoed wings to the side of the memorial chapel; this felicitous arrangement carries the eye beyond the central body to visually embrace the large surface behind.

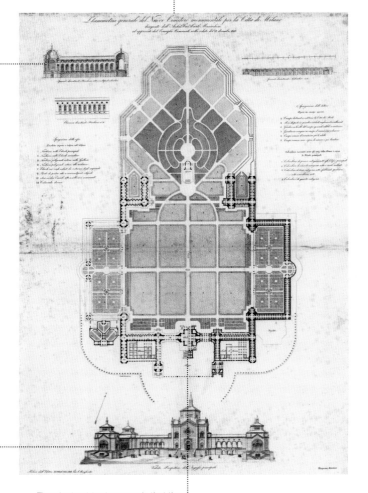

The planimetric view reveals that the buildings are arranged according to precise geometric spaces that make possible later additions and integrations. There is the opportunity for further aggregations that will not alter the overall appearance of the project, in which the large central building acts as a hinge for the composition.

The wings extend outward symmetrically to octagonal chapels, located at regular intervals at points of intersection or at the far ends of buildings, thus becoming true modular joints that permit the various parts of the building to rotate 90 degrees.

Elevation and Section

An elevation is a face of an architectural structure, or of a part of it, in projection on a vertical plane. It can be both external and internal and is not necessarily identified with the façade, although it often coincides with it. Widely used by architects in both the conceptual and final design phases, an elevation can also present a structure that will never be built.

Creation of the elevation is a descriptive procedure that provides an indispensable reference tool for use during the work of design, that facilitates the work and ensures its conformity to the design, and that explicates the geometrical and spatial relationships of the building. It need not be a technical drawing, and it can make use of different techniques, such as, for example, the excellent drawing by the architect and city planner J.J.P. Oud, which represents all the aesthetic qualities of the façade of the Café De Unie in Rotterdam. This is a simple, white plaster surface on which the squares of the windows and doors, painted in the primary colors of Mondrian, stand out clearly, following the shapes of abstract Cubism.

A section is the graphic rendering of a building through a vertical plane, sometimes oblique, used to display the interior. It provides information on the thickness of walls and the character of vaults, the shapes of roof structures, and so forth. Also called a vertical section, it is a fundamental tool for understanding the spatial relationships of an architectural work.

Related Entries
Plan and Planimetry;
Architectural Drawing;
Project

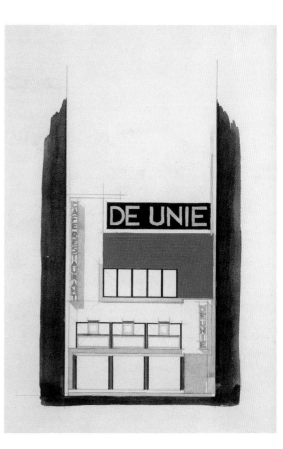

J.J.P. Oud, elevation of the Café De Unie, Rotterdam, 1925. Architecture Institute, Rotterdam, the Netherlands

Filippo Juvarra, design
for a central-plan church,
1707. Accademia
Nazionale di San Luca,
Rome

The elevation of the façade of
this church, designed by Juvarra,
perfectly illustrates the articulation of
a large Baroque religious building,
beginning with the ground-floor row
of Corinthian pilasters, the regularity
of the flat panels, the portals,
and the triangular tympanum.

In the upper areas of the building, the
Baroque lexicon is apparent in the
geometric alignment of the belt
courses, cornices, and balusters, as
well as in the dome, set on a high
drum with windows ending in an
aerial lantern; there are also twin
side bell towers.

The plan of the
building makes
clear the
complexity of
its volumes and
spatial cells,
aspects not
perceptible in the
elevation. The
church is revealed
to be centrally
planned around an
octagon. Also
presented are the
mixtilinear outline
of the façade and
the related shape
of the stairways,
the presence of
a columned
portico, a series
of radiating
semicircular
chapels, and the
circular outline of
the bell towers.

Jacques Lemercier, view
of the Farnese Palace
at Caprarola, 1607.
Biblioteca Apostolica
Vaticana, Vatican City

In this engraving Lemercier unites
a perspective view of the palace
with a section of it; this reveals the
building's octagonal plan, dictated by
the remnant foundations of a fortress
begun by Antonio Sangallo the Younger,
which had polygonal bastions.

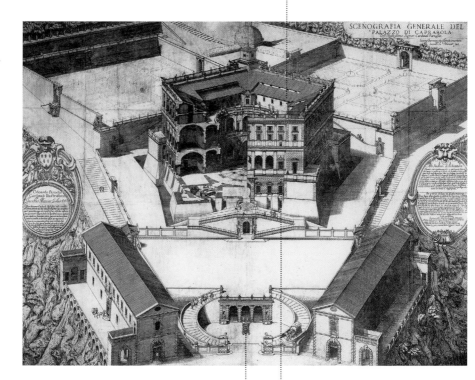

The perspective view presents
the point of contact between the
aristocratic residence and the
medieval settlement: the road that
cuts the town in two ends at a
series of terraces flanked by two
structures arranged diagonally; the
connections are made by two sets
of stairs, the first pincer shaped
and the second with double ramps.

The austere exterior—with its stately
articulation of angular rustication,
pilaster strips, and the sharp
horizontal lines of cornices and belt
courses—corresponds internally to
a central circular court. The section
reveals Jacopo Barozzi da Vignola's
skill at diminishing the weight of the
compact structure of the building
through the chiaroscuro effects
of windows and arches and the
rustication of the two-floor loggia
overlooking the inner court.

Étienne-Louis Boullée, proposal for the reconstruction of the theater of the Paris Opéra, 1781, section of the amphitheater. Bibliothèque Nationale de France, Paris

Boullée's drawing illustrates the internal structure of the theater of the Paris Opéra, with its large auditorium open on a proscenium and covered by a hemispherical coffered dome; in the background is a colonnade, and above are four rows of boxes, an arrangement made clear by the side section.

The interior space is generated by the rotation of a semicircle on its diameter. Lying flat, it defines the shape of the hall; standing, it creates the area of the stage.

Visible to the sides are such service areas as foyers, hallways, and rest areas.

There is also an indication of the row of gigantic Corinthian columns that were to frame the exterior faces.

A circular plan is an unusual choice for a building designed for performances, and it seems to have been derived from the shapes of ancient temples with round plans. Determination of the ideal shape for a theatrical space was of enormous interest to theoreticians of the second half of the eighteenth century.

Architectural Drawing

The architectural drawing, perhaps the most spontaneous and immediate expression of the architect's planning activity, establishes the principal aspects of the project while also indicating the distinction between artistic and technical activity. It can take various forms—technical drawing, freehand drawing, sketch—and can address the totality of the building or its parts; it may also bear handwritten notes and second thoughts from the architect. As early as the thirteenth century, the *Livre de Portraiture* by Villard de Honnecourt established the role of the architectural drawing in its dual function of formal investigation and executive program. Over the course of the fifteenth century humanist culture, most notably Alberti in his *De re Aedificatoria*, codified the idea of the design as an intellectual operation by the artist-designer, separate from the execution, which was delegated to others, thus emphasizing the new status acquired by architects.

From then on the architectural drawing underwent various fundamental transformations that reflected the conquest of the geometrical laws of perspective, the codification of the architectural orders, the seventeenth-century definition of the analytical and mathematical laws of depiction, the scientific foundation of descriptive geometry, and the eighteenth-century formulation of the method of central projection, which is the basis for double projection and three-dimensional drawing. With the advent of the industrial age the architectural drawing was transformed from a conceptual and cognitive tool into a project. Recent trends in architectural design assign to architectural drawing a communicative role, leaving analysis of the project's data to computer-based systems.

Related Entries
Plan and Planimetry;
Elevation and Section;
Project

Villard de Honnecourt, choir of Saint-Étienne, Meaux, from the *Livre de Portraiture*, c. 1220–35. Bibliothèque Nationale de Paris

Andrea Palladio, Greek house, from *The Four Books of Architecture*, book 2, Venice, 1570, p. 42

Over the course of the sixteenth century Palladio used the architectural drawing to codify the architectural orders. His purpose was to standardize construction elements in terms of their morphological and structural components. In this way he sought to configure a building suitable for all periods.

This elevation illustrates the front of a Greek house set upon a colonnade; Corinthian columns support an entablature and above it a balustered balcony. The floor above is marked off by a regular series of pilaster strips and ends in a triangular tympanum in which, thanks to a vertical section, the trusses that support the sloping roof are visible.

A partial plan presents the arrangement of the columns around the central peristyle and the differing shapes of the niches that hold the statues, alternatively rectangular and semicircular.

Hector Guimard, drawing of Castel Béranger, Paris, from *Le Castel Béranger*, Paris, 1894–98

The architectural drawing of the Art Nouveau period emphasizes the typically urban character of artistic and intellectual elaborations, devoting equal attention to the themes of public and residential architecture as well as to interior furnishings and objects of daily use, ranging from the overall layout to individual decorative elements.

The design of Castel Béranger—a residential complex in the heart of middle-class Paris—illustrates the structure of the building, with its projections, indentations, and embellishments, including the highly original matching of such materials as wrought iron, brick, stone, and ceramics. The various elements are emphasized by elegant, naturalistic decoration that signals the exuberant triumph of plant motifs.

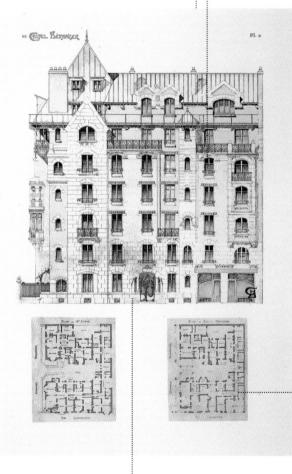

The pair of plans demonstrate the absolute regularity of the building lot and the traditional interior arrangement of the apartments; only the façade was revolutionary—a fact that in no way diminishes the artist's considerable originality.

With its soft, pastel tonalities, the finely painted watercolor emphasizes the use of stone and plaster for the exterior surfaces.

The image depicts the pleasing combinations of windows—some mullioned, others not—with a medieval sensibility, combined with the proliferation of wrought iron in the balconies and the fairytale towers.

Frank Lloyd Wright, *Office Building for the National Life Insurance Co.*, Chicago, 1924–25. Seymour H. Persky Collection

Beginning with the modernist movement, the architectural drawing underwent a transformation in accord with the dominant functionalist ideology. It sought to rationalize the growing complexity of the subjects of architecture and urban planning through the typological investigation of residential architecture and its projection on an urban scale, as well as through the use of construction materials and techniques derived from industrial production.

The drawing presents the articulation of the building as interpenetrating masses. It is an architecture of cantilevered masses anchored to the ground—a sort of metaphysical interpretation of architecture.

Thanks in part to the use of colored pencils and inks, Wright's drawing gives a perspective view of the large multistoried office building that at the same time reveals his habit of designing on a modular grid and making use of simple geometric forms.

Alvar Aalto, perspective
drawing of the residential
complex of Kauttua,
Finland, 1937–38.
Alvar Aalto Foundation,
Helsinki

The concept of the green city led
Alvar Aalto to elaborate a form of
urbanization called the city-forest,
in which terraced houses follow
the slope of a hillside, marking a
significant break from the traditional
row house and also from the urban
model based on city blocks.

The beautiful freehand drawing shows
the Kauttua residential complex for
employees of the Ahlström Company:
architecture based on the concept of
a housing development in a forest,
calling for an ecologically responsible
type of residential building suitable for
high-density living and characterized
by low construction emphasizing
horizontal lines.

The drawing illustrates a group of
terrace houses with bodies and bases
made of concrete (only one house was
ever completed), which perfectly
conform to the natural qualities of the
site, emphasizing the desire for light,
air, and sun. It is an urban plan that
represents a serious investigation into
resolving the construction challenges
of industrial communities.

Le Corbusier, sketches
from *Carnet* N56,
folio no. 49, 1959

Le Corbusier, known for his multi-faceted and highly original personality, here generated an architectural drawing that is evocative and notable for its spontaneity and immediacy of execution. The sketches from the *Carnets*, made during his travels, are freehand drawings that illustrate architectural ideas and include handwritten comments.

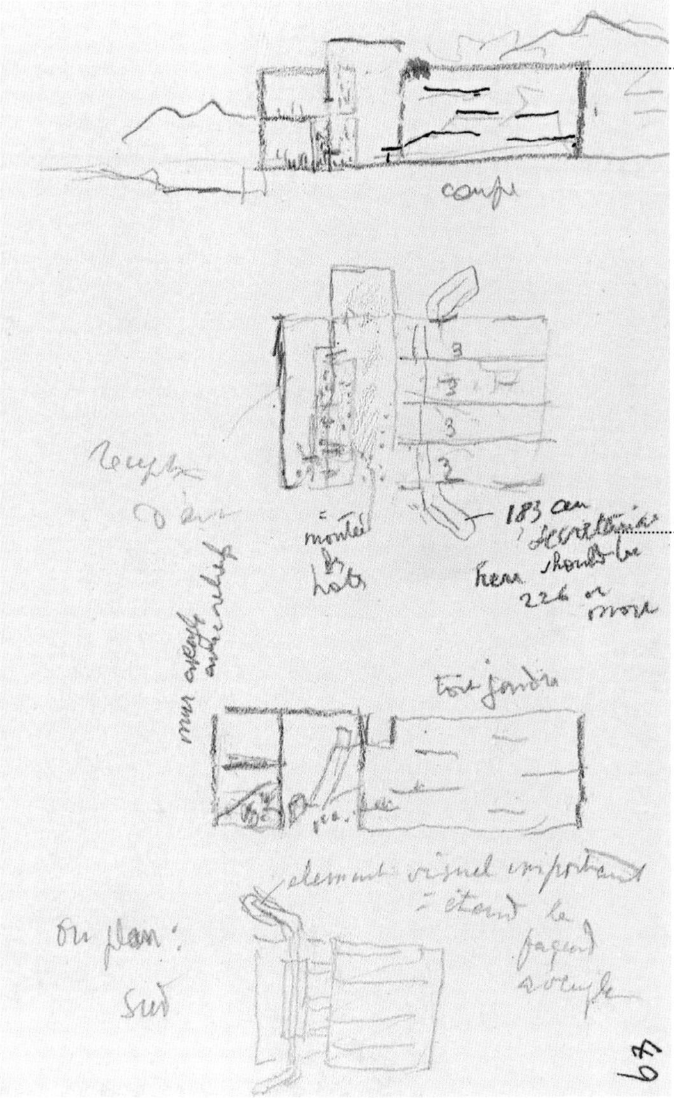

The sketch of a building being used as a hotel includes a vertical section of a very simple structure, composed of the kind of regular geometric modules typical of modernist architecture.

The notation "183 cm Secrétariat" seems to suggest the application of the Modulor, a study of modular coordination that Le Corbusier published in 1948, which was based on the size and movements of a man 1.83 meters tall. The Modulor led to an architecture based on the human scale, not (or not only) on structural demands and purely compositional rules.

Project

The project is a method of theoretical and methodological elaboration using a variety of instruments—from technical drawings to models to computerized three-dimensional images—that precedes the execution of an architectural work and is associated with creativity. The architectural project always falls within the dimension of aesthetics: it is never merely technical or instrumental but rather more resembles a discussion. The project must not only offer proof of technical proficiency—from the structural calculations to the physical plant, from the topographical representation to the unification of the sizes and the scale of representation—it must also show respect for the urban setting and for social conventions, as well as knowledge of building types and their compositional, economic, and distributional optimization. Specifically the project must respect, interpret, and resolve, both artistically and technically, every aspect of living in the proposed structure.

For centuries the classical style represented the model of aesthetic perfection to which any project had to conform, but today form no longer draws inspiration from past styles, nor even from the imitation of nature. Architectural studios have become centers for the transmission of architectural knowledge, organized around a unity of thought that is more methodological than stylistic and is capable of confronting the various demands of the social fabric. At the same time, postwar reconstruction made necessary the formation of studios that bring together various specialists trained to meet the construction challenges posed by large-scale urban and territorial transformations. The internationalization of techniques, information, and mass communication clashes with diversification as a value, and with the new subjectivism that promotes an architecture—postmodern and deconstructivist—that is seen as the "spectacularization" of modern society. In more recent times attention to context seems to have reaffirmed itself, and thus we may find a project that respects the identity of its location even as it takes a critical stance vis-à-vis that location.

Origin of the Term
The term *project* appears for the first time in the 1838 edition of the *Dictionnaire Historique d'Architecture* by Quatremère de Quincy, to distinguish the architectural drawing from an artistic drawing.

Related Entries
Descriptive Geometry; Plan and Planimetry; Elevation and Section; Architectural Drawing; Model; Rendering

Charles Percier, project for a Palace for the Meetings of the Academies, Grand Prix 1786, École Nationale Supérieure des Beaux-Arts, Paris

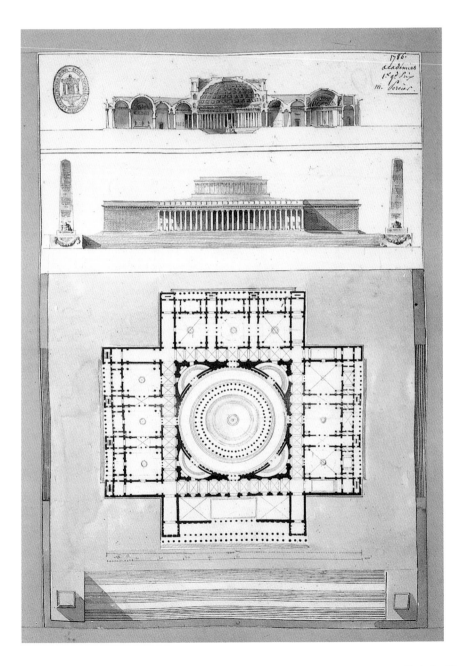

Carlo Scarpa, project for the Gallerie dell'Accademia in Venice, 1945–59, planimetric study of the second floor. Archivio Carlo Scarpa

Scarpa used different colors to indicate the chronological arrangement of the works, with pink for the fifteenth century, blue for the sixteenth, and yellow for the seventeenth to eighteenth, as indicated by the circles above right. There is also an indication of the scale in meters: 1/200.

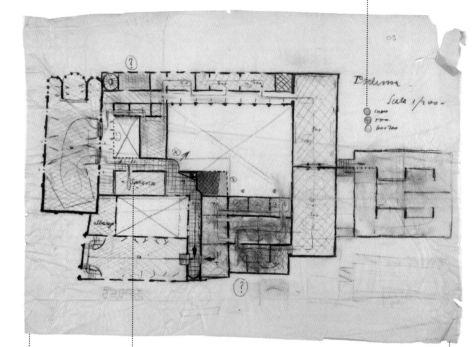

Displaying skillful use of graphite and colored pastels on glossy paper, the drawing—as indicated in the autograph inscription—is a first sketch for the reworking and enlargement of the Gallerie dell'Accademia prepared by Scarpa with the collaboration of Vittorio Moschini during the postwar period. The project was never undertaken.

With the intention of creating a sequence based on chronology, Scarpa proposed a new route that would lead from the end of the first hall to the so-called Sant'Orsola Hall, then to the former Church of the Carità, and then to the rooms destined for eighteenth-century oil paintings and to the halls of fifteenth-century paintings.

This preliminary project for the rearrangement and presentation of the second floor makes very clear the artisanal nature of Scarpa's formal thinking, reminiscent of De Stijl–like (assymetrical balance) and Wrightian ideas. It also demonstrates his genius for details and his refined sensibility. All his work is characterized by a stately, classical layout, despite the continuous decomposition of volumes, materials, and colors.

Aldo Loris Rossi,
Vincenzo Torrieri,
Emma Buondonno,
"Due Teatri di Verzura"
project, Schindler Prize,
Naples, 1997

This project
illustrates the
Capodimonte
parking garage and
the Teatro di Verzura
in Naples as the
perspective con-
clusion of the
Murattiano axis.
It presents a route
that leads from the
Capodimonte
Museum to the
Albergo dei Poveri;
the Torre Palasciano
acts as the point of
orientation for the
image. There is also
indication of a well-
equipped park.

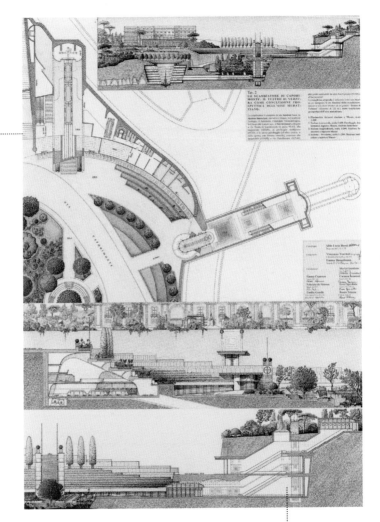

The project is distinguished
figuratively by the use of perspective
drawings following the plan-
elevation-section method that is of
such fundamental importance
to architectural design.

Model

The model is a small three-dimensional construction that reproduces a building to scale to verify its composition or to clarify the architect's intentions to the patron. As such, the model is one of the most immediately understandable means of architectural representation. The materials used to make models include plaster, wood, metal, and plastic. Since the nineteenth century distinctions have been drawn between the general model, understood as a relief representation, usually small in size, of a work to be undertaken; the conceptual model, understood as a representation not made strictly to size and not of any use to the builder, serving only to clarify the architect's thinking; and the scale model, the parts of which are in proportional dimension to the work to be built, for the use of the workers who will eventually construct the building.

The cutaway model of the restoration and enlargement of Milan's La Scala Theater demonstrates how the architect Mario Botta added two volumes to the rear of the original eighteenth-century structure: a scenic tower shaped like a cube, housing the new rehearsal halls, and an elliptical body to house dressing rooms and various service spaces. In contemporary usage the model preserves all the meanings and implications that have been layered onto it over time; however—and particularly in terms of industrial design—the model is also used as a tool for investigating production methods and as a means of forecasting and verifying. There are also models of infrastructure works, such as bridges, that can be subjected to various tests to check their resistance to stress.

Origin of the Term
Alberti used the term *modulus* to indicate prototypes used as supports for the creation of a work, but only in the following century was the term used definitively to designate an example to which the artist would refer in the execution of an architectural work, as was clearly explained by Baldinucci in the *Vocabolario* (1681).

Related Entries
Elevation and Section; Project; Rendering

Mario Botta, enlargement and restoration of the La Scala Theater in Milan, 2004, wooden model of the project made by Ivan Kunz

Model of the Tempio
Malatestiano in Rimini,
made for the show "Lo
splendore dei Malatesta
a Rimini," Rimini, 2001

The model reconstructs the upper
part of the façade with Venetian-style
crowning and the volutes designed
to hide the pitch of the roof. These
architectural solutions were never
implemented; the unfinished
structure above the central bay in
the actual version may have been
meant, in Alberti's original design,
as a triumphal arch.

The wooden model does not present
the temple as it was actually built;
instead it is based on its depiction
on a medallion made by Matteo
de' Pasti, which reveals that the
original design called for a large
hemispherical dome not unlike that of
the Pantheon, probably meant
to accentuate the building's
monumental appearance.

In his ingenious reconstruction of
the sepulchral church of the Malatesta
family, Alberti incorporated the original
building within a sumptuous classical
marble temple; the façade repeats
the Vitruvian order of the nearby Arch
of Augustus, and the arcades on
the sides are reminiscent
of Roman aqueducts.

Antonio Labacco, model of the basilica of Saint Peter's following the project by Antonio da Sangallo the Younger, 1539–46. Museo della Fabbrica di San Pietro, Rome

This wooden model of the Vatican basilica faithfully reproduces the project designed by Antonio da Sangallo the Younger during the years 1520–27. It includes the transept by Bramante already installed at the time—an apsidal Greek cross with the four enormous piers and arches that were to support the dome—to which the new longitudinal building with a nave was applied.

The shape of the trefoil apses framed by square structures at the sides is clear, as is the dome, set atop a high drum lightened by two rows of arcades. The lantern, however, seems particularly massive and heavy.

The entire side is marked off horizontally by belt course cornices; it is scored vertically by pilaster strips and engaged columns that frame niches and windows with tympanums. The façade is framed by twin bell towers.

The model of Saint Peter's is a work of microarchitecture that occupies a surface area of about 45 square meters and is 4.5 meters high, making it possible for visitors to enter it to study its spatial articulation and examine the smallest decorative detail.

The refined execution of a model of this size, with such precise renderings of architectural details, is a further demonstration of the importance of the debate concerning the basilica—a discussion of such import at the time that it made this expensive creation acceptable.

Antonio da Sangallo's plan, with its forced overlapping of the central and longitudinal layouts, reveals that the discussion regarding the appearance of the new Saint Peter's was still far from a definitive conclusion; at the same time it indicates that the papal curia was still strongly animated by a conservative drive, favoring traditional models with a Latin-cross layout.

Rendering

Derived from the descriptive geometry applications used most often in the construction of manufactured products for architectural use, the rendering makes it possible to replicate and monitor the proportions and visual features of a given design concept. The computerized application of the concepts of descriptive geometry today allows the architect not only to create a three-dimensional view of a highly complex architectural object but also to check every shape and dimension beyond all reasonable doubt. The data on which such electronic depictions are based are not rigid, as they were in traditional methods, but are instead changeable—not only individually but in their relationship to the whole.

The rendering is one of the most important applications of three-dimensional computer graphics. In architecture it is used for the visualization of a project and to ascertain the effective impact of a building— its insertion into the urban context, the anthropomorphic scale, the environmental impact, and so on. Put simply, it could be called a virtual model.

In the representation of the headquarters of the National Assembly of Wales at Cardiff, designed by Richard Rogers, the rendering illustrates the lightness of the transparent structure—fabricated using avant-garde technologies and materials—at the end of a ramp and raised upon thin cylindrical pylons. At the same time it presents the relationship of humans to the building as well as the context of the setting.

For many of today's architects, a rendering is not merely a pure and simple digital image of the architectural object. Given his highly unusual design requirements, Frank Gehry has trademarked a computer program that permits him to make a digital transcription of data and thus to check effective structural strengths of his construction.

In Depth

A rendering is the outcome of a process that begins with a mathematical description of a three-dimensional scene, interpreted by algorithms that define the color of every point of the image. The description includes the geometry, point of view, and information on the optical characteristics of the visible surfaces.

Related Entries
Descriptive Geometry; Project; Model

Richard Rogers,
The Senedd, headquarters
of the National Assembly
of Wales at Cardiff,
Great Britain, 2006,
rendering of the project

Zaha Hadid, Phaeno
Science Center,
Wolfsburg, Germany,
1999–2003, rendering
of the project

All the shapes
seem to be
generated from
a continuous
intersection of
lines; the spaces
are articulated
without visual
interruption
between the
different areas.

The digital rendering of the Phaeno
Science Center designed by Zaha Hadid
presents the horizontal shape of the
building, its complex volumes, and the
open areas through which the public
is to move. At the same time it depicts
the intersection of the volumes and the
alternation of full and empty spaces.

The new Science Center reflects
Hadid's unmistakable and dynamic
aesthetics: the building has a
sinuous, flowing profile, meticulously
defined, with a compact and elegant
main volume that seems to have
been just popped from a mold.
From a distance its shape is monolithic but not looming, and its
proportion, even if the building hardly
touches the ground, seems flattened
in the horizontal sense. It is
essentially a quadrangular slab
suspended 8 meters off the ground
and supported in this position by ten
"cones" that descend to the ground
like the feet of an outsize insect.

The rendering is here used to
explicate both Hadid's exploration of
the spatial dimension of the building,
as well as a concept of architecture
as a field of energies and flows that
create new landscapes.

Architecture and Engineering

The creation in 1747 in France of the École Nationale des Ponts et Chausées confirmed the new professional figure of the engineer—marking a schism destined to make its way across the entire field of architectural culture. By taking structural precision as its objective, engineering spurred the search for new construction technologies, transforming the architectural project into a means to achieve the greatest economy of materials, to organize the worksite in a rational way, and to design buildings around a structural skeleton. The terms of architecture's theoretical debate were changed, no longer revolving around the classical orders and seeking instead to interpret the expressive possibilities of a variety of diverse languages, prefiguring the overturning of the historical models on which the field had depended.

Jean-Nicolas-Louis Durand addressed the relationship between architecture and engineering in *Précis des leçons d'architecture données à l'École Royale Polytechnique* (1802–5, 1823–25), a work that had a great influence on professional training during the first half of the nineteenth century. The refocusing of architecture's attention from problems of representation to those of construction meant distancing it from the ideal of the architect as intellectual that dated from the Renaissance.

Today's architect, confronted by an explosion of forms, a constant flow of innovative materials, and demands for increasingly tall structures, cannot do without the technical support of an engineering studio to calculate the constructive possibilities of buildings, testing designs to the point of collapse. The British engineer Ove Arup has come to be recognized as one of the leading specialists in reinforced concrete and steel construction, and in particular in structural consulting.

In Depth
Beginning in the early nineteenth century the dispute reflected in the opposition between the École Polytechnique and the École des Beaux-Arts mirrored the cultural, technical, and functional separation between engineering, understood as the technical science of construction, and architecture, seen as the stylistic and decorative side of construction.

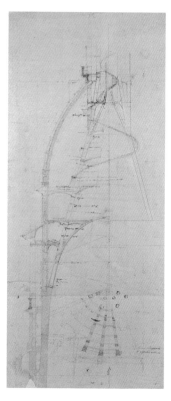

Alessandro Antonelli, study for the dome of the church of San Gaudenzio at Novara, 1861. Archivi Alessandro Antonelli, Museo Civico, Turin

Jørn Utzon, Sydney
Opera House, 1956

The shells of the roof of this building became feasible to build only when the architect came up with the solution of deriving their shape from a single geometric figure, in this case a virtual sphere with a diameter of about 75 meters.

The shells are quarter sections of a single sphere supported by double-curved ribs composed of prefabricated elements, while the cladding is composed of more than a million white ceramic tiles manufactured in Höganäs, Sweden, applied to panels in prefabricated vibrated concrete, which was raised and anchored to the superstructure.

The vaults, following a daring construction principle, constitute a novelty in the field of reinforced concrete prefabrication.

The highly original design by the Danish architect rests on a giant stepped podium in stone—which houses, side by side, the two main halls and all the technical and functional rooms—over which rise the large reinforced concrete shells of the roof, extending up to a height of 60 meters.

During the execution of the building, the complexity of the roof vaults (which are of a composition completely different from the articulation of the internal spaces) led to so many structural problems that the London engineering studio of Ove Arup and the engineer Peter Rice were called in to assist Utzon. Arup's studio, an inter-disciplinary team of collaborating architects and engineers, is one of the most respected in the world in terms of structural calculations.

Architectural Theory

Architectural theory began to flourish in the fifteenth century in the wake of the only architectural treatise known from the classical age, the *De architectura* by Vitruvius. During the Middle Ages this text had served primarily as a source of erudition. The figure of the architect it presents was extraneous to the organization of the medieval building site: there, architecture was relegated to the *artes mechanicae* and required no technical knowledge not already included among the professional secrets in manuals and *schedulae*. The fifteenth-century restitution of the dignity of art to the craft of the architect resulted in a profusion of treatises investigating the representation and objective construction of space through proportional systems and the control of perspective. In his *De re aedificatoria*, Leon Battista Alberti asserted the preeminence of planning and of the project. The fifteenth-century treatises had been written for intellectuals and lords; those of the sixteenth century—from Serlio's meticulous typological-formal approach to the practical method of Vignola's *Regola* to Palladio's more elevated theoretical elaborations—were fashioned expressly for the professional architect.

In the seventeenth century the literature of architecture abandoned the presentation of methodologies and all-encompassing critical systems to assume more autobiographical forms, and the treatise as such, given the training of architects in art academies, lost its function. It was France that now took a systematic approach to the various themes of the discipline, from technological and functional progress to city planning and garden design, in an attempt to identify the essential construction elements and to make form correspond to function. Throughout the eighteenth century the principles of architectural rationalism were developed in the form of the essay; at the same time publications about archaeological discoveries and the reliefs on classical monuments began to take on particular importance in the sphere of architectural debate.

Developments in nineteenth-century architecture—with its adoption of new techniques and new materials and its need to cater to the eclectic tastes of the middle class—resulted in publications that took the form of theoretical essays or specialist technical manuals. The fragmentation of architectural theories in the twentieth century resulted in works that dealt with the concepts and purposes of architecture, design, and method, but in a nonsystematic way, using the forms of the manifesto, the autobiographical work, and the article. Magazines and conference proceedings have also played a fundamental role.

In Depth
Until the nineteenth century, the *De architectura* by Vitruvius Pollio of the first century BCE was the primary didactic tool in architecture, a resource for explanations, a conversational model, and a source of inspiration. In addition to providing precise compositional and proportional principles, Vitruvius offered theories on optics, acoustics, geometry, mathematics, and music, thus focusing on the interdisciplinary nature of architecture.

Related Entry
The Figure of the Architect

Anonymous French artist, *Vitruvius Presenting His Book to Augustus* and *Vitruvius Teaching Disciples*, illuminated page from the *De architectura* of Vitruvius, fifteenth century. Biblioteca Medicea Laurenziana, Florence

Vitruuii de architectura prologus libri incipit feliciter ..

Jacopo Barozzi da Vignola, frontispiece to the *Regola delli cinque ordini d'architettura*, Rome, 1562

An architect and theorist, Vignola (1507–73) was trained in painting and perspective. After a short stay in Rome, where he studied the ancient monuments, and at Fontainebleau, where he worked with Primaticcio, he became the architect of the Farnese family.

Vignola occupies a particularly important place among the treatise writers of the Renaissance. In the effort to interpret Vitruvius's canons and classical architecture, his work established rigorous rules based on the so-called architectural orders and presented a synthesis and codification of the classical architectural lexicon. It was held in great esteem by architects until well into the nineteenth century.

The Renaissance understanding of the figure of the architect is made explicit in representations of architects: Vignola did not hesitate to have himself portrayed on the frontispiece of his treatise, presented inside an elaborate architectural aedicule; the new identity attributed to the profession is made clear through its emblems: the square and the compass.

The *Regola delli cinque ordini d'architettura* has a markedly practical character as a manual that establishes the norms of a formal lexicon, taking for granted that lexicon's universal value.

Its deliberately comprehensible character and didactic clarity as a handbook have made Vignola's text indispensable to designers for more than two centuries.

Eugène-Emmanuel Viollet-le-Duc, *The Ideal Cathedral* from the *Dictionnaire raisonné de l'architecture française du XIe au XVIe siècle*, Paris, 1854–68, vol. 2, p. 324.

Over the course of the nineteenth century specialist technical manuals began to take up questions of a distributive nature.

As a theorist and architect, Viollet-le-Duc attempted to free the Gothic from Romanesque notions in order to propose the Gothic as a rational construction system for meeting modern building needs. As a restorer, he worked on many important monuments.

For Viollet-le-Duc architectural theory was no longer a speculative system of aesthetics, but the result of empirical-scientific research. Favoring the use of industrial products, he encouraged architects to explore all the new tools and materials available to them.

In 1838 Viollet-le-Duc was appointed auditor to the Conseil des Bâtiments Civils and began inventorying and restoring France's medieval patrimony. At the same time he compiled his *Dictionnaire raisonné*, in which he presented his ideas on medieval architecture along with a clear explanation of his architectural concepts.

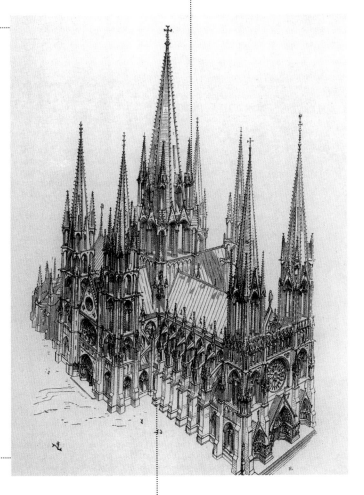

This ideal cathedral represents a synthesis of the great buildings of the Flamboyant Gothic style, a result of Viollet-le-Duc's interpretation of "true" Gothic architecture.

Viollet-le-Duc saw the "skeletal" architecture of the Gothic as the height of progress in its ability to express the qualities of materials and to transform static relationships into a dynamic one based on balances between opposing tensions.

Stability and Form

Wall / Column / Capital / Entablature / Pillar / Pilaster Strip and Lesene / Buttress / Arch / Roof Covering / Vault / Dome / Façade / Portico and Loggia / Doorway, Door, Portal / Window / Stairs, Staircase, Ramp

Erechtheum, Athens,
420–406 BCE,
porch of the caryatids

Wall

The wall is an artificial structure that may be made of various materials. It vertically delimits space and often serves a bearing function as well. Walls can be rectilinear, curved, or in any other shape, provided they are perfectly contiguous, so as to create a building complex in which thrusts and stress are transmitted without interruption.

The oldest examples of walls date to the Neolithic period; their shapes are based on the use of the elementary materials available in nature. Two methods were used to build walls in the ancient world: dry masonry, and the use of mortars and binders. In dry masonry the cohesion among the parts depends completely on the force of gravity and the level of adherence between one element and the next. The heaped-up rough-hewn boulders of Roman walls were followed by early Greek walls, with smaller blocks counterbalanced by the insertion of stone chips. Later walls display progressive improvement in the shaping of contact surfaces (Incan walls being an outstanding example). The use of mortars and binders ensured greater cohesion among the various parts and made possible the use of small elements such as bricks, which were easier to manufacture and transport and more adaptable to different structural and spatial applications.

The technique of brickwork found its highest expression in Roman constructions. The arrival of reinforced concrete and metal alloys, used in the creation of an independent load-bearing skeleton, finally freed the wall from any support function, reducing it to a curtain (nonbearing) wall. This approach has led to the development of new construction techniques and to new materials for walls that are extremely light but also well suited for thermal and acoustic insulation. Such walls, including those made with prefabricated panels, can be built quite rapidly.

In Depth

If a wall serves a structural function—meaning it transfers to the ground the weight of the structures above it—it is called a bearing, or main, wall. An interior bearing wall whose primary function is that of separating a space can be called a division wall. A nonbearing wall that serves to delimit space and protect it from external agents is called a curtain wall. A wall built to absorb and contain pressure from earth or water is called a retaining wall.

Incan wall at
Machu Picchu, Peru,
late fifteenth century

The Domus Augustana—the residential part of the great palace commissioned by Domitian on the Palatine Hill—was built entirely of concrete with tiles inserted between brick surfaces. Its remains still manage to suggest the grandness of its proportions, the technical skills of the workmen, its planimetric variety, and its nontraditional design.

The basic element in the Roman wall technique was the brick. Bricks were produced in a range of sizes and could be combined, enabling a construction method that became essential to the exportation and spread of brick technology.

The structure of the Domus reveals the application of a brickwork system based on the technique of laying linear rows of bricks arranged with the long side running in the longitudinal direction of the wall itself. The use of bricks as reinforcement—arranged radially over doorways or windows to form relieving arches that disperse the weight of the walls—also makes an aesthetic contribution to the walls.

The Domus codifies the building type of the dynastic palace, with private areas strictly separated from public reception areas. The great lower peristyle—once surrounded by porticos on two levels and today stripped bare of its dressing—is occupied at the center by a large fountain with a motif of opposing *peltae*, inserted in a pleasant garden that is one of the most evocative spaces in the palace, because of both the complex articulation of its parts and for its secluded and quiet atmosphere.

Fachwerk is an ancient building
technique based on the use of a
support structure of timber framework with the spaces filled with
nonstructural materials, like daub
or wattle or brickwork, or more rarely
with stones bound with mortar. The
façade of a timber-framed house
displays the wooden framework
structure, while the filled-in areas
are usually plastered.

Variations characteristic of
regions or historical periods can be
recognized by the materials used to
fill in the spaces, the arrangement
of the timber beams, the use of
diagonal wooden elements, or the
use (or not) of a brick podium.

Over the course of the fifteenth
century a fundamental evolution
took place: the use of vertical
beams reaching from the ground
to the top floor was supplanted by
constructions of independent floors.
This made possible the use of short
beams that could be arranged with
a certain aesthetic sense; it also
made possible an increase in
the height of buildings.

An ancient and widespread technique—
used as early as Roman times, as indicated by various examples preserved at
Herculaneum and Pompeii—*Fachwerk*
spread during the late Middle Ages
across certain areas of central-northern
Europe: in particular Germany, between
the fifteenth and seventeenth centuries
France, where it was called *pan de bois*
or *colombage*; and England, where
it was called timber-framing and,
colloquially, half-timbering.

Ludwig Mies van der Rohe, Seagram Building, New York, 1956

The curtain wall, a widespread building system in contemporary architecture, involves the use of exterior nonbearing walls, often composed of repetitive, prefabricated, modular panels.

These panels, put in place on site, not only separate the interior from the exterior but more importantly protect the interior from atmospheric agents, providing thermal and acoustic insulation and also regulating the flow of light and air.

Modernist architects performed a series of experiments that are now seen as progressive movements toward use of the curtain wall. The technique was adopted on a large scale in the United States only in the postwar period, with the first attempts at the industrialization of building construction on a vast scale. Innovative expressive possibilities were made possible by the introduction of new materials and construction techniques.

The Seagram Building, with its glimmering external elevations in bronze and marble, is emblematic of the application of these new building techniques.

Today the use of the curtain wall is enormously widespread, particularly in office buildings. Glass is one of the primary materials in such structures, and has become a defining element of high-tech architecture.

The panels, which are fixed to the framework of the bearing structure, can be made of metal alloys, glass, or plastic. The use of the curtain wall saves a great deal of time and expense because it is mounted in series and the elements are light in weight.

James Stirling
and Michael Wilford,
Neue Staatsgalerie,
Stuttgart, 1977–83

The complex interpenetration of volumes, the inclined surfaces, and the visible pathways of the Neue Staatsgalerie are emphasized by the use of materials assembled in a sort of collage: the two-color stone walls constitute the continuous dressing of the building and at the same time connect it to the older buildings, while the entrance is indicated by the undulating glass wall.

Stirling introduces the concept of the museum as an open space designed for group participation and public life. Playing on the contrast between the empty public space and the density of the urban fabric, he opens a pedestrian passageway that leads through the entire museum, the faces of which present an eclectic collage of forms designed to match the context of surrounding structures.

The use of perfectly squared and mounted ashlars required highly refined technical and constructive skills. This is in fact the most costly type of wall, as well as the most highly esteemed, uniting as it does great strength with expressive qualities that make all decoration superfluous.

Great Wall, China,
begun third century BCE

The Tao religion is responsible for the ecological sensibility of Chinese architecture, as proven by the colossal work known as the Great Wall. With its slow meandering that follows the undulations of the landscape, it represents an outstanding example of an accord struck between a human creation and its natural surroundings.

The Great Wall, built beginning in the third century BCE, is one of the finest Chinese architectural creations. It was reworked more or less completely during the Ming period to defend the empire's northern borders.

Although there are notable differences in particular areas and periods of construction, the Great Wall is primarily composed of large blocks of earth and stone dressed in bricks and forming a battlemented wall about 10 meters high and 6 meters wide. It is often interrupted by guard towers, and a paved road runs along its upper level.

Column

The column is a vertical, usually circular, architectural element serving primarily a support function, although it can also serve decorative or celebrative functions. Rarely made from a single monolithic block, it is composed of a series of three distinct elements: the shaft, composed of different lengths, or sections, joined in a row; the base, which connects the shaft to a support element (sometimes a stone plinth); and the capital, which connects the shaft to the structure above and which becomes the identifying element for the column.

The proportions and decorations on columns vary according to the period, type of construction, use, and civilization. An element typical of ancient architecture from the Mediterranean to India, the column was later widely used in both Christian and Islamic architecture. It was in Greek architecture that the column was given definitive and constant characteristics. The establishment of its principal elements led to the definition of the "architectural orders," destined to play a fundamental role in later developments, first in Roman architecture and then in the Renaissance and Neoclassical periods. The late Hellenistic period saw the introduction and spread of unusual forms, from the twisted column to rusticated columns and those with tendrils. During the Early Middle Ages ancient columns were often reused, but by the later Middle Ages the column was breaking with the proportional and morphological norms of the past to assume new and fantastic forms—from the knotted corner column, in which the ends of two columns knot to form a unit, to the twisted columns of San Michele in Foro at Lucca.

During the Renaissance, as during the Neoclassical period, the column was assigned a specific architectural role, returning to the classical rules of the orders, but in the Baroque age the column was again subject to free interpretations in terms of not only form but also size. During the nineteenth century the use of novel construction materials and techniques suggested the development of new types of support structures of great agility and lightness, such that the modern movement began to eliminate every reference to the traditional type of column from the architectural language. In contemporary architecture the column is present only for its functional or structural value and often ends up disappearing altogether.

Origins
The column, from the Latin *columna*, was originally made of wood and probably derives its shape from that of a tree trunk. Over time it evolved technically and stylistically, leading to the origin of its complementary elements, the base and capital, and to their later differentiation.

Related Entries
Capital; Entablature

Church of San Michele in Foro, Lucca, Italy, begun 1070, detail of the façade with twisted, knotted, and decorated columns

Sebastiano Serlio, the five orders, from *I cinque libri dell'architettura* (The five books of architecture), book 4, Venice, 1537, folio 127r

In classical civilization the column assumed clearly defined and constant characteristics, with two distinct types, Doric and Ionic. From these certain variations were derived, notably Tuscan and Corinthian. The relationships of column, capital, and entablature, and of their component parts, all of which have established forms and proportions, are necessary elements of the architectural orders.

The result was a consolidated architectural approach that saw the orders as a way to predetermine the dimensions of a building, establishing the proportional and symmetrical relationships among the elements.

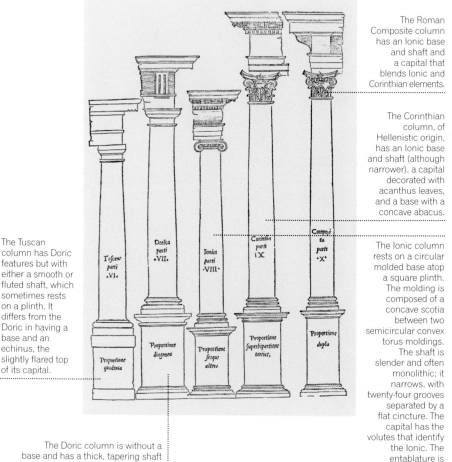

The Roman Composite column has an Ionic base and shaft and a capital that blends Ionic and Corinthian elements.

The Corinthian column, of Hellenistic origin, has an Ionic base and shaft (although narrower), a capital decorated with acanthus leaves, and a base with a concave abacus.

The Tuscan column has Doric features but with either a smooth or fluted shaft, which sometimes rests on a plinth. It differs from the Doric in having a base and an echinus, the slightly flared top of its capital.

The Ionic column rests on a circular molded base atop a square plinth. The molding is composed of a concave scotia between two semicircular convex torus moldings. The shaft is slender and often monolithic; it narrows, with twenty-four grooves separated by a flat cincture. The capital has the volutes that identify the Ionic. The entablature is decorated with a continuous frieze.

The Doric column is without a base and has a thick, tapering shaft composed of a series of sections, with entasis (a swelling at one-third of its height to correct the optical illusion of concavity). It is scored by twenty vertical sharp-edge flutes.

The Doric capital is distinguished by a circular, expanded echinus and a thick, square abacus. The entablature bears a frieze composed of metopes and triglyphs.

Church of Santa Costanza, Rome, 350 CE, interior with coupled columns

The classical orders were still being used inside buildings during the late Roman empire, although the trilithic system had been abandoned, and the traditional flat architrave had been replaced by arches. The elimination of the entablature as the connecting element between a wall and its supports led to significant structural problems, since the wall being supported tends to be thicker than the column and its capital.

In the mausoleum of Santa Costanza architects solved this problem by reinforcing the support structure through the adoption of paired columns set so close to each other that their capitals and bases almost seem to touch. The architectural orders constitute a decorative feature that has little to do with the building's load-bearing structure.

The rotunda is crowned by a dome resting on a wall, supported in turn by a series of arcades built with coupled columns made of granite. This results in spatial continuity between the central area and the ringed vaulted ambulatory. The radial arrangement of the coupled Corinthian columns and their heavily molded entablatures suggest a multiplicity of directions, foremost among them the convergence toward the visual focus of the building: once the sarcophagus of Costanza, today the altar.

A variation of the coupled column is the paired column, meaning one joined to another, sometimes both resting on the same base and terminating in a shared capital.

Cathedral of Chartres, France, Port Royal, 1140–50, detail with columnar statues

The Port Royal of Chartres is considered the departure point for Gothic sculpture. The slender and austere jamb figures are columns with biblical personages; although still connected to the architecture, they assume a life of their own.

The human figure returns to central importance in Gothic architecture; thus the column becomes symbolic of the relationship between humans and the cosmic order and can assume anthropomorphic features.

With its almost total negation of any structural involvement, the sculpture makes clear the rediscovered centrality of the human story in the world.

Colonna Santa,
Museo della Fabbrica
di San Pietro,
Vatican City

Gian Lorenzo Bernini,
baldacchino, Basilica of
Saint Peter's, Vatican
City, 1624, detail of a
Solomonic (spiral)
column

When he set about the rearrangement of the area of the main altar in
the basilica of St. Peter's, Bernini was
not insensible to earlier ideas and
decided to evoke the 12-columned
pergola Constantine had put at the
end of the nave by setting the bronze
baldacchino on Solomonic columns,
with their chromatic tones of black
and gold. Like their oldest relatives,
these have fluted bases and plant-like
decorations. He contrasted the
twisted form with the pillars of the
transept; in this way the baldacchino
both dominates and centralizes the
enormous space around it.

The Colonna Santa has a spiraling or
twisted shaft, composed of alternating
sections that are fluted and bear
vinelike decoration (suggesting vine
shoots wound around the shaft),
ending with a Composite capital; the
echinus has a single strand of
acanthus leaves and a grooved
background, ending in two volutes.

During the period of Constantine's
patronage the six twisted columns
were arranged above the tomb of
Peter. Another six were later added to
these, gifts of the governor of Ravenna;
their fame is based on their legendary
provenance from Solomon's temple
at Jerusalem, and hence they are
called Solomonic columns.

The vine leafs and shoots of the
decoration are symbolic references
to Jesus Christ, understood as the
"true vine" of the Lord.

Augustin-Charles D'Aviler, comparative table of columns, from *Cours d'architecture qui comprend les ordres de Vignole*, Paris, 1691

Since antiquity it has been customary to use a column as an autonomous monument connected to religious or civil rituals, serving a celebrative or commemorative purpose; in ancient Greece, for example, it was common practice to raise votive columns in sanctuaries.

The erection in public places of columns commemorating events or personages or their deeds was typical of the Roman era. Isolated columns were also erected during the Baroque period, assuming a special importance in city planning.

Structural support is not the only function of a column. Symbolic meaning can be given a column through decoration on the shaft or at its apex. D'Aviler illustrates all the possible variations permitted within the orders and interprets their formal repertoire as a true language, in which the individual architectural elements can be assembled or disassembled as desired.

The twisted column has a spiraling shaft.

The commemorative column, understood as an isolated monument supporting a statue, traces its origins to republican Rome. Its various types include the historiated, the triumphal, and the rostral column, and it can have a shaft decorated with figures.

The cochlear column, which also serves a celebrative function, is erected as an isolated element in an urban setting. Its name is derived from Trajan's Column in reference to the spiral staircase inside it (from *cochlea*, "snail shell"), and the name was later applied in general to all columns with a spiraling relief. If it bears a narrative relief, it is also referred to as being historiated.

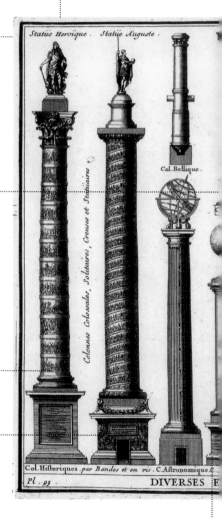

The milestone, about 150 centimeters high, was a column used to mark off miles on Roman roads.

With its purely decorative function, the baluster column is characterized by its contoured outline.

The triumphal column, which enjoyed such great popularity during the Baroque period, often bears an equestrian monument.

The marine column has a rusticated surface covered with seashells.

The rings on the so-called ring column are located at the junctures of the sections of the shaft; in addition to being decorative they are also a means of reinforcement.

The rostral column was the celebrative column from which the Romans hung the rostrums (prows) of captured enemy ships; such columns were erected on the occasion of naval victories.

Claude-Nicolas Ledoux,
Maison du Directeur,
Saline de Chaux, Arc-et-
Senans, France, 1775–79

The façade culminates in a simple
triangular pediment, framed by
dentils, that follows the slope of
the roof and encloses a smooth
tympanum with a circular window.
The entire building appears to have
been constructed by combining
elementary geometric forms.

The hexastyle
portico of the
director's house
has rusticated
columns (of late
Renaissance
derivation), used
with extreme
formal freedom.

Ledoux presents a colonnade that
is apparently of the Tuscan order,
with Attic bases resting on plinths.
The shafts of the columns are
composed of alternating smooth
and rusticated sections.

The columns are completed by a
capital with an expanded circular
echinus and a square slab of an
abacus; the Doric matrix of the
entablature is made clear in the
frieze, alternating smooth metopes
with triglyphs, and there is a
dentiled cornice.

Jain temple, Ranakpur, India, begun 1439, detail of the carved marble columns

Indian architecture makes frequent use of polygonal columns, usually decorated in the Hindu tradition, that present relief figurations very similar to lace. They are embellished by the use of marble as a construction material.

The prevailing aesthetic is the striking dynamism of the architectural mass, revealed in the linked series of different spaces defined by the forest of trabeated columns. On the architraves, statues of dancers depict the movements of the sacred devotional dance that accompanies Jain rites.

A slightly tapering shaft that bears a figural capital stands on a richly molded base. The decorative display is of unequaled richness and covers every available surface. The iconography blends floral and geometric decorations with images of Jain and Hindu divinities.

The temple, dedicated to Adinatha, has an unusual cross-shaped plan and is divided into twenty-nine rooms with different shrines and fully 1,444 columns of carved marble, each different from the next.

Capital

The capital is the building element that identifies the different architectural orders and serves as the connection between the vertical elements of the support structure (column, pillar, pilaster) and those that rest on it (architrave, arch). It is called a hanging capital when it is set against the wall to emphasize the impost of an arch or vault. In its simplest form the capital is composed of two elements with different functions: the upper part, called the abacus, with a geometric form, and the lower, called the echinus, used for decoration. The point of connection to the vertical support is called the necking.

The proportions and types of capitals remained unchanged throughout antiquity, destined to be revived and reworked during each period of classical revival. The Middle Ages were a period of fecund creativity, but the heritage of classical culture was also acknowledged, as demonstrated by the great quantity of decorative elements, especially foliate ones; the custom of reusing ancient examples (spolia) also continued until well into the late eleventh century. This period saw the full affirmation of the figural capital, with fantastic compositions that involved the mixture of zoomorphic and vegetal motif

and the introduction of new iconographic themes, some with a narrative flavor.

The systematic revival of classical culture during the Renaissance—which inspired a great deal of treatise writing—saw the classical orders revived, along with the canonical types and proportions of capitals. The Corinthian and Composite capitals became the object of the most fantastic interpretations, while the Doric was reworked over the course of the sixteenth and seventeenth centuries, finding excellent expression in Bernini's colonnade in Saint Peter's Square at the Vatican. The capital of the Baroque age was distinguished by a true explosion of decorative elements—the insertion of shields, plaques, zoomorphic protomes, masks, plant motifs—along with elements drawn from the canonical types—abacus, echinus, volute, acanthus leaves—but always with respect for codified proportions and schemes.

The nineteenth century, with its neoclassical and eclectic trends, was the last great age for the capital, which like the column itself has become detached from all reference to traditional types in the architecture of the contemporary world.

In Depth
The creation of the capital as an element autonomous from the column resulted from the technical necessity of improving the connection between the upright support and the structure being supported. The capital's privileged position in terms of visibility made it an architectural element suitable for decoration, and it was the element most subject to stylistic and symbolic variation.

Related Entries
Column; Entablature; Pillar; Pilaster Strip and Lesene; Arch

Monastery of Sant Pere de Galligants, Gerona, Spain, eleventh to twelfth century, capital in the form of a siren

Temple of Neptune,
Paestum, Salerno, Italy,
c. 460 BCE, Doric capital

The smooth architrave bears
guttae, small truncated-cone
elements beneath the tenia, the
fillet separating the architrave
from the frieze.

The Doric capital was in widespread
use as early as the sixth century BCE
and is characterized by the more or
less total absence of decorative elements. It is composed of a projecting
echinus, similar to an upside-down
truncated cone, separated from the
shaft by vigorous rings (the necking)
and topped by a square stone tablet
abacus. The Doric is found primarily in
continental Greece and in the colonies
of Magna Grecia.

In his effort to establish standards,
Vitruvius, in book 4 of *De architectura*,
identified the particular traits of the
three principal orders—Doric, Ionic,
and Corinthian—in relation to their
geographical areas of diffusion.

A necking with
annulets connects
the capital to the
column with its
sharp-edged
fluting.

Of Etruscan origin, and comparable
to the Doric capital in shape and
robustness, the Tuscan capital was
widely used in the Roman age.
It is based on the combination of
geometric elements: an echinus with
a very flat convex shape and a high
and heavy quadrangular abacus.

Temple of Apollo at
Delphi, Greece,
550–525 BCE, Ionic capital

Temple of Octavia,
Corinth, Greece,
end first century BCE,
Corinthian capital

The Ionic capital has an echinus decorated with a ring of *ovolos* topped by a strip with two corner volutes and necking decorated by astragals. The somewhat narrow abacus can bear molding or incised motifs. Being finished only frontally, it presents problems in terms of its side working; the two opposing volutes are connected by a channel that narrows at the center. There are, however, Ionic capitals with four equal faces; in such cases, the volutes are positioned diagonally. The Aeolic variant has two simple opposing volutes.

An Ionic column with fluting separated by flat listels.

The Corinthian capital is the one richest in decorative motifs. Tradition attributes its invention to the sculptor Callimachus, who was inspired by the sight of a wicker basket deposited on the tomb of a girl, around which an acanthus plant had grown.

A double row of acanthus leaves decorates the conical bell (the central part of the capital), which is also distinguished by the presence of caulcoles (the main stalks of the leaves), from which extend the inward-turning volutes and those on the corners that support the abacus. The abacus is concave and molded and is divided in half by a floral motif. This is the so-called abacus flower. This capital is very common in Hellenistic and Roman architecture.

Henri Labrouste, drawing
of the order on the
portico of the Pantheon,
Rome, *c.* 1828

Francesco Borromini,
church of San Andrea
della Fratte, Rome,
1653–65, capital

In the Baroque period Borromini
designed Composite capitals with
reversed volutes and anthropomorphic protomes in the vegetal
crown. If too much freedom is
allowed in refashioning a classical
capital, however, the process can
completely reverse the logic of the
canonical type.

The Composite
capital was a
creation of Roman
architecture, made
from a combination
of Ionic and
Corinthian ele-
ments. The central
bell, with its double
crown of acanthus
leaves, is topped by
an echinus with
ovolos of the Ionic
type. Between the
echinus and the
abacus, which is
convex and divided
by its flower, are
two large corner
volutes.

The Composite capital enjoyed
great favor, particularly during
the Flavian age, and was widely
repeated, with fantastic variations,
in later periods.

Church of San Vitale, Ravenna, Italy, begun 532, Byzantine capital

Le Corbusier, drawing of a capital at San Vitale, 1907, Fondation Le Corbusier, Paris

In the Byzantine–Ravenna area a new type of capital was created through the addition of a stone called a pulvin. It was shaped like an upside-down pyramid and set on top of the abacus of the true column so that its top became the impost of the arch. An ideal place for rich and fanciful decoration, it is here carved with a pair of birds drinking from the fountain of life.

Le Corbusier's drawing, created during a trip to Italy, faithfully reproduces one of the capitals in San Vitale and testifies to the deep impression that the decorative-sculptural solutions of Byzantine architecture made on the imagination of the great modern architect.

A true capital, with a simple geometric shape, is here enlivened by dense geometric decoration across its surface.

A revolution took place in the concept of the capital, the structural aspects of which were no longer masked by mimetic naturalistic elements. On the contrary, thanks to an abstract geometric language, the capital assumed a central role in the system of thrusts and counter-thrusts that support a vault.

The use of the pulvin prepared the way for the cube-shaped capital with rounded corners at the point of connection to the column—a type that led directly to its use in the complex medieval world, in the Ottonian and late Romanesque periods.

Abbey of Cluny,
France, c. 1110–20,
figural capital

In the fervid religious and cultural climate of Europe during the eleventh through thirteenth centuries, the figural capital assumed a position of central importance as one of the many elements of church architecture that could embody important and complex iconographic cycles.

The recurrent themes of such cycles were scenes from the Old and New Testaments: the lives of saints, parables, and legends were presented to make use of the instructional and persuasive power of the image; particularly rich in this regard were Spain, Italy, and certain areas of France, including Burgundy.

The musical capitals from the choir of the church of the abbey of Cluny, illustrating the tonalities of Gregorian chant, reveal particular refinement and compositional freedom. A mandorla appears against a classical-style background of acanthus leaves bearing the inscription TERTIUS IMPINGIT CHRISTUMQUE RESURGERE FINGIT ("The third strikes and represents the resurrection of Christ"). Within the mandorla is a personification of a Gregorian tone, a young man playing the psaltery.

The figure of the musician emerges with great sculptural clarity against the background. The other three faces of the capital bear other musical personifications: a lute player, a dancer beating a small drum, a young man ringing chime bells. In this way the capital, at least visually, abandons its structural function, and is transfigured by its strongly symbolic decoration.

Saint Augustine's *De musica* was a strong influence throughout the Middle Ages, and it defined the musical art as the "science of proper modulation," meaning the arrangement of the musical units following a strict formula expressed in mathematical relationships, first among them the interval of the perfect fourth.

Georg Gottlob
Ungewitter, studies of
capitals, from *Lehrbuch
der gothischen
Konstruktionen* (Manual
of Gothic construction),
Leipzig, 1859–64

In the Gothic period, especially within
the sphere of monastic architecture,
the exuberance of the Romanesque
made room for the creation of works
distinguished by greater formal simpli-
fication, as discernable in the type called
the crocket capital, decorated with
stylized leaves with tips folded over
in the form of hooks or bulbs.

The broad range of
the Gothic capital
was by no means
limited to the
crocket type;
examples were still
being produced that
involved the use of
figural elements,
along with those
with fanciful
combinations of
naturalistic leafy
elements derived
from the Corinthian.

The so-called Gothic flora, which
began taking shape in Île-de-France
in the middle of the twelfth century,
reflected a desire to imitate nature.
The result was perfectly naturalistic
leaves, as pliable and soft as those in
nature. This was only one of a vast
variety of details used to serve the
monumental decorative demands
of the great cathedrals.

Around the
years 1230–40, the
crocket capital
was composed of
three flowers.

Temple of Horus, Edfu,
Egypt, 237–57 BCE,
plant-shaped capitals
in a detail of the portico

The columns and capitals of the
portico of the temple of Horus support
a smooth entablature with torus and
cyma molding. Between the capital
and the architrave is a somewhat
heavy quadrangular stone abacus.

The column with
a palm-shaped
capital refers
back to ancient
structural and
symbolic customs:
the shaft ends with
a ligature on which
rests a capital,
imitating a bundle
of palm branches
with their ends
rounded and
curved outward.
It recalls the poles
decorated with
palm branches that
were stuck into the
ground to mark off
the precincts of
ancient funeral
ceremonies.

The columns and
capitals of Egyptian
architecture repeat
in stone the vegetal
forms typical of the
region; bundles of
palm leaves,
papyrus plants, or
lotus flowers rest
on circular bases
joined to the base
of the capital, which
in turn imitates the
shape of the flower,
with a prismatic
abacus making the
connection. The
motif of bundles of
plants used as a
support element
harks back to pre-
historic building
methods.

In monumental
architecture, plant-
shaped columns
constitute the most
widespread shape
of support: the
papyriform
columns with
capitals depict
the open calyx of
the flower that is
the heraldic plant
of Upper Egypt.

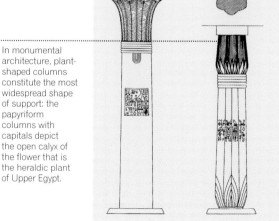

The lotus-shaped
column presents a
bundle of six
stylized stalks. The
capital is shaped
like a flower com-
posed of six calyxes,
slightly open, and
is topped by a
heavy abacus;
between the shaft
and the echinus
are six small steles
with buds. In
Egyptian mythology
the lotus is tied
to the figure of the
sun god, who
rose from the
primordial waters
on a lotus flower.

Fatehpur Sikri,
near Agr, India,
c. 1571–85, Hall of
Private Audience,
capital of the
central column

The Hall of Private Audience, also
known as the House of the Jewel, is
distinguished by a splendid central
column that bears the throne on
which the emperor sat. The enormous
capital that supports the circular
platform is finely carved with typical
Hindu symbols, such as lotus flowers,
elephant trunks, and geometric
designs of an Islamic flavor.

The powerful artistic appeal is
highlighted by the use of red
sandstone, worked with great precision
and lightness in a sophisticated
technique based on
the local woodworking traditions.

The connection to the shaft of
the column, which is very thin
compared to the capital above it,
is less pronounced by means
of an expanded neck.

This trilithic structure is joined to the
second floor of the palace by aerial
stone footbridges with balusters
decorated with lacelike piercing.

Entablature

The entablature, or trabeation, is the horizontal element in the trilithic system (post-and-lintel system), composed of two vertical members that support a third horizontal member. This third member bears the weight of the structures above it, transmitting that weight to the vertical bearing elements (columns or pillars). The entablature is composed of the architrave, frieze, and cornice. It can be made of a variety of materials, from the most elastic, such as wood, iron, or reinforced concrete, to the most rigid, such as ashlars.

The architrave is the lowest part of the entablature, positioned over the opening between the uprights. In classical architecture the entablature became a distinguishing element of the architectural order; precise laws of proportion established its harmonious relationship to the diameter of the column and the distance between the columns. In the Doric order the architrave is smooth, with small guttae below the projecting strip of the crowning; in the Ionic, and thus in the Corinthian and the Composite, it is divided into a series of strips that increasingly project outward.

The frieze is located between the architrave and the cornice; in the Doric order it is composed of metopes and triglyphs; in the Ionic, of a continuous strip called the zophorus. The term *cornice*, which dates to the fourteenth century, indicates the projecting strip of molding above the frieze and thus the conclusive element. Molding forms the outlines of the connections among the elements. If it is convex and half-round in profile it is called astragal; if it is concave with a curve like a quarter circle it is cavetto; if it is composed of a double-curve shaped like an inverted S it is called cyma (also ogee).

Origins
The trilithic system originated in primitive megalithic dolmens.

In Depth
In the Christian age the entablature often bore inscriptions that emphasized the symbolic aspect of Christ as a "door" or as "he who bears the weight."

Related Entries
Column; Capital; Pilaster Strip and Lesene

Dolmen of Fontanaccia at Cauria, Corsica, 2500–1800 BCE

Temple of Amun, Karnak, Thebes, Egypt, 1530–323 BCE, detail of the columns and entablature of the hypostyle hall

The trilithic system assumed monumental forms in Egyptian architecture: the height of the central columns with the architraves, constructed of hewn ashlars that were later decorated, reached 23 meters.

In temples and tombs the architrave symbolizes eternal creation.

The hypostyle hall, with its 134 colossal papyriform columns, is one of the most famous sites of Egyptian architecture. The two central rows, each with six columns, are higher by a third than the others and constitute a sort of access portico to the temple.

Giulio Romano,
Palazzo Te, Mantua,
Italy, c. 1524–35,
detail of the Doric
entablature of the
courtyard

Parthenon, Athens,
447–438 BCE, detail
of the pediment with
Doric frieze

The cornice includes a projecting upper
part decorated along its
inside face with square blocks
called mutules.

Giulio Romano's Palazzo Te is a
fascinating work that was significant
for the cultural climate of its time.
It is an entertaining and astonishing
theatrical structure, with themes based
on the dialectic between the irrationality
of nature and the rationality of humans
as artificers. The Doric entablature of
the court includes triglyphs that slide
out of place, alluding to an unstable
structure but also to the possibility
of varying established schemes,
to a freedom from the classical
rules that nonetheless were still a
language so vital that they could
be continuously reinvented.

In the case of the orders set into
a wall—supported by engaged columns
or semicolumns—the entablature is
composed not of blocks but of slabs of
dressing of various thicknesses applied
to the wall that repeat the standard
divisions and decorations, but that
perform no real support function.

The entablature here assumes a
conspicuously decorative aspect and is
free to have a more articulated
structure; in such cases it is called
a projecting entablature.

Above the entablature is the tympanum, the triangular surface enclosed in the molding of the cornice, the uppermost ridges of which are called the cyma. In the case of the Parthenon the tympanum is decorated with sculptures.

The frieze is composed of an alternation of metopes and triglyphs. The metopes are the open areas between the triglyphs. They can be left smooth, carved, or even be painted; they were originally a way of filling in the open spaces between the beams supporting the roof.

The triglyph is a square stone block bearing three vertical grooves or flutes; Vitruvius calls the smooth part between the grooves the femur. He gives very precise information on the ideal size of triglyphs, which he thought originated as the ends of wooden support beams.

The Doric entablature is composed of a smooth architrave with small guttae below the tenia.

Andrea Palladio,
outline of the upper
external entablature of
the Hadrianeum, Rome,
detail of the architrave,
1545–47, Museo Civico,
Vicenza

In its version of the classical orders,
Roman architecture adorned the
architrave with a great wealth
of decoration and carving.

In the imperial age the entablature
often included strips separated by
smooth or decorated molding in
proportions that tended to vary
according to the style of the period.

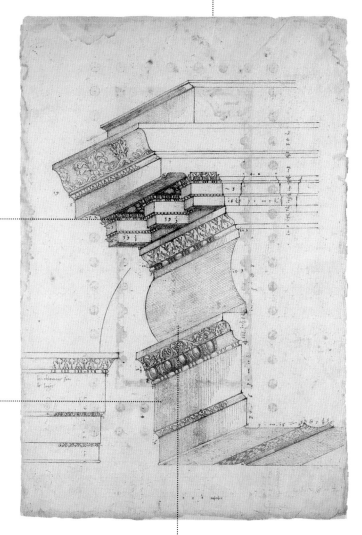

The cornice is
decorated with
dentils and
strips of vegetal
ornamentation.

The architrave is
divided into strips
that progressively
project outward;
its crown is
composed of a
smooth fillet
topped by a
reverse cyma
molding decorated
with an Ionic
egg-and-dart
cymatium.

The continuous
frieze has a
convex shape.

Balthasar Neumann,
church of Neresheim,
Germany, 1745–92,
detail of the broken
entablature

Late Baroque architecture witnessed a continuously changing array of structural combinations. For example, the pairs of freestanding columns in the church of Neresheim support an entablature with distinct outlines, free of decoration but with an almost neoclassical sensibility.

This is combined with the extreme dynamism of its curved concave-convex outline, which matches the shape of the wall. By wrapping around the column, the entablature not only serves as its top but also becomes the vertical support member, with significant structural value.

The plan—composed of a series of transverse oval spaces covered by domes that are connected dynamically—is expressed by the line of the cornices, which curve or break at the sites of structural junctions.

Pillar

The pillar is an architectural and structural element that provides vertical support, sometimes including a base and capital. Although substantially preserving the shape of a symmetrical solid, it can take on different appearances through the combination of geometric forms and can be monolithic or composed of a series of blocks. Its function is similar to that of the column, but it can support greater amounts of compression.

The use of materials like steel and reinforced concrete—far more resistant to compression and most of all to tensile stresses—rather than stone or brick makes possible very interesting structural creations that once would have been unthinkable. Steel pillars are usually composed of metallic sections joined by stiffening cross brackets—steel plates arranged perpendicularly to the axis of the pillar—which are bolted, riveted, or soldered to the sections and are usually prefabricated. Reinforced-concrete pillars are made by incorporating a metallic armature into concrete poured into a mold made of various materials—for example, wood or metal—that is called a formwork. The armature is composed of reinforcing rods, arranged longitudinally and united by

transverse bars, that extend up to about 3 centimeters from the external surface of the pillar and that run parallel to the axis of the pillar to provide structural continuity. Sometimes pillars are made with a circular or octagonal section in which the vertical armature is tied to a continuous spiral from the base to the top; this increases the pillar's strength by working against transverse stress.

Origin of the Term
The term *pillar* is derived from the Latin *pila*. As an architectural element, the pillar has been in use since the earliest recorded architecture.

Related Entries
Capital; Entablature

Pier Luigi Nervi, Palazzo del Lavoro, Turin, Italy, 1960–61, detail of a mushroom pillar

Robert de Luzarches, Cathedral of Amiens, France, begun 1220, nave with compound piers

The plasticity of the compound pier, which permits the central column to rise to the vault without interruption, accentuates the sense of verticality and speeds the compositional rhythm.

The column loses its formal and structural autonomy to integrate, by way of engaged semicolumns, with the pillar; it serves the structural function of transferring downward the thrusts of the vault. In later, more elaborate Gothic architecture this takes place without any intermediate elements like cornices and capitals, thus creating a visual structural unity between supports and vaults.

The compound or clustered pier is a complex unit composed of distinct construction elements joined in a single body and shaped in accordance with the element it is designed to support. This type of support element is at the base of the so-called active-resistance system, the construction system in which the rigorous play of thrusts and counterthrusts permitted Gothic builders to compose a thin and graceful support skeleton with wonderful results.

Donato Bramante,
plan for the basilica of
Saint Peter's, 1505–06.
Uffizi, Florence

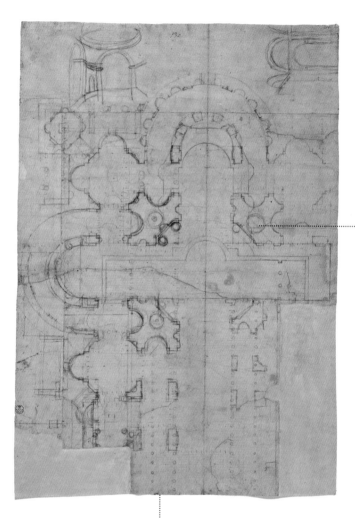

The four enormous pillars of the transept of the basilica of Saint Peter's have a mixtilinear outline designed to bear the arches supporting the dome. Their size is such that in 1628–40 Gian Lorenzo Bernini opened niches in them large enough to hold colossal statues. They were further enriched with the loggias for reliquaries, framed by the twisted columns of the ancient Constantinian *pergula*.

Bramante assembled his symbolic and liturgical design on the basis of ideas drawn from earlier buildings and research into the spatial values of regular geometric bodies, thus confirming that the Renaissance artists' use of the central plan was not merely the application of a preferred aesthetic but the result of research, at once theoretical and formal.

No other building comes close to Saint Peter's in the presentation of the idea of the centrality and universality of the church, translated in the visible forms of celestial Jerusalem.

Lorenzo Mattielli, telamons in the atrium of the Upper Belvedere, Vienna, 1721–22

The telamons support a complex entablature unrelated to the classical orders, that is in turn supporting a vault carved with the arms, armor, and exploits of the family of the patron, Prince Eugene of Savoy.

In the Baroque age the pillar was often so radically transformed that it seemed to lose its structural function in the exaltation of its aesthetic potential. The ground floor of the Upper Belvedere is decorated by these powerful telamons, male figures of super-human size carved out of marble that support the ceiling vaults.

The figure of the telamon is based on the Titan Atlas from Greek mythology, condemned to support the vault of the sky; the telamons are designed to visually express the exertion to which Atlas was subjected. According to Vitruvius, a telamon should symbolize defeated enemies, for which reason the telamons in eighteenth-century Baroque residences in Austria were often given Turkish features.

The telamons in the Belvedere rest on high plinths with moldings and decorations.

Peter Behrens, AEG
Turbine Factory, Berlin,
1909, detail of steel
pillars

The sides of the building, erected as
a plant for the production of turbines,
are marked off by regularly spaced
steel pillars that taper groundward
and support, along with the corner
pylons of masonry, the weight of
the iron and glass structure.

Pillars serve
the static function
of providing
vertical support for
the weight and
thrust transmitted
by horizontal
structures.
Pillars undergo
compression and
are also subject
to flexing tension
because of the
limited size
of their section
in relation to
their height.

The terminus of the pillar, a joint in
riveted steel designed to direct the
thrust to the base of reinforced
concrete, is hinged to a metal mount.

Le Corbusier,
Villa Savoye, Poissy,
France, 1928–31

Reliance on a very strong material
such as reinforced concrete makes
possible the visual contradiction
between the thin supports and
the body of the villa.

The use of a similar structure
inside permits the absence of
bearing walls, also allowing for the
open façade and the use of large
ribbon windows.

For Le Corbusier it is not possible
to separate the support elements of
a building from those that do not
support; for this reason, in place of the
old-fashioned base on which the walls
rested, reinforced concrete permits
the use of a small base, with thin
pillars, called pilotis, taking the place
of walls. They lift the house off the
ground, freeing it from the dampness
of the earth and increasing its
access to light and air.

Borrowed from the ancient
construction method of pilework,
pilotis are made of reinforced
concrete with a circular section.
They open up the ground floor and
make it usable; the area gained
can become part of the garden,
as is also the case with the house's
roof terrace.

Eugène-Emmanuel Viollet-le-Duc, market roof supported by iron pillars, from *Entretiens sur l'architecture*, Paris, 1863–72

Richard Rogers, Terminal 4 of Barajas Airport, Madrid, 2005

Over the course of the nineteenth century iron replaced stone as a support for roofs, an idea drawn from the principle of the elastic skeleton in Gothic constructions.

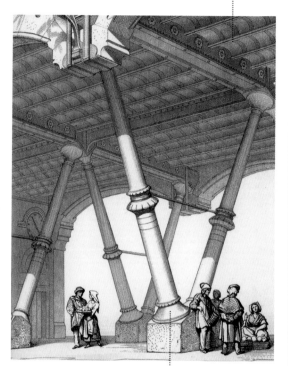

The engraving illustrates a structure free of decoration, simple and functional; the powerful inclined pillars, connected at the middle and set in cement bases that collect the downward thrust, support simple horizontal beams on which the undulating roof rests.

Almost 130 years later Richard Rogers applied similar structures in the design of inclined steel pillars, branching out from bases of reinforced cement, in a terminal at the Barajas Airport. The pillars support an airy, undulating roof of steel beams clad in bamboo strips.

Receiving light from large circular skylights, the roof creates a transparent expanded space that exploits sunlight: in fact, the 1-kilometer-long terminal has no need for artificial lighting during the day. The pillars vary in color, a feature that enlivens the impressive length of the terminal.

Inclined pillars are often used in modern and contemporary architecture, from the works of Gaudí to the Car Park and Terminus in Strasbourg by Zaha Hadid.

Santiago Calatrava,
Gare do Oriente,
Lisbon, 1998

For the roof of the Lisbon transportation hub, Calatrava adopted steel "tree" pillars similar in shape to palms. The pillars become trunks that bifurcate into the branches that support the roof, forming a forest-like structure.

Attentive to the most unusual forms drawn from the natural environment, Calatrava infuses his works with a highly personal style, blending architecture and engineering in a seamless unity.

The use of tree pillars recurs periodically in the history of architecture, showing up in many projects that draw inspiration from natural forms. The idea of a pillar designed to resemble a tree can be found in the works of Gaudí and of Victor Horta, as well as in the airports at Stansted and Stuttgart.

Charles Lavigne,
Normandy Bridge,
Honfleur–Le Havre,
France, 1995

The decision was made to erect a cable-stayed bridge because such a structure is more resistant to wind than a suspension bridge. The cables are centrally supported by two enormous pylons made of prestressed reinforced concrete, with steel caissons enclosed in the concrete at the heads to provide rigidity.

The metallic sections are each composed of two beams and a series of vertical prefabricated diaphragms inserted into the panels that form the ribs, which absorb the vibrations and provide an anchorage for the stays.

The pillars look like a pair of compasses open to form an A, supported by two legs under which the traffic moves and that transmit the thrusts to the base. They are joined at the top to form a single supporting anchorage that is 210 meters high and 50 meters wide at the base.

To avoid a high number of supports (which would have interfered with navigation along the Seine), the Normandy Bridge is a cable-stayed bridge with central supports and a span of no less than 856 meters.

Akashi-Kaikyo Bridge,
Honshu–Shikoku,
Japan, 1998

The large steel towers, about 283 meters high and 35.5 meters wide at the top, were put together using elements about 7 meters in length. They support the bridge deck, which in turn is composed of three spans of diagonal reticular beams with parallel reinforcements that are intended to reduce the spacing of the truss girder system; the latter is 14 meters high with hinged elements.

With its six-lane deck and roadway, the bridge is currently the longest suspension bridge in the world: its total length is 3,911 meters, of which the central span accounts for 1,991 meters.

The structure of the bridge—which is located in a seismically active area that is also subject to typhoons—proved its great strength even while it was still under construction: it suffered only slight damage from the 1995 Kobe earthquake.

The bridge has a three-span, two-hinged stiffening girder system. Its construction necessitated several improvements in steel strength, including the development of a new kind of cable wire that improved safety. The bridge's corrosion-protection system is unique and incorporates a dehumidifying system to reduce moisture.

Pilaster Strip and Lesene

The pilaster strip is a vertical structural element: a half-column or half-pillar set into and projecting from a wall. It serves a support function and follows the decorative scheme already seen in columns and piers, with a base, capital, entablature, fluting, and whatever else distinguishes the various architectural orders.

The pilaster strip is sometimes confused with the lesene, which instead serves an exclusively decorative function. Thus the distinction between the two is made on the basis not of morphology but of function.

Within the complex of the Medici church of San Lorenzo at Florence, Michelangelo used lesenes to serve three-dimensional and chromatic purposes. All the rooms in the complex, including the beautiful reading room of the library, are marked off by strong frameworks around niches, windows, and mirrors. The architectural forms in pietra serena stand out against the pale walls; the walls themselves are treated as sculptural surfaces, animated by continuous projections and entrances.

Origin of the Terms
Pilaster is derived from the Italian *pilastro*, which in turn comes from the Latin for pillar. *Lesene* is probably derived from the medieval Latin *lauxema*, in turn originating from the Greek *lauxema*, meaning "work in stone."

Related Entries
Wall; Capital; Entablature

Michelangelo, Laurentian Library, Florence, begun 1524, reading room

Buttress

The buttress is a vertical building element used to reinforce a structure by absorbing some of the thrust it is receiving. Usually located on the exterior of a building, a buttress can also be built inside a wall—most especially in military works and fortifications—to confer greater strength. The buttress assumes particular importance as the support for a simple or complex vault, since vaults involve thrusts concentrated on the points of stress instead of being distributed along perimeter walls.

In Roman architecture buttresses are most often placed inside buildings. During the Romanesque period there was a growing tendency to put them outside, as the principle of inert stability—so-called passive resistance—gave way to the principle of the balance of thrusts. In that period the buttress sometimes took the shape of a semicolumn. More often it had a quadrangular section and took the form of a thickening of the wall at a point where thrusts were concentrated.

In the skeletal structure of Gothic architecture, the thrusts of groin vaults were often supported by external buttresses extended upward with pinnacles, in keeping with the theory that additional loads should be concentrated on supports that were separate but joined and transversally strengthened, but without the need for a continuous wall to unite them. In the Gothic balance of thrusts, the buttress served a preeminent role, making it possible to replace perimeter walls with large expanses of stained glass windows.

Buttresses assumed different shapes in later centuries, in keeping with changing architectural typologies. Thus they range from the side chapels of sixteenth-century hall churches to the great eighteenth-century volutes of Longhena's church of Santa Maria della Salute at Venice to the oblique buttress-like supports beneath the upper section of the Torre Velasca in Milan.

Related Entries
Wall; Vault; Façade

Baldassare Longhena, church of Santa Maria della Salute, Venice, 1631, external buttressing of the dome

Cathedral of Palma de
Mallorca, Spain, begun
1306, south side

Seen from the sea, the cathedral rises
like a sort of containment wall for the
urban fabric behind it. On the south
side the static construction scheme
is based on a system of buttresses
and double rampant arches with the
addition of masonry walls arranged
at right angles to the axis of the main
body. This system, frequently found
in Gothic cathedrals, lightens the
masses of the walls while absorbing
the lateral thrusts of the vaults.

The unitary archi-
tectural mass of the
south side looks
something like a
fortified structure
overlooking the sea.

A second lower row of buttresses
runs along at the level of the side
chapels; these are prolonged upward
by reinforcing towers. The static
arrangement seems to follow the
well-known methods of French
Gothic architecture, but the dense
series of walls of the buttresses on
the lower level is transformed into
a single massive stone wall grooved
by lines of shadow, with dramatic
visual results.

Arch

The arch is an architectural structure used to span an opening; it is composed of separate units called voussoirs arranged along a curved surface and given stability by mutual pressure. Made of stone or brick, wedge shaped or rectangular, joined by a binder or not, the voussoirs rest on two uprights and fulfill their function through compression: they are directed toward the center of the curve, exercising lateral thrust.

With its ends located at the two points that flank the opening and receive the thrusts, an arch makes it possible to span large spaces with an agility unknown to the lintel or architrave, enabling the creation of architectural effects of particular grandeur. Together with and in opposition to the beam, the arch is one of the most important static figures because of the multiplicity of its applications. Its stability depends directly on the curve of the thrusts, that is, the distribution of thrusts on every transverse section of the arch and on the uprights.

In its two-dimensional form the arch is used to make openings in walls; however, it is also used at the base of the three-dimensional structures of vaults and domes, which are obtained geometrically by the translation or rotation of an arch.

The applications of the arch are vast and various, from spanning doors and windows to major city-planning and infrastructural functions, as in the architecture of bridges and aqueducts—not to overlook the typically medieval decorative function served by arches, arcades, and blind arches.

Construction of an arch requires the use of a temporary framework (centering) usually made of wooden or steel elements connected to one another to give form and support to the structure.

The arch has been known since antiquity, although its function was not always fully exploited, except in the Mesopotamian and Indian worlds. Although Greek architecture remained faithful, for the most part, to the post-and-lintel system, Roman architecture made systematic and original use of the arch, applied in technically innovative and daring structures with great monumental value. During the Middle Ages new forms were spread by Arabic culture and became widespread, reaching their apex in Gothic architecture. Used widely throughout the Western world until the nineteenth century, the arch has lost its structural preeminence in contemporary architecture because of the availability of new building materials and techniques, and today its applications are purely aesthetic.

In Depth

From the Latin *arcus*, the arch was the outstanding theme of an architecture based on support structures for a period of some three thousand years. Today, with the advent of such new materials as steel and the evolution of building techniques, the arch is no longer a necessity; it is used instead to give expression to walls and bring them to more human scale.

Related Entries
Wall; Vault; Dome; Architectural Gilding

Roman aqueduct, Segovia, Spain, first century, detail of the sequence of round arches

Defining the component parts of an arch

The two parallel faces of the arch are the archivolts.

The keystone is the top of the intrados and often coincides with the central voussoir, which, because of the force of gravity, pushes to the sides, lending stability to the arch.

The voussoirs are the elements arranged along the curved surface; those closest to the impost are called springers.

The curved inner surface is called the intrados or soffit; the external surface, the extrados. The distance between the two is the arch's width. The orthogonal projection of the curved inner surface is called the curve.

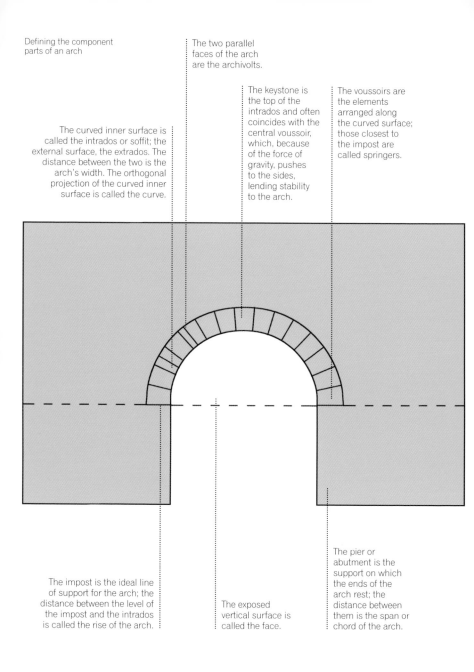

The impost is the ideal line of support for the arch; the distance between the level of the impost and the intrados is called the rise of the arch.

The exposed vertical surface is called the face.

The pier or abutment is the support on which the ends of the arch rest; the distance between them is the span or chord of the arch.

Types of arches

Every static arrangement calls for a different shape of arch, so in addition to any aesthetic or stylistic value, an arch also serves a precise structural function. The main types of arches are produced by beginning with a circle or other curve whose path very rarely corresponds to the actual direction of the thrusts.

The pointed or equilateral arch is produced from the intersection of two curves that meet to form a point at the keystone and whose centers lie along the same impost line. Given equal-size spans and equal weight, this solution has the advantage of putting less horizontal thrust on the imposts.

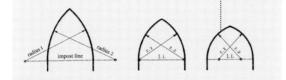

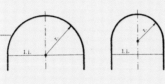

The round arch is produced when the curve of the intrados forms a semicircumference whose span corresponds to the diameter from the center of the imposts. The simplest arch, it is a distinguishing characteristic of Roman architecture; commonly used in the Romanesque period, chiefly for its aesthetics, it was revived in the Italian Renaissance and in the Neoclassical age.

The segmented or depressed arch is produced when the curve of the intrados is part of a semicircumference. More rational from the static point of view, more economical, and less difficult, it was adopted after the tenth century, most of all in the construction of bridges. If the uprights continue past the impost line, it is said to be raised.

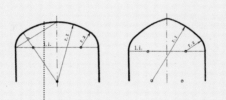

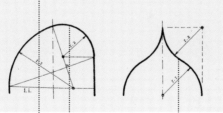

The elliptical arch has several centers of curvature and is composed of the juncture of several arches, creating an elliptical outline that does not correspond to the geometry of its generation. The Tudor arch is a polycentric depressed arch composed of four arches with different radii, two of which curve upward to form a point at the keystone. It is typical of English architecture of the fifteenth through seventeenth centuries.

The rampant arch has an asymmetrical shape and is used for counterthrust; it is typical of Gothic architecture.

The ogee arch is produced by four shanks of arches; the centers of curvature of two are inside the arch, and two lie outside the face of the arch, one convex and the other concave. Its opposite in terms of concavity/convexity is the Flamboyant arch.

Filippo Brunelleschi,
church of Santo Spirito,
Florence, begun 1444,
interior

The aesthetic value of the round arch,
joined to the grammar of the architrave
system, was revived during the Italian
Renaissance, most of all by Filippo
Brunelleschi, who was able to bring
innovation and evolution to the
architectural role of the arch.

Roman architecture was the first to give
deep significance to the round arch—
typologically the simplest type of arch,
and one valued from the beginning for
its practicality—developing it to its full
aesthetic sense. To emphasize the
compositional rhythm of buildings,
Roman architects invented the
architectural motif—later to become
symbolic of Renaissance architecture—
of the round arch inserted into the
pilaster-entablature system. This formal
invention probably owes its origin to
a structural necessity, given the fact
that, when working primarily in brick, the
construction of arches was more
economical than reliance on the
trilithic system.

Brunelleschi repeats this solution in Santo Spirito, making a
splendid colonnade of round
arches. The rational and easily
understandable division of the
space and its surfaces leads to
a rebirth of the architectural
orders, proposing once again their
characteristic shapes and sizes.

Cathedral of Wells, Great Britain, c. 1338, strainer arches of the crossing tower

This solution brings to church architecture a building technique common in civil architecture—mostly in the construction of bridges—with new formal results, obtained through the introduction of curves. That introduction was to characterize much of English production, not only in the late Gothic period.

The base of the great crossing tower of the Cathedral of Wells presents an unusual stone support system consisting of two enormous molded strainer arches inserted between the walls of the nave, one pointing up, the other down. Two oculi are inserted into the resulting side spaces.

Cathedral of Chartres,
France, 1194–1221,
detail of rampant arches

The rampant arch is an asymmetrical architectural element used to contain and direct downward the lateral thrusts of the upper parts of a building; to that end the impost line on the buttress is located lower than the impost line on the wall.

The rampant arch plays an essential role in the aesthetic-formal definition of the "skeletal system" of Gothic architecture, contributing to its elevation.

The use of rampant arches, built over the aisle roofs to better absorb the thrusts, made possible the elimination of internal tribunes, thus unifying the elevation and raising the roofs to heights of up to 40 meters.

The design of the rampant arches—with the weight of the vaults passed along double arches joined by arcades of round arches on short columns—reflects the size of the double ambulatories. The third, thinner arch may be a later addition to better balance the upper area of the walls.

Basilica of Saint Mark's, Venice, 1063–94, detail of the façade with composite arch

The crowning part of the façade of the basilica of Saint Mark's includes a series of complex arches created by inserting a round arch with a finely carved archivolt inside an ogee arch that bears a row of statues and ornamental motifs, like pinnacles, along its extrados.

This arrangement is a hybrid between the cathedral's original Byzantine and Romanesque forms and the more fanciful expressions of Venetian Gothic; the area of the face between the round arch and the ogee is decorated with a starry sky; standing atop the extrados is a statue of the lion of Saint Mark.

Peter Parler, cathedral
of Saint Vitus, Prague,
Golden Gate, 1367, detail
of the vestibule with
flying ribs

In the south porch of the cathedral
of Saint Vitus at Prague is the portal
called the Golden Gate; in the
vestibule Parler used the English
solution of flying ribs, further
complicated by the ribbing of the
portal, which spread outward with
three interaxes and inward with two,
a result of the creation of the
contiguous Wenceslaus Chapel.

The flying rib does not necessarily
follow the curve of an arch and is
instead shaped independently; it is
not even part of the wall. There is a
clear difference between the ribs set
into the wall and into the vaults and
those that lift off the pillar.

King's College Chapel, Cambridge, Great Britain, 1508–15, fan vaulting of the bays

The fan vaults, and thus the upward movement of the bays, are produced through the translation of a depressed four-centered arch. This shape makes possible great technical and formal expression through the clear articulation of the structure.

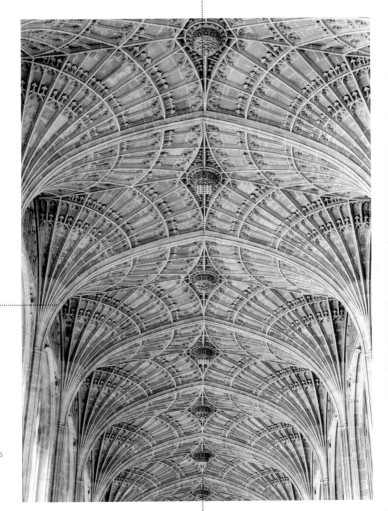

The chapel of King's College, Cambridge, has very high walls completely filled with broad surfaces of glass. The structure's verticality is accentuated by thin columns that lead the eye upward to the vault and its series of fan vaults.

The depressed four-centered arch is typical of English architecture of the late Gothic period.

Juan Guas, San Juan de
los Reyes, Toledo, Spain,
1479–80, detail of the
cloister

The complication of the arch is typical
of Spanish Isabelline architecture,
which drew forms from the late
Gothic and merged them with typological, functional, and linguistic
elements from the local Mudéjar
tradition, along with adaptations
of Renaissance styles.

The upper level
of the loggia of the
cloister of San Juan
de los Reyes has an
elegant series of
arches, aesthetically
and formally
delineated by their
overlapping lines.
On the uprights is a
complex arch
created from the
presence of convex
and concave edges
at the top, with
a molded and
lobed intrados.

The cloister is notable for its
rich decoration of piers and
buttresses, culminating in
feathery pinnacles.

Antoni Gaudí, Casa Milà, called La Pedrera, Barcelona, 1905–7, detail of the mansard with parabolic arches

Lover of the curving line as a generator of forms, Gaudí introduced the parabolic arch to modern architecture. His work is distinguished by the elaboration of extraordinary and unpredictable forms, made from the most varied materials, from which he drew the maximum possible expression.

Gaudí used the parabolic arch as an element of a truly plastic architecture; in the convexities and curvatures of the arch, light creates surprising chiaroscuro effects.

The parabolic arch is extremely rational from the static point of view, generated as it is by the translation of a parabola. Widely used in contemporary architecture, it represents the most recent innovation of one of the most ancient architectural elements.

Mosque of Cordoba,
Spain, prayer hall,
987–88

Inside the mosque is a hall with more than
850 columns made of marble and granite
that rework the shape of provincial
Roman columns, with smooth monolithic shafts and Composite capitals.

The considerable height of the
ceilings, about 13 meters, resulted in
a double row of arches. The lower
horseshoe arches serve as tie beams,
and above them are round arches, all
of them supported by a column or by
the pier atop the column, thus
repeating a system the Romans used
in the construction of aqueducts.

The Moresque or horseshoe arch is
produced when the angle of the arch
is created by one or more curves with
the center above the impost line of
the arch itself; it narrows downward,
ideally following the curvature of
the circumference. Here it is given
particular clarity through the use
of two colors in the voussoirs,
alternating white and red.

The horseshoe arch is typical of
Islamic architecture but is also often
used in Gothic architecture and
in Art Nouveau.

Red Fort, Agra, India,
1627, Hall of Public
Audience (Diwan-i-Am)

An arch is called polylobate when
the intrados is composed of a series
of equal intersecting lobes; in this
case the keystone has countercurves
that form a small inflected arch, while
the dynamic profile is emphasized
by a darker line.

The Diwan-i-Am is the Hall of Public
Audience. It consists of a large
hypostyle loggia on three rows of
polygonal marble columns with
carved capitals. Resting on these
are arches whose curves are
embellished by nine lobes, the
apical one being polycentric.

The royal loggia
on the west side is
enclosed by *jali*,
finely carved
stone screens.

The many-lobed arch
is very common in
Mogul architecture,
which unites local
forms with those of
Islamic art.

Roof Covering

The roof is that part of a building arranged to upwardly limit the internal space and to protect it from atmospheric agents. In architecture it is defined as an upper horizontal boundary. It is composed of a bearing structure that supports an impermeable mantle, called a covering mantle, which can be made from a variety of materials, from tiles to metallic panels, from synthetic resins to sheets of stone or glass. The covering should provide protection, impermeability, thermal and acoustic insulation, and structural stability; it should deflect rainwater and, not the least, present an aesthetically pleasing exterior.

The most traditional form of roof is composed of one or more inclined planes, whose pitch is based on the climatic conditions of the site and local traditions. Even so-called flat roofs have a slight inclination, about 1 to 2 percent, to permit the drainage of water. The planes that compose a sloping roof can be continuous or discontinuous; the first are true attics, inclined according to the angle of the roof; the second are composed of a main framework in wood or steel with a triangular section to provide rigidity and a secondary framework above it that constitutes the true roof. The principal roof structure is composed of inclined diagonal beams, called rafters, which are subject to combined compressive and bending stress; horizontal transverse beams, subject to traction; horizontal joists; a central vertical, called the queen post or truss post, joined to the beams; and two braces at an angle opposed to the rafters that connect to the beams, also subject to flexing tension.

In Depth
The oldest roof shape is the pitched roof, which has remained functionally unchanged from the primitive hut to today. In Neolithic villages structures were covered with roofs or cones to rapidly deflect precipitation, and for this reason the angle of roofs varies according to the local climate.

Basilica of Santa Croce, Florence, begun 1295, ceiling of the nave with wooden trusses

Westminster Palace,
London, Hall of Richard II,
1377–99

The Hall of Richard II is covered by
a complex wooden structure whose
construction recalls shipbuilding
techniques and uses rafters in the
shape of pointed arches more for
decorative than for structural reasons,
although in place of the tie beams
there are hammerbeams.

The master carpenter Hugh Harland
made use of hammerbeams—
projecting brackets connected to
vertical members called hammer
posts—with sculptural embellishment in the lunettes and at
the ends of the beams.

As complex and articulated as the
carpentry is, it seems to present itself
as an autonomous structure, not
related to the areas beneath it—an
additional element not architecturally
integrated with the whole.

Despite the impressive three-
dimensional impact of the structural
elements and the organic articulation
of the supports, which intersect in
a complex system of beams, the
result does not succeed in overcoming the discontinuity among the
architectural structures.

Ludwig Mies van
der Rohe, Neue
Nationalgalerie, Berlin,
1962–67

The Neue Nationalgalerie, a glass-and-steel box, has a flat roof structure, a square that is almost 65 meters across, constructed of a grid framework composed of thin steel double-T beams with a height of 1.8 meters.

With such high beams, the roof grid provides rigidity to the entire structure and makes it possible for the roof to be supported at the sides, leaving the corners free.

The roof framework is supported by eight slightly tapering steel pillars with the typical cruciform cross section, located two on a side and with none at the corners.

Despite the weight of its roof, nearly 2 meters thick, the Neue Nationalgalerie seems incredibly "light" thanks to the use of glass, to the tendency to see structures in steel essentially as skeletons, and to the almost total absence of decoration.

With this version of an open-space museum, Mies overcame the traditional concept of the museum—with its established ways of being read—and created a dynamic space free of restrictions, based on the transparency of the glass walls.

A skylight is a glass fixture for a roof space, providing air and illumination. Its use is of fundamental importance in this case, as it eliminates the need for windows in the walls of the exhibition spaces.

The introduction of building techniques using iron and the invention of reinforced concrete made it possible to cover increasingly large spaces; one method for providing diffuse and uniform light inside large buildings is the use of large skylights as roofs.

The simplicity of the skylight—which can take a variety of shapes and sizes and can also be produced from such transparent plastic materials as polycarbonate or methacrylate—is balanced by certain negative aspects, such as the difficulty of eliminating glare, the necessity for periodic maintenance, and the noise produced by pounding rain.

The Guggenheim's large skylight provides bountiful light to the large central hall with its spiral ramp.

Renzo Piano, Pinacoteca
Giovanni e Marella
Agnelli, Turin, Italy, 2002

This futuristic structure, with its parallelepiped shape suspended in the air over the roof of the Lingotto car factory, has a flat roof made with transverse metallic walls supported by longitudinal beams—a grid system customary in the construction of such roofs.

Like all flat roofs, it has only a minimal slope, enough to ensure proper drainage of rainwater.

When a flat roof is inaccessible, as in this case, the insulating and weatherproofing materials can be located in the external part of the roof structure and need not be particularly resistant to mechanical stresses, such as those posed by trampling feet. When, on the other hand, a flat roof is accessible, as is the case with Le Corbusier's creations, it is also called a roof terrace.

Temple of Heian Shrine, Kyoto, Japan, 1895, pagoda roofs

The pagoda is a structure typical of Buddhist architecture. It is composed of various floors, each of which has its own roof, usually in a quadrangular or octagonal shape with sloping, projecting sides, and with the entablatures and the ridges curved upward and the eaves supported by complex brackets.

Because of its height and the presence of the pointed plume on the ridgeline—often decorated with religious motifs that also act as lightning rods—one of the functions of the pagoda was in fact to attract lightning. Drawing lightning to the pagoda helped protect the other areas of the shrine, which were mostly made of wood.

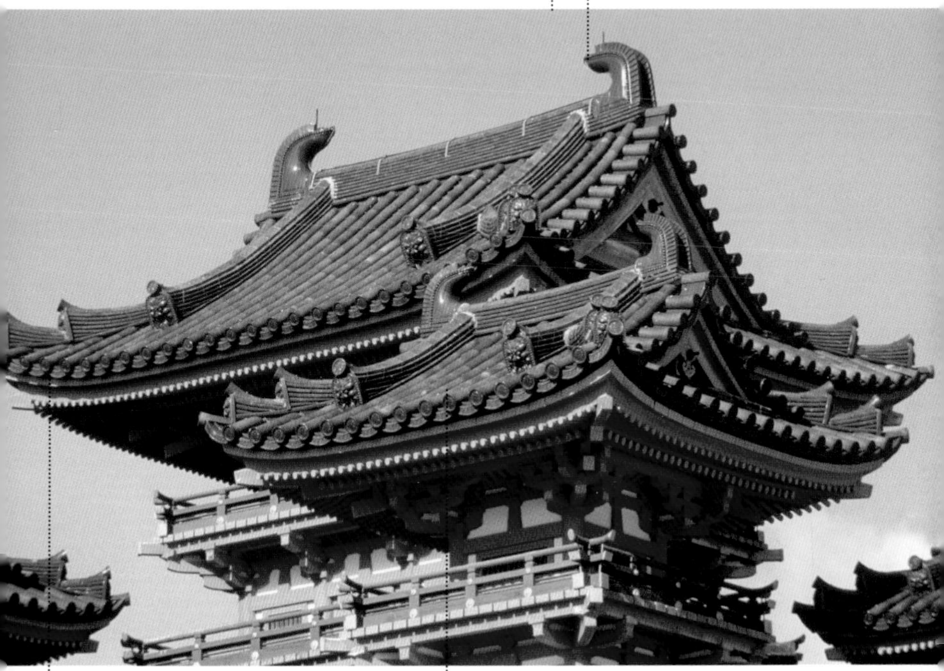

The sloping roofs of pagodas, and their complex wooden structures, are typical of the architecture of the Far East.

The polychrome wooden structure is topped by an upward-curving roof with finely carved diagonal beams that emphasize the slope of the roof as well as carving along the ridgeline and under the eaves.

Vault

A vault is a covering for a structure, with the concavity of its curved surface turned inward. The material used is primarily subject to compression; the vault transmits laterally the thrust that must be contained by its supports. With its great variety of types, the vault makes it possible to cover vast spaces, often using small construction elements, and to do so without recourse to intermediate supports. The continuity of the material and the covering serve to emphasize the unity of the covered space.

The most important vaults in terms of use are composed of surfaces generated by the translation or rotation of an arch; there are a wide variety of formal solutions, and the terminology clearly indicates the type.

Not coincidentally the vault first appeared in regions that were poor in wood and stone but rich in clay, such as Mesopotamia in the third millennium BCE, where brick was more or less the only construction material. For similar reasons the vault came into early use in Egypt and Persia. It was, however, Roman architecture, after the invention of concrete, that perfected the various types of vaults, from the barrel vault, with all its derivations (used for monumental buildings), to the cross vault, revived by Romanesque builders and in Gothic architecture, in particular in its ribbed version. The delicate elegance of these elaborations, which tend to treat the vault as an autonomous expressive element, has reappeared in contemporary architecture in the technique of thin vaults, which permit the creation of coverings of various forms through the use of a thin layer of reinforced concrete.

Origin
Among the most ancient uses of vaults are those in certain tomb chambers in the Royal Cemetery at Ur (third millennium BCE), followed by Egyptian and Persian examples.

Related Entry
Arch

Westminster Abbey, London, Henry VII Chapel, 1502–12, detail of the barrel vault with pendants

Leon Battista Alberti,
Church of Sant'Andrea,
Mantua, Italy, begun
1470, detail of the portico
with barrel vault

Geometrically a barrel vault is
generated from a linear sequence
of arches, assuming a semicircular
shape. Typical of Roman architecture,
it was systematically reprised by
Renaissance architects.

One of the simplest
systems of nonflat
covering, the barrel
vault is generally
used to cover rec-
tangular spaces.
Unlike the cross
vault, it is not
divided into bays
and thus does not
require a close
relationship
between length
and width; it can
expand, theoreti-
cally, to infinity.
According to the
type of arch from
which it is gen-
erated, it can be
fully round, ogee,
depressed, and so
on. The crossing of
two barrel vaults
with different
curves and com-
planate horizontal
axes—one larger
than the other
that acts as true
covering, the
smaller serving to
create an opening
in the surface of
the larger—creates
a lunetted barrel
vault.

Alberti arranged the semicylindrical volumes
of three round barrel vaults, which unload
their weight in a uniform way along the
perimeter walls, alternatively in longitudinal
and transversal directions. They rest on a
molded entablature and bear coffer decoration.

Church of the Madeleine, Vézelay, France, 1104–1215, choir with cross vault

The cross vault results from the intersection of two barrel vaults; the internal surfaces, called cells, are marked off by four perimeter arches and by two crossed diagonal arches.

The convergence of arches makes it possible to concentrate the supports for a vault at that point, but it also implies, in terms of covering elongated spaces, the necessity of marking off the distance between the supports following the modular rhythm of the bays.

The choir emphasizes the diagonal shape of the arches with projecting ribs that are decorative but that also serve the structural function of reinforcement. In this way the vault becomes self-supporting, unloading its weight on the supports.

The downward thrusts of the vault are transferred to the ground by means of a compound pier; the difference in size between the ribs and the thin columns (worked against the vein to increase their strength) is mediated by the presence of a crocket capital and a molded cornice.

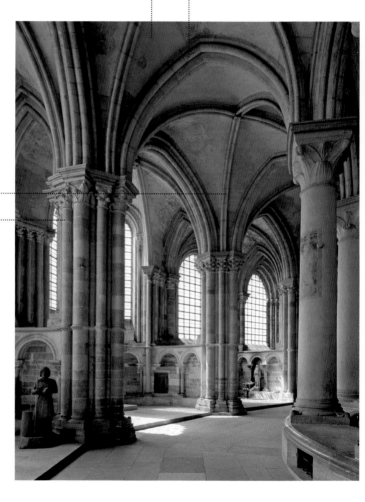

Cathedral of the Holy Cross, Schwäbisch Gmünd, Germany, begun 1317, detail of the reticular vault

The Cathedral of the Holy Cross has a slightly raised barrel vault intersected by small lunettes, also pointed, on both sides; hence the name, lunetted barrel vault.

Positioned along the center line of the vault are varied keystones that serve no structural function.

The vault loses its typological legibility, transfigured by a grid of ribs that intersect in a complex manner. The obsessive reiteration of the geometric shapes (rhombus and triangle) and the use of polychromy indicate the exclusively decorative function of this spiderweb; the space is enclosed below a surface that is uniformly curved and molded.

The presence of a transverse ogee arch visually marks the module of the bay that is demarcated by pairs of cylindrical pylons.

Hôtel de Cluny, Paris, 1485–98, detail of the chapel vault

The chapel has a Flamboyant Gothic vault supported by a polygonal mushroom pier, from which rises a dense web of ribs with sharp-edged extradoses that form a vault combining umbrella vaults and cross vaults.

Definition of the theoretical lines of force along the various members has clearly been abandoned in favor of a new formal sensibility that makes reference to naturalistic decorative themes.

Flamboyant architecture is primarily characterized by the embellishment of technical and decorative elements, without structural inventions of any importance; the decorative outlines of the cells are provided by the undulating combination of curving lines.

Cathedral of Gloucester, Great Britain, 1337–60, cloister with fan vaults

The cloister at Gloucester presents a new static and formal structure: the fan vault. A system of ribs springs upward from engaged piers to form a conical pattern that at the middle of the vault becomes tangent to the conical pattern generated by the pier on the opposite side.

The conical surfaces as well as the remaining open spaces of the vault are decorated with motifs—mouchettes, keel arches, trefoils, quatrefoils, rose windows—that create outlines similar to those of the cloister's mullioned windows.

The fan vault is one of the leading typological inventions of the late English Gothic. Replacing the traditional intertwining ogee arches, the conoids—double-curved surfaces created through the rotation of a curve on its axis—join above, at the center of the space. The ribs are no longer part of the structure but are simply carved into the surface and arranged in rays.

The fan vault is generated by many conoids arranged one beside the next. This is an important technical advance, as it places the mechanical elements of a structure on the same conceptual plane as the more properly decorative.

Antonio Basoli, design
for the decoration of the
lunch room in Palazzo
Rusconi, Bologna, 1816.
Accademia di Belle Arti,
Bologna

The cavetto vault is created by
sectioning a pavilion vault with a
horizontal plane above the impost
line. Because of the horizontal plane
it is not usually used as a support
structure and is not able to support
a roof. It is instead a "false vault,"
often used in reed structures or with
tiles placed on edge and plastered
on the intrados.

The cavetto vault has often been
adopted as a support for frescoes
and decorations and was used in the
past for inexpensive structures, as
for example in Campania. In Basoli's
design for the decoration of a room,
the cavetto vault is decorated with
grotesques of exquisite elegance
presented in a wide range of versions, from the candelabra to a frieze
with lovers and dancers set in fields
of bright colors.

Jean Prouvé, CNIT,
Rond-point de La
Défense, Paris, 1958

The Center of New Industries and
Technologies hall in Paris, a triangular
building 230 meters on a side, has a
vault with an unmistakable structural
matrix characterized by three triangular curved cells 50 meters high.

The building was made using
ferroconcrete, invented and
trademarked in 1943 by Pier Luigi
Nervi, who was structural consultant
on the project. Ferroconcrete made
possible the construction of a
delicate vault with a wavy profile,
resulting in a single, vast space—
consisting of prefabricated elements—that clearly demonstrates
the integration of structural and
architectural inventions.

Light, strong, and elastic, this type of
roof does not weigh on the perimeter
walls, which makes it feasible to
replace the walls with large expanses
of glass and thus provide efficient
internal illumination.

Felix Candela,
Oceanographic Museum,
City of Arts and
Sciences, Valencia,
Spain, 2001

The use of reinforced concrete
enables the construction of thin
shell structures. The Oceanographic
Museum in Valencia has double-
curved hyperbolic parabolic roofs—a
geometric expression of which
Candela is a leading exponent,
using it with great skill to
generate sinuous coverings.

Adoption of this shape, instead of another type of vault, makes it possible to use ordinary wooden planks in formworks for casting the concrete. The technique is therefore extremely competitive economically.

These are truly thin vaults, with a light elegance that allows for the insertion of large glass walls in the face of the arch.

Eladio Dieste, parish church of Atlántida, Uruguay, 1955–60, interior with undulating vault

The church of Atlántida presents a thin vault of bricks laid on edge in a light shell with longitudinal undulations inspired by the industrial use of sheets of corrugated materials.

Atlántida is the best of Dieste's works in exploiting the concept of variable undulation. The tie rods necessary to compensate for the horizontal thrust are concealed in the troughs of the smaller undulations of the vault, which is built like an overturned parabola that "hangs" from the side arches.

To solve the not merely formal problem of the support elements and to deal with the functional question of drainage, Dieste used a variable width for the wave, putting the maximum width in the keystone—site of the greatest amount of inertial force—and nothing on the sides, where the support elements are of the same (minimal) thickness as the vault.

Dieste thus fashioned a memorable work of architecture in reinforced brick, applying an innovative technology that confers a new lightness on what has become the material par excellence.

Frank Gehry, DG Bank, Berlin, 1994–98, atrium with curving skylight

The metal-frame structure permits the creation of a thin, transparent shell. The curving skylight on a structure of steel cables covers the full length of the 61-meter-long space.

The atrium of the DG Bank is distinguished by abundant and diffuse illumination from above, thanks to the installation of an undulating skylight.

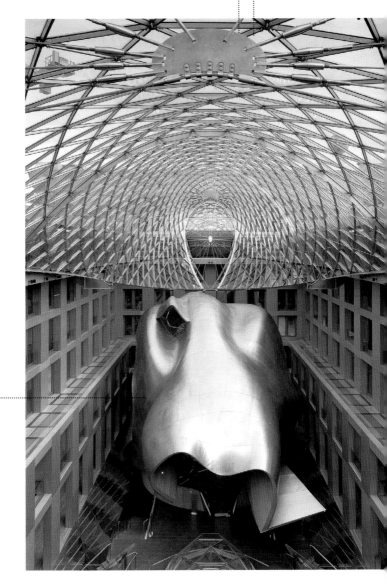

In ideal correspondence to the vault and resting on a glass floor that is also curved, Gehry's hollow steel-clad structure recalls the skull of a horse and houses the conference room.

Great Mosque, Cordoba,
Spain, 961–76, dome of
the *maqsura* of Al-Hakam

Islamic architecture often makes
use of ribs interwoven to form the
shape of a star; these are supported
by a central octagon into which
a segmented dome is inscribed.
The ribs form two squares shifted
45 degrees from one another.

The space is thus divided into sixteen
smaller sections that are easy to vault,
each having a triangular section, their
cells decorated with mosaics with
delicate floral motifs in gold
and glass-like paste.

A series of
squinches
connects the
square outline
with the
octagon above.

Kharazi House, Isfahan,
Iran, twentieth century,
vault with *muqarnas*

The use of *muqarnas*, or stalactite
ornamentation, spread rapidly
throughout the Islamic world beginning
in the twelfth century. They were used
in all types of vaults, in niches and in
portals, and as a connecting element
between walls and cornices. They were
made of stone, brick, stucco, wood,
or ceramics.

What had originally been used on
a large scale to serve a structural
function was later adopted on a
smaller scale for its ability to create
a decorative scheme—most of all on
ceilings, arches, vaults, and domes,
where it was repeated in a beehive-
shaped structure often painted in
bright colors and gilt.

Arab architecture transfigured the
vault through *muqarnas* decoration, a
succession of deep contiguous hollows
that create the impression of stalactites.
This decorative motif began as the
division of the surface into angular
niches, connecting the zone of transition between the impost line of the
dome and the square or polygonal base
by means of many smaller niches.

Dome

The dome is a type of covering, most often with a circular base, generated by the rotation of an arch around a central vertical axis. Depending on their curvature domes can be hemispherical, ellipsoidal, depressed, ogival, parabolic, or raised. The internal surface of a dome is called the intrados; the external surface is the extrados. If the extrados is visible the dome is said to be extrados; otherwise it is masked by an external prism covered with a roof called the lantern.

A dome can rise from continuous walls or from arches and columns. When the shape of the base differs from the shape of the dome it is necessary to use connecting elements, such as squinches or pendentives. Between the dome and the perimeter of the vaulted base a cylindrical or prismatic body called the drum may appear, which usually has windows. The interior of a dome is often illuminated by a hole at the top that may be closed by a skylight (oculus or *opaion*) or topped by a lantern, a crowning element similar to a small temple. A dome can be illuminated internally by opening oculi in the surface of the shell or small windows above the impost line.

Primitive forms of domes were used widely in antiquity to resolve static problems, but it was the invention of concrete in the Roman age, the introduction of the double-shell dome in the Renaissance, and the structural opportunities later offered by new building techniques that led to the true affirmation of the dome. Engineering has explored the increasing possibilities of reinforced concrete, enabling the replacement of pendentives with simple longitudinal planes in concrete. In the twentieth century the dome acquired new symbolic and functional meanings, becoming the characteristic spatial expression of many forms of public architecture. Improvements in techniques and the use of sophisticated materials have led in recent years to the elaboration of extremely thin membranes and increasingly surprising creations.

Origins

Dome-shaped coverings were already known in the sixth millennium BCE. The Neolithic homes of Choirokoitia on Cyprus present early forms of domes, which later spread to the Mesopotamian and Mediterranean areas.

Related Entries

Arch; Vault

Jain temple, Ranakpur, India, begun 1439, intrados of a dome

Treasury of Atreus,
Mycenae, Greece,
c. mid-thirteenth century
BCE, interior

Trulli at Alberobello,
Bari, Italy, detail of
domes

The tholos of Mycenae is a semi-subterranean chamber with a circular plan and a covering with an ogival section. It is composed of progressively projecting rows of stones held in place solely by the force of gravity. It is 13 meters high, with a diameter of 14.50 meters. The arrangement of the enormous stones gives the vault the stability to withstand the forces of compression caused by its weight and also creates a perfectly smooth interior surface, which was once decorated with gold, silver, and bronze.

Above the door, with jambs and a monolithic architrave, is a triangular exhaust opening.

Ancient primitive cones were the original source for the building techniques of the *sesi* (tombs) of Pantelleria and the *nuraghi* of Sardinia, which led to the typical architecture of the trulli in Apulia.

The trulli are ancient conical constructions of dry-wall stone, topped by a primitive dome composed of a double layer of limestone—an interior one of rocks, an exterior one of slabs—often surmounted by decorations with an exoteric character, spiritual and superstitious. At the top is a stone that serves as both the keystone of the roof and an ornamental function.

Pantheon, Rome,
117–30 CE, interior

The intrados of the dome is lightened by coffers arranged like ribs, which rise to the top of a circular oculus, the single source of illumination and air. The wall of the dome tapers upward, going from a thickness of roughly 6 meters at the base to 1.5 meters at the top.

At the same time the aggregate used to make the walls grows lighter from bottom to top, mixed at lower levels with travertine, then with tufa, then with fragments of brick; the uppermost "cover" wall is of bricks alone.

The support wall is composed of two parts. At the bottom areas of solid wall alternate with eight niches faced by columns; above this is a circle of blind windows. The thickness of the wall is mitigated not only by the niches but also by eight invisible interior spaces, with arched shapes to better relieve the stress of the outward thrust of the dome.

Section and plan
of the Pantheon

Visible along the exterior part of
the cylinder are restraining cupolas
built into the wall; at the level of the
impost of the dome are the typical
stepped reinforcement rings.

The hemispherical
Roman dome
reached its highest
formal and static
expression in the
Pantheon, in which
the concept of
lightening the
construction
materials was
perfected. In fact
the section of the
building reveals five
different annular
levels resting on
side walls made
of an *opus
caementicium* of
tufa and travertine
rubble. At 43.3
meters in diameter,
the dome is
supported by a
cylindrical body as
high as its radius,
so that a perfect
sphere could be
inscribed within the
building's volume.

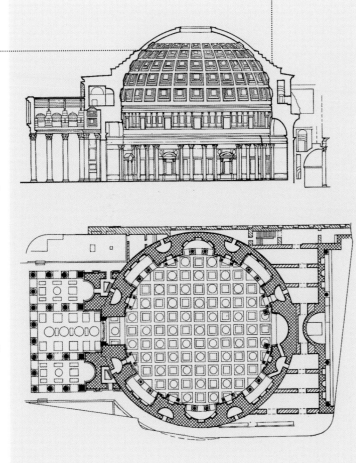

Panagia Parigoritissa,
Arta, Greece, 1282–89,
intrados of the dome

The dome rests on
eight supports
composed of the
shafts of *spolia*
columns that rise
projected from the
wall to be inserted
in pairs into solidly
anchored brackets.

Byzantine architecture combined
different expressive methods with new
technological contributions, creating
the system Richard Krautheimer
called the "canopy" style: the dome
acts as the covering of a polygonal
space, connected with the support
arches by means of angular
squinches or pendentives.

The pendentive is a connecting
element, usually hemispherical in
shape, between a support structure
with a regular shape and the dome
above; it is necessary when the
architectural elements have
different geometric matrices.

The pendentive was used in Egypt and
Mesopotamia as early as the second
millennium BCE. The Etruscans used a
"false pendentive," created by gradually
projecting rows of ashlars; this technique
was perfected by the Romans with the
opening of niches above the structure,
and it later came to be called the
squinch. In later centuries the pendentive
became a choice spot for rich decoration,
whether pictorial, mosaic, or sculptural.

Alhambra, Granada,
Spain, second half of
the fourteenth century,
dome of the Sala de los
Abencerrajes

The base of the dome of the Sala de
los Abencerrajes is in the shape of an
eight-pointed star; the problem of
connecting it to the square support is
resolved through the architectural
expedient of *muqarnas*, which, thanks
to the stalactite niches, accomplish
the transition between the two
different geometric shapes.

The dome of the room reflects
the Islamic call to introspection;
the room is fragmented in an
almost obsessive repetition of the
decorative element.

The dome is transfigured by hundreds
of *muqarnas* and stands
on a high drum pierced by sixteen
clerestory windows that let in the rays
of the sun at dawn and sunset;
these in turn strike the conical
beams of the intersection, creating
kaleidoscopic effects of golden light.

Filippo Brunelleschi, cathedral of Santa Maria del Fiore, Florence, begun 1418, axonometric projection and exterior view of the dome

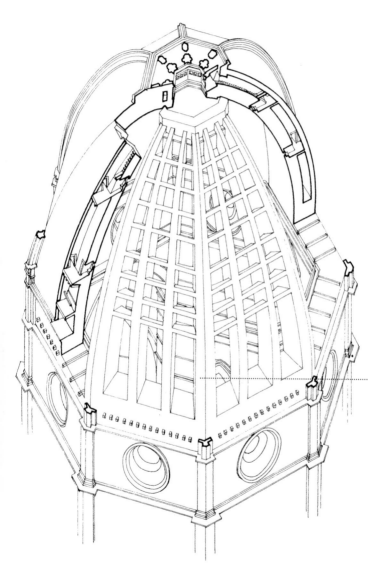

The dome was built from the inside, without the use of centering and using special techniques, including the creation of concentric self-supporting rings; the use of a double shell to reduce weight; the use of the curve of a "quarter-acute arch" in the upper part to taper its thickness from 5.8 to 3.6 meters; the use of bricks laid in a herringbone pattern to give solidity to the curtain wall; the lightening of the wall through the use of blocks of stone in the lower part, gradually replaced by bricks.

Since its construction, the dome of Santa Maria del Fiore has ranked among the most famous domes in the world. It was built following explicit instructions that no one before Brunelleschi had dared to implement, because they were not considered feasible: these called for the ogival section of a "fifth-acute arch" and specified the height of the impost and its gigantic dimensions (45 meters in diameter on the exterior, with a predicted height of more than 100 meters, including the lantern).

The structure concludes with a high and heavy marble lantern, the weight of which stabilized the entire structure, opposing the visual tendency of the eight sections to close the ring at the top. This octagonal temple draws light inside the structure while ending the upward curve of the ribs.

Michelangelo, dome of
the basilica of Saint
Peter's, Vatican City,
begun 1546

The dome of Saint Peter's is a
hemispherical dome about 43 meters
in diameter and standing on four
powerful arches, which rest on the
same number of piers, with a
perimeter of 71 meters. Giacomo
della Porta completed the project
with construction of the dome,
raising it about 10 meters higher
than Michelangelo's design and
thus changing the intended shape
of the original project.

Michelangelo brought the basilica
of Saint Peter's back to Bramante's
original idea of the central plan,
concentrating his attention on the
dome, which was understood as the
concluding element of the building
and also its coordinator. The clear
Brunelleschian geometries—which
Michelangelo was well aware of and
which he reworked in adopting the
double-shell dome—are transformed
in a plastic and dynamic tension
that involves all the compositional elements.

The debate over
Saint Peter's
established the
canonical char-
acteristics of the
Renaissance dome:
a pure spherical
outline, the use of
ribbing, the double
shell, and the drum
supporting the
concentrated
thrusts of the ribs.

The piers are
connected to the
dome by decorative
pendentives.

Guarino Guarini,
Chapel of the Holy
Shroud in the cathedral
of Turin, Italy, begun
1666, interior of the dome

A massive drum pierced by six large windows, which is part of the internal skeleton in a double-shell construction, holds the extraordinary dome-spire, composed of superimposed arches joined by sections of ribbing. This architectural motif is repeated six times to generate a system of thirty-six curving ribs that create six hexagons rotated 30 degrees, three at a time. Small windows opened between the ribs give the interior a transparent light.

The dome is flooded with vibrant light and is marked off by a complex system of symbols that recall divine perfection. The structure's extremely complex symbolic character is emphasized by the use of black marble.

To give stability to such a daring work of architecture, fully 60 meters high, Guarini used a stonecutting technique that made it possible for the interior dressing to participate in the structural work of the walls. The marbles that form the drum are not an applied ornamentation but a gigantic support structure composed of thousands of carved cubes mounted using metal cramps.

The structure is conceived geometrically on multiples of the number three, symbolic of the Trinity, and of the perfect figures of the circle, triangle, and star—an explicit reference to the cosmos that moves toward the light of the sun, seen as Christus Triumphans guiding humanity to salvation. The space concludes with a large twelve-pointed star.

Francesco Borromini,
church of Saint Ivo
alla Sapienza, Rome,
1642–62, exterior and
intrados of the dome

The lantern is composed of
six concave parts with double
columns that terminate in
very high pinnacles.

The shape of the exterior does not
correspond perfectly with the internal
structure, and the dome is masked
by a high convex and many-lobed
drum marked off by Corinthian
pilasters; above that, the top of the
dome is dressed in a step motif
marked off by buttresses that support
the vertical rush of the spiral lantern,
and is surmounted by a delicate
structure in iron. The accumulated
energies from the building rise along
the spiral and the metallic cage to
finally achieve liberation in the sky.

The pointed-arch dome is without structural transition elements. Instead it rests directly on the complicated outline of the chapel, the geometric scheme of which is based on the superimposition of two equilateral triangles to form a hexagonal star-shaped space with a contoured profile.

The transition is accomplished in a gradual way through the transformation of the unusual shape at the point of departure into a perfect circle by a series of fluted pilaster strips; very narrow cornices; a heavy cornice that acts as the entablature; and finally thin ribbing that converges in the lantern.

The internal space is enclosed in a wrapper, the basic geometry of which is generated from the mixture of rigid forms and concave-convex forms with the symbolic shape of the bee, the heraldic emblem of the Barberini family.

The result is a vertical play of dynamic expansion and contraction—a series of interwoven centrifugal and centripetal movements.

Ismail Khan,
Taj Mahal, Agra, India,
1632–54

A masterpiece of Mogul architecture, the Taj Mahal has a large central onion dome; in keeping with Persian tradition it is enclosed at the four corners by four smaller domes, each of which rests on an octagonal pavilion formed by arches.

Rising up to about 60 meters, the dome is dressed—as is the entire building—in shiny white marble that changes color according to the hour of the day, ranging from blue to white to gold.

The onion dome is distinguished by its raised, swelling body and its pointed top.

John Nash, Royal
Pavilion, Brighton,
Great Britain, 1815–23

Culminating in a delicate pinnacle,
the dome is partitioned by thin
ribbing and perforated by a
horizontal series of windows that
provide light to the interior; it rests
on a high, decorated drum.

Western culture's
fascination with
Mogul India peaked
in the nineteenth
century. Islamic
styles were being
imported to
England just as
that country was
involved in colonial
expansion. So it is
that the series of
onion domes on the
exterior of the Royal
Pavilion closely
resemble their
Indian sisters.

The palace makes
structural use of
such modern
materials as cast
iron and exploits
all the newly
developed technical
methods of its
day, including a
primitive form of
concrete for the
pale external
dressing.

Buckminster Fuller,
United States Pavilion,
Expo '67, Montreal, 1967

A geodesic dome is the result of the intricate combination of prefabricated triangular elements, arranged so as to be self-supporting without the need for interior walls or pillars. Based on modular elements, it is the only structure that becomes proportionally stronger as it is made larger.

Fuller drew on the natural shapes of crystals to make a structure in which compressive forces are distributed among elements in tension, putting it together with a complex of regular tetrahedrons in light steel.

A geodesic dome can be erected very rapidly and, being aerodynamic, is able to withstand strong winds. Used with success for industrial purposes, the structure has proven less successful in residential applications because of the increased design complexity.

Called "geodesic" because its shape resembles that of the earth, Fuller's dome unites the ability to cover enormous areas with lightness, ease of assembly, and economy. The principal advantage of a dome-shaped construction is that it can provide the same amount of internal space as a conventional rectangular structure with an exterior surface that is 38 percent smaller.

The dome in Montreal measures 76 meters in diameter and 41.5 meters in height.

Norman Foster, dome of
the Reichstag, Berlin,
1994–99

The dome of the Reichstag is 23.5 meters high and 40 meters in diameter. It weighs 1,200 tons, 700 of which are the result of its steel structure. It is dressed in two layers of glass with an intermediate layer of PVB (polyvinyl butyral).

The dome is a fundamental element in the architectural composition, outwardly communicating the themes of lightness, transparency, permeability, and public openness; it is also a key element in the building's strategies for the use of energy and light.

Inside the dome is a spiral ramp, with an open width of 1.6 meters, that acts as a ring providing structural rigidity.

At the center of the dome is the so-called light sculptor, a truncated cone—2.5 meters wide at its lower end and 16 meters wide at its top—that perforates the ceiling of the plenary chamber and extends upward to reach the top of the dome. The light sculptor, which weighs 300 tons, is dressed in 360 highly reflective inclined glass mirrors that reflect natural light into the chamber. It also has a mobile sun-following screen, powered by photovoltaic cells, that regulates the penetration of the sun's heat and light.

Façade

The façade, or front, is the external structure of a building that includes one or more sides of its perimeter, serving symbolic, artistic, and planning functions. In particular the façade is the principal elevation of the building and contains the entrance. Its articulation is based on the arrangement of the windows, portals, and floors, often with the assistance of modeling and decoration related to the material used.

Some types of buildings, such as Gothic cathedrals, can have side façades; others have two façades of equal importance, such as the Baroque palace, in which the elevation overlooking the garden is considered as representative as that of the entrance. The façade can reflect the internal articulation of the building or it can mask it; in the latter case it is called a blind façade. In Christian basilicas, if the façade corresponds to the internal distribution of the nave and its aisles it is said to be salient; if instead it slopes to follow the shape of the nave it is called gabled.

During the Renaissance the façade assumed an autonomous conformation open to inventive solutions of great artistic character. In the Baroque period it became an element of fundamental importance, giving the external face precise articulation and a scenographic effect. The concept of the façade as a

structure separate from the rest of the building and from its internal organization remained practically unaltered until the modernist movement, in which the façade became expressive of the building's function. Contemporary architects design using several external faces undifferentiated in importance; thus the idea of a "main" façade is fading. All the external surfaces delimiting a building become different aspects of a single plastic object.

In Depth
The façade has always been at the center of architectural debate, since it is the focal point for questions relating to the relationship between external and internal spaces, static vision and movement, and form and function.

Related Entries
Portico and Loggia; Doorway, Door, Portal; Window; Stairs, Staircase, Ramp

Charles W. Moore,
Piazza d'Italia,
New Orleans, 1977–78

Abbey church of Maria Laach, near Coblenz, Germany, begun 1093

Maria Laach is based on the model of the double-ended German plan with opposing choirs and side entrances. The result is a façade with a ponderous *westbau*—a massive turreted body located in front of the western side of the church—framed by small side towers and the lantern tower at the crossing, in a pleasant, geometrically balanced composition.

The decoration with flat pilasters and blind arches, presented in two colors with thin outlining of calligraphic delicacy, provokes something akin to a visual doubling between the architectural volumes and their ornamentation.

The entire elevation is symmetrically articulated through the insertion of windows of different types, with single-opening apsidal windows, fan-shaped windows in the transept, and elegant windows with two lights in the towers.

The *westbau* is preceded by a low portico with an arcade with thin columns and a strongly splayed central entrance.

Robert de Luzarches,
cathedral of Amiens,
France, c. 1220–36,
façade

Amiens has a "harmonic" façade,
meaning one framed by two towers,
a style typical of Gothic architecture.
The primary generator of the composition is the large Flamboyant rose
window, located next to the main
interior keystone and thus placed in
an elevated position because of the
unusually high and narrow shape
of the nave.

The façade is
completely
dressed in the
usual Gothic
ornamentation of
trilobed arches,
gargoyles
(waterspouts
in carved stone),
pinnacles, and
pediments
(cusped elements
crowning doors
and windows). The
result is a highly
articulated front
cut by deep
shadows and
loaded with
elements at
different levels.

The lower area of
the façade with
the portals is
connected to the
height of the
triforium by two
superimposed
galleries—an
ambulatory with
elegant two-light
windows and the
galerie des rois
(kings' gallery)—
that further
emphasize the
close relationship
between the
exterior and
the interior.

The façade is divided by four
pilasters and has three strongly
splayed and finely carved ogival porches.

Luzarches greatly diminished the
depth of the façade by inserting
enormous projecting buttresses, with
side portals, in front of the two towers.

Andrea Palladio,
Villa La Rotonda,
Vicenza, Italy,
begun 1567

The exceptional Greek-cross plan of the Rotonda begins with a clearly delineated central cube, dominated by a flattened dome externally masked by a drum and by a stepped roof; from this extend the four arms with their porticoed faces.

The external elevations of the Rotonda unmistakably express its essence—the villa is designed to be seen from every side, with no preferred axis.

Palladio's primary compositional intention in terms of this building's structure and type was to reproduce the model of the classical temple. The theme of the villa, so dear to humanist thought, was of central importance to much of Palladio's highly productive career, and he demonstrated great originality even as he made precise references to the Vitruvian model.

On each face the hexastyle Ionic pronaos is raised on high stairs. On the entablature is a dedicatory epigraph, and the tympanum is pierced by two oculi.

Guarino Guarini,
Palazzo Carignano,
Turin, Italy, 1679–85

A work of true urban theatricality,
Palazzo Carignano enlivens the traditional
layout of the palace with the insertion
along its longitudinal axis of a large
elliptical tower that is slightly pushed
back, culminating in a drum without a
dome visible from both sides.

The central convex area is cut away
to accommodate an aedicule; the
portal is framed by two rustic
columns bearing an entablature
that supports the balcony of the
piano nobile. Two columns continue
upward, through the mediation
of the cornices, to the corbels
supporting the convex pediment,
the pointed tip of which visually
interrupts the flowing curve of the
palace's upper frieze.

The façade exhibits a splendid
dressing in molded brick that
celebrates the feats of the noble
Carignano family, demonstrating
outstanding artisanal mastery
in every decorative detail.

Also completely original is the
shape of the windows, which
present a variety of mixtilinear
tympanums and cornices. A powerful dentiled cornice closes the top of
the façade, crowned by a pediment
with an outline that is, once again,
concave-convex.

The articulation is based on the
superimposition of two gigantic orders:
the lower has pairs of surreal Doric
pilasters, while the upper has equally
free pairs of Corinthian pilasters.
The façade has a complementary
relationship with the interior and at
the same time forms a continuous
covering, with a wavy movement
resulting from the fluid alternation
of concave and convex volumes.

Leo von Klenze,
Propylaeum,
Munich, 1846–50

The programmatic revival of classicism gives the façade a static, almost draftsmanlike image, imprinted excessively with a rhetorical monumentalism. The Propylaeum in Munich, designed as the entrance to a new city of culture, imparts a triumphal and original conclusion to the theme of the original Propylaeum in Athens.

The passage from classical to neoclassical turns the ancient into a metaphor for public magnificence. A Doric hexastyle pronaos bears a carved pediment on the model of the Athenian Parthenon.

To the sides stand sharply profiled rectangular towers, each with an airy loggia formed of an architrave on pillars. Below this opening runs a frieze in relief; above it is decoration in vertical bands with a molded cornice.

The white splendor of the marble unifies this "isolated" structure, amplifying to the maximum its monumental prominence.

Josef Hoffmann,
Palais Stoclet,
Brussels, 1905–14

Constructed with almost perfect bilateral symmetry, with its center indicated by the large bay windows on the façade, the house presents the interaction of all its elements arranged in a conventional way. It is constructed on a basic square module, chosen because it is directionless and thus unable to produce even the most minimal dynamic effect.

The visual result is highly effective: Palais Stoclet can be taken as the herald of a new deconstructivist concept of space. The surfaces are presented as defined spaces; even when framed, they have their own separate existence and do not emphasize the plasticity of the volumes or the sharply outlined insertion of the windows.

The verticality of this face contrasts with the horizontal tendency of the projecting body that houses the entrance and reduces the volumetric importance of the polygonal bay window.

The long façade on the street is not immediately visible in all its impressive extension; it is as though the main elevation were the western, "stepped" front, topped by the high telescope-shaped tower.

Continuity is provided by the use of molding in gilt bronze that emphasizes the external outlines of the façade.

In the external elevations of Palais Stoclet, Hoffmann reached the height of simplicity and geometric abstraction, making use of elementary forms that are nevertheless enlivened by discreet decorative elements.

Frank Lloyd Wright, Fallingwater (Kaufmann House), Bear Run, Pennsylvania, 1934–37

The suspended floors of the external elevations of Fallingwater mark the triumph of modernist language—which is then contradicted by the use of color; by synergy with the landscape, which influences the construction; and by the metaphoric interpretation of the relationship between humans and nature. In fact, finding himself forced to deal with the contours of the landscape, Wright inserted a landscapist element into his design.

The exteriors make clear that the design followed a modular system and also demonstrate Wright's fondness for geometric forms, which, variously combined, enable an extraordinary manipulation of space.

The projecting floors that are the building's distinguishing characteristic are an abstract repetition of the stone stratifications around the waterfall and in the area near it. The main entrance is at the end of a path that leads through the woods and over a small bridge, putting the visitor in direct contact with all the primary elements of nature.

Wright originally wanted the large projecting floors—made of reinforced concrete and painted yellow ocher—to be dressed in gold leaf so as to shine out among the trees. This was an explication of the "organic" concept of harmonizing nature and technology, also reflected in the dynamic contrast between the airy suspension of the projecting floors, interpreted abstractly, and their material nature.

Peter Cook and Colin
Fournier, Kunsthaus,
Graz, Austria, 2003

The Kunsthaus presents an
unusual composition made up of an
older building in cast iron and glass
and a biomorphic, shiny, warm-blue
volume through which the architect
gave life to a synthesis between a
historical presence and an experiment
in form: a floating cloud, unconnected
to the ground, suspended over the
ground floor and delimited by
a continuous glass façade.

The bubble is covered by a skin
of 1,066 panels of acrylic resin
wrapped around a metallic interior,
whose mesh is interrupted by
cylindrical protuberances that face
north to capture sunlight.

The organic construction is expressed
in an innovative language, as form
becomes space. The body is an
autonomous element whose surface
is conceived as a translucent outer
skin integrated with a system of
luminous communication.

The digital technology of pixels is
thus joined to the industrial technology of the first structures in
prefabricated cast iron. It is a daring
step, and the compositional division
has great communicative effect.

The BIX façade system, which
consists of 930 forty-watt fluorescent
rings embedded in the outer skin,
changes the color of the skin,
transforming it into an oversize, low-
resolution screen able to project
pulsating film sequences and flowing
text. Each light ring functions as
a pixel, and the entire system is
controlled by a central computer.

Norman Foster, Swiss Re
Tower, London, 2004

The 180-meter-high skyscraper—
known for its audacious architecture
and for its unmistakable cone shape,
designed to reduce air turbulence—
eliminates any sense of a visually
privileged axis. The building makes use
of energy-saving methods that use half
the energy that would otherwise have
been necessary. In the so-called ventilated façade system, spaces between
the walls on every floor serve as a
system of natural ventilation, which is
durable and resistant to the damage
caused by atmospheric agents,
especially dampness.

In a large-scale application of
double-pane glass technology, air is
channeled through two layers of glass
that insulate the interior offices, while
still permitting sunlight to penetrate
the building. Conduits remove warm
air from the building during the
summer—thus cooling it—and warm
the building in the winter, using a
system of passive solar heating.

With the help of the structural
engineers at Arup Associates, a fully
triangulated perimeter structure was
developed for the Swiss Re Tower
that makes it sufficiently stiff
without extra reinforcements and
counterweights. Despite the building's curvilinear shape, it has only
one piece of curved glass: the
lens-shaped cap at the very top.

Herzog & de Meuron,
Library, Cottbus,
Germany, 2004

A building that defies all conventions, it expresses a new way of experiencing libraries as multi-media centers, giving them central importance as research centers for the scientific community.

On the broad expanses of the external walls, thousands of pixels show the characters of the Latin alphabet and other writing systems, both ancient and modern, emphasizing the continuous evolution of universal culture.

In the evening the building is illuminated from within. The symbolic message is clear: books, like electronic media, are a vehicle for both history and contemporary reality, for reflections and continuous progress.

The external elevations evoke an amoeba that rises and towers provocatively above the grim structures of the industrial city, formerly part of East Germany. It is a hyper-glassed building, full of curves and movement, without corners and edges, deliberately surreal, always changing according to the visual angle, the weather, and the colors of the sky.

Hawa Mahal
(Palace of Winds),
Jaipur, India, 1799

The Hawa Mahal, or Palace of Winds,
is a five-story structure whose pink
sandstone façade is decorated with
hundreds of aedicules and windows
outlined in white and diminishing
in size as one moves upward.

Facing one of the
principal streets of
the city, the Palace
of Winds is distin-
guished by its
elegant windows,
originally designed
to allow the women
of the royal house-
hold to observe
the activity of
processions and
everyday life in the
streets without
being seen.

The windows
are closed by
perforated grids—
the *jali*—that
prevent views of
the interior while
increasing venti-
lation and screen-
ing the inner rooms
from the direct rays
of the sun, thus
keeping them from
overheating.

The elegant mixtilinear profile is a
result of the compacted sequence of
convex bodies, with aedicules and
windows in symmetrical alternation.

Portico and Loggia

The portico is an open gallery with columns or piers that provides shelter and also serves a decorative function. The portico's entablatures or arches rest on supports; the roof can thus be flat or vaulted. It can project outward from the façade of a palace or church, as an entry or ornament; it can recede into a building; or it can face onto a court or square. There are also four-sided porticos.

The portico was widely used in the Greek and Roman civilizations—as the stoa in Greece and the forum in Rome—as a location for religious or civil functions. The narthex of the early Christian basilica—the long, narrow, covered passage running along the façade, reserved for the penitent and the catechumens—is considered a type of portico. It is called an exonarthex if located on the exterior of the façade and an esonarthex if instead it occupies a part of the nave, where it is set off by a transenna (a screenlike construction). In the Ravenna region it is called an *ardica*.

Since the fourteenth century the term *loggia* has been used to indicate an architectural element composed of a gallery supported by columns or pillars and serving different functions—providing a location for everything from the town assemblies of the medieval period to the benedictions delivered from church façades. During the Renaissance the loggia often served as a richly decorated area for entertainment. If a loggia is a covered terrace that does not project from the body of the building and is instead raised above the roof, it can also be called an altana.

The cryptoporticus is a hidden or covered portico, very common in Roman architecture, consisting of a semisubterranean gallery with a vaulted covering that gets light from side openings. It was used as a passageway, sheltered from heat in the summer and from cold in the winter. In contemporary architecture the use of networked structures and those covered with glass permits solutions of great airiness and luminosity, presenting versions of the portico that go well beyond the traditional models.

In Depth
Its name derived from the Latin *porticus*, the portico saw extensive use in Christian architecture, with many forms designed to serve different functions.

Related Entries
Column; Pillar; Arch; Vault; Façade

Roman theater at Arles, France, inaugurated 12 BCE, ruins of the portico

Basilica of Saint Ambrogio, Milan, begun 1080, four-sided portico

Inserted in the façade, with its sloping roof, is a stately and monumental series of round arches that form a loggia, from which the interior draws light.

The motif of the arcade is repeated on the ground floor, where it becomes the eastern wing of an elongated four-sided portico with vaulted corridors.

The entire structure is made of attractive red bricks that contrast with the pale tones of the columns and the elements composed of inserted stone.

Closed off from the outside by a continuous wall, the four-sided portico presents an elegant arcade of round arches supported internally by piers with engaged semicolumns.

The four-sided portico is a cultural reference to early Christian tradition—no longer an assembly point for religious training and instead a monumental atrium used for civil and religious assemblies.

Use of the four-sided portico declined as the custom of giving churches an atrium or narthex was abandoned, and was gradually replaced by a cloister located to the side of the church.

Abbey of Saint Pierre,
Moissac, France, c. 1100,
detail of the cloister

The wonderful carved capitals illustrate
stories from the Old Testament, scenes
drawn from Revelation and from the
lives of saints, in many forms.

As the center of monastic life, the cloister is a place of prayer and meditation, but it also serves as the connecting element among the various buildings. It usually runs along the south side of the church, with various monastic spaces opening off from it. It has the form of a porticoed court, its shape derived from the atrium of the Roman *domus* and from early basilicas.

The corner decorations include quadrangular brick piers, with marble reliefs carved with figures of the apostles framed inside arches. This decoration recalls the ivory plaques and gold-working art of the same period.

The cloister of Moissac is the oldest example of a completely preserved historiated cloister. Four corridors covered with wooden beams open onto a garden through an ogival arcade supported by alternating single and double marble columns with separate bases and shared capitals.

Alhambra, Granada, Spain, Patio de los Leones, 1354–77

The succession of the columns is determined by the formation of symmetrical groups of arches that alternately join and separate as parts of intersecting geometric systems.

The extraordinary complex is unified by the skillful tracery of the stucco decorations and by the many-lobed pointed arches with their stalactites, which dissolve the form of the architectural structures. The fine carving of these decorations captures light, seeming to slow its passage and expand the outlines of objects.

With its rectangular plan, the inner courtyard of the Alhambra is surrounded by a portico set on 124 thin columns of white Almería marble, with elongated cubic capitals inlaid with Kufic inscriptions. Curtains could be draped between these columns, filtering light or cutting it off altogether.

Giulio Romano,
Palazzo Te, Mantua, Italy,
Loggia of David, 1530–34

The large barrel vault rests on four powerful piers and on tetrastyle groups of Doric columns in turn connected by small barrel vaults resting on large square corbels.

Located between the courtyard and the garden of the exedra, the loggia acts as a filter between the architecture and the landscape through the typological variation of the Serlian motif, an architectural structure composed of columns supporting a round arch flanked symmetrically by two architraved openings. It is named for Sebastiano Serlio, who first illustrated the motif.

According to the dictates of Vitruvius, the loggias of palaces—as distinguished from the winter rooms—were meant to be summer settings par excellence.

The loggia expresses the contrast between the powerful authority of the architectural orders and the variety of the pictorial and stucco ornamentation, which involved biblical themes, putti, figurines of monsters, pergolas, and whatever else was part of the late Renaissance repertoire.

Pedro Machuca,
Palace of Charles V in the
Alhambra, Granada,
Spain, begun 1550,
porticoed court

The ground floor
of this corridor is
covered by a
depressed barrel
vault; the floor
above has a flat
covering.

The two-story columned portico
makes use of the orthodox Doric
order on the ground floor and the
Ionic on the floor above, with
rectilinear entablatures and friezes
with bucrania (a decorative motif of
an ox skull garlanded with plants).

The large circular court of
the Alhambra, about 30 meters
in diameter, clearly displays an
arrangement based on the precepts
of Roman classicism tied to a
uniform geometric decoration.

The great continuous row of the colonnade is Doric in the vertical supports and Ionic in the entablatures. The curving arrangement necessitated the gradual increasing of the diameter of the columns from the first to the fourth row to compensate for the increase in the spacing between the columns, causing a proportional difference in the columns that would have been clear in the decoration of the Doric frieze.

The use of a triple portico was related to the structure's function as a location for processions, but it also represents a theme drawn from the Old Testament, in which the court of the Temple is described by Ezekiel as a "porticus incta portici triplici."

The enormous colonnade of Saint Peter's is composed of a quadruple row of 284 columns and 88 piers that form two hemicycles that wrap around the vast elliptical piazza. The long row of statues of saints—each corresponding to a column, like so many individual triumphal columns—represents the *ecclesia triumphans*.

Antoni Gaudí, Güell Park, Barcelona, 1900–14, detail of the portico

In the portico of Güell Park, Gaudí displays a version of rupestrian, or rock, architecture generated by telluric motions that rend the earth—presenting a rustic, tumbledown series of terraces.

The architecture of the portico is supported by parabolic curves that support one another, contradicted by the rustic leaning pillars, that Gaudí seems to fashion directly from nature.

Gaudí's talents as a builder led him to a keen awareness of materials and of the relationship between nature and artifice, as well as toward the exploration of certain morphological-constructive principles. This included the use of the parabolic arch, which helped reinforce the dynamic sense of his never-straight lines, animated by strong curves and movement.

The static arrangement makes clear the structural complexity with which Gaudí elaborated this new construction method, which nevertheless relied on artisanal techniques in working the very stone of which the mountain was made.

Massimiliano Fuksas,
Nuovo Polo Rho-Pero,
Milan Trade Fair, 2005,
Ponte dei Mari

An innovative structure from the point of view of architecture applied to engineering, the veil is an arrangement of suspended volumes, reflections, and transparences of light.

The central covered passageway—warmed or cooled according to the season and flanked by a conveyor belt—is suspended 6 meters off the ground and covered by a revolutionary "veil," a reticular bolted structure supported by tree-shaped steel pylons.

The line of the veil is distinguished by continuous variations in height resulting from the shape of the natural landscape around it.

The Ponte dei Mari presents a long central axis that makes it possible to cross the full 1.5-kilometer length of the complex on its upper level.

Doorway, Door, Portal

The doorway is an opening made in a wall to permit entrance and exit from a building or passage from one area to another. If it is monumental or embellished with decorations, the doorway becomes a portal. In modern architectural terminology the doorway is a structure composed of two uprights or jambs—whose axis can be either vertical or inclined and which serve the static function of supporting their own weight and any thrusts transmitted to them from structures above them—on which rests a transverse element of closure, an architrave, forming the rectangular trilithic doorway, or over which springs an arch.

With the doorway there is also the door, the mobile element that closes off or opens the entryway. In the field of interior design, the door is a fundamental element in finishing a space and ranks as a true design element. The many typological and formal differences among doors over the span of architectural history make it possible even today to identify a setting within a certain stylistic canon.

Doorways can be used as elements in creating plays of light. Not to be forgotten is their importance in establishing size relationships within settings:

the shape, size, and location of a door helps determine the use and functionality of a space as well as the definition of exterior and interior passageways. In archaeological terminology, the *porta urbica* has particular significance, indicating as it does a construction in the form of a passageway, usually inserted into a city's wall, that is often the subject of monumental treatment and architectural dignity and that has a sacred value.

In Depth
From the grand portals with arches or tympanums that stand out on the façades of palaces and churches, to internal doors with or without modeling and made of natural materials, to those that are high-tech and artificial, doors and portals offer architects and designers an infinite range of stylistic and formal options.

Related Entries
Wall; Façade

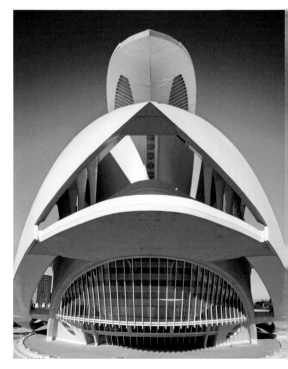

Santiago Calatrava,
City of Arts and Sciences,
Valencia, Spain, 2005,
entrance to the Palacio
de las Artes

Lion Gate, Mycenae, Greece, fourteenth century BCE

The polygonal wall has a thickness that varies from 6 to 8 meters and is built of stones, some squared and some left irregular. Up to a certain height these are simply piled one atop the next, entrusting the stability of the structure to their weight alone.

The gate is part of a system of fortifications using cyclopean walls. It makes use of a trilithic system in which four colossal monolithic uprights support a massive architrave that in turn is topped by a large triangular stone carved with two lions on either side of a column.

The Lion Gate gave access to the acropolis of Mycenae, the ancient center of the Mycenaean civilization, one of the leading cultures of the Bronze Age.

The Lion Gate is the most complete extant expression of Mycenaean art. The naturalistic treatment of the two animals does not in any way diminish the sobriety and rigor of the architecture, which has the fundamental role of expressing a sense of monumentality.

Ishtar Gate of Babylon,
seventh century BCE.
Vorderasiatisches
Museum, Berlin

The double circle of walls at Babylon
was interrupted by the Ishtar Gate, a
porta urbica through which passed the
main road giving access to the city.

The glazed-brick decoration presents, on a dark blue background,
naturalistic images of dragons,
aurochs (extinct cattle), and lions
modeled in relief. The lions probably
refer to the figure of the goddess
Ishtar; the dragons and aurochs
represent the gods Marduk and Adad.
The gate was once decorated with
more than 120 statues of lions with
gaping jaws.

Located at the end of the processional
road, the Ishtar Gate has a wide, round
arch flanked by four quadrangular
towers and a rectangular space;
along its top were found the vaulted
structures that supported a series of
elevated and terraced gardens.

Church of the Madeleine, Vézelay, France, 1104–1215, portal

The archivolt bears one of the most common iconographic subjects of the medieval age: the signs of the zodiac and their respective labors in the fields.

The lunette, carved with an image of Christ sending the apostles on their mission to evangelize the world, and the architrave, with small figures representing the pagan world, constitute one of the high points of Romanesque sculpture. The almost fully round work is intensely dynamic, with great visionary power.

The beautiful carved *trumeau*—the central pillar dividing the portal and bearing the weight—supports, along with the columns of the jamb, the architrave and the tympanum.

The Madeleine has a central double doorway framed by the arcade of the narthex.

Federico Zuccari,
Palazzo Zuccari,
Florence, 1590–98,
entrance

The door is composed of a large
mask with a giant open mouth,
as though to swallow those who
enter, with a nose not unlike a
keystone, cheeks like jambs, and
eyebrows that form a tympanum.

The transformation
of an architectural
element into a
capricious, gro-
tesque invention
testifies to the
lengths to which
the Mannerist
fondness for the
bizarre would go.

Louis Le Vau and Jules
Hardouin Mansart,
Palace of Versailles,
France, 1661–98,
Marble Court

The front of the palace overlooking
the Marble Court contains three rows
of French windows, each with a different configuration. On the ground floor
are simple rectangular windows
between paired columns; the windows
on the piano nobile are arched and
open onto a balcony; on the top floor
the windows are again rectangular,
but here they are smaller and fronted
by a low balustrade.

The French window
offers access to
balconies and
gardens; it has a
glassed frame and
usually can only be
opened from the
interior. It has the
great value of letting
in abundant light.

Versailles presents
itself as a palace
"between court
and garden," exem-
plified by the close
ties between the
building and the
park. It is precisely
for this reason that
the rear façade and
the façades on the
courtyard present
compacted rows of
French windows.

Hector Guimard,
Castel Béranger,
Paris, 1894–98,
wrought-iron door

Within an arched structure—similar to a thermal window except for the vertical supports resting on bases—Guimard expresses the metamorphosis of architecture and nature in the fantastic metal creation of a door, linking decoration to function.

An *architecte d'art*, an expert in the techniques of all the arts, is what Guimard aspired to become; the essence and the meaning of a building are its "decoration."

Wrought iron was the material par excellence for Guimard; it could assume elongated, sinuous forms in designs based on lines drawn from nature—always and everywhere avoiding any type of symmetry or parallelism.

In creating the front door of Castel Béranger, Guimard made the structure dynamic though the highly original matching of materials such as wrought iron and stone. White, refined naturalistic decoration emphasizes the different elements, marking a triumph of the most exuberant kind of plant-inspired design.

Otto Wagner, Villa
Wagner II, Vienna,
1913, front door

In Villa Wagner II, the presentation of
an isolated, symmetrical composition
combined with the restrained use
of decoration—which is strictly
functional in defining the volumetric
forms—produces a "classicist"
architecture.

The villa's front
door is composed
of a simple rec-
tangular opening
that draws its
raison d'être from
the two decorated
doors. Wagner
loosens his ties to
the style of the
Viennese Secession
in favor of sharper
forms, cubic blocks
made to stand out
by the blue geo-
metric decoration,
and by the metallic
bolts—almost an
anticipation of
protorationalist
forms. The deco-
rative geometric
motifs are empha-
sized by the white
plaster of the walls.

Window

The window is an opening made in the wall of a building to bring illumination and air to the interior, while offering a view of the exterior. The window has a very close relationship to the conformation of the façade. Architectural treatises contain numerous prescriptions concerning the sizes, distribution, shape, and decoration of windows.

Window sizes vary according to function and type, from French windows, which extend to the level of the floor, to skylights opened in roofs. Windows are composed of the same elements as doors, but their bottom element can be elongated toward the exterior in the form of a sill.

Throughout antiquity windows had simple shapes and somewhat small sizes. The Middle Ages had mullioned windows—windows divided into units by slender vertical members—with two, three, or more lights, as well as large circular rose windows with ornamental tracery. The sixteenth century returned to the sobriety of classical forms, using rhythm to infuse façades with great balance, in particular with architraved windows based on the proportions of the double square, as in the aedicule and the Serlian window. The range of types was enriched in the Baroque age through the use of oval, semicircular, or star-shaped windows framed with a wealth of decoration. In modern and contemporary architecture the introduction of reinforced concrete and steel has made large openings possible. The notable thinness of metal skeletons and progress in glass fabrication have enabled windows to be transformed into window-walls in response to the demand for maximum natural illumination.

Related Entries
Wall; Façade

Charles Rennie Mackintosh, detail of a false window from the Charterhouse of Pavia, 1891

Westminster Abbey, London, begun 1245, rose window of the south transept

The rose window, usually opened on the façade of a church or at the head of a transept, is a decorative window based on a pattern of elongated foils extending from a center.

The rose window at Westminster is set tangential to the side walls of the transept and, because of its size, becomes itself a wall. It is composed of a radial pattern of foils extending from a central circle. The marble tracery is further complicated by the addition of such decorative elements as trefoils and quatrefoils.

Historiated windows create surprising effects of light related to the medieval symbolism of theophany (divine disclosure to man). Thanks to the skills of master glass artists, the decoration varies from geometric motifs to iconography of sacred texts to the lives of saints.

The rose window is a characteristic element of Gothic architecture. Such windows grew progressively in size in response to the development of daring construction techniques that used walls whose structural roles were reduced to a secondary collaboration with the building's primary framework.

In the lower order is a row of elegant mullioned ogival windows with bundled columns and trefoil arches filled with stained glass.

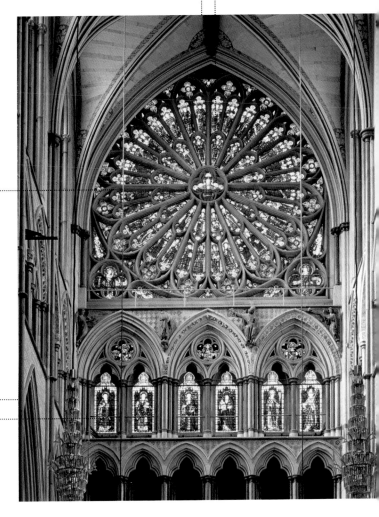

Convent of Christ,
Tomar, Portugal,
c. 1510–15, window of
the chapter house

The window of the chapter house
blends Renaissance elements with
an inventory of forms typical of
the Manueline style, an extremely
original period of Portuguese
architecture, free of any linguistic
or structural references.

The knots and
twisted ropes are a
visual reference to
the great period
of Portuguese
seafaring, while the
naturalistic motifs
reveal the play of
an unbridled
imagination.

The perfectly
rectangular window
is draped in a
complex decorative
system that erases
the window's shape,
all of it based on
naturalistic and
seafaring imagery.

Francesco Primaticcio, Château Fontainebleau, France, begun 1528, dormer window of the Cour du Cheval Blanc

The dormer window (also called a lucarne) is a window opened in a floor below the roof with a height equal to that of one of the floors of the building. It is very frequent in northern European architecture, given the size of the attic spaces under sloping roofs.

This dormer window follows to the letter an architectural drawing taken from the *Quarto libro* by Sebastiano Serlio.

The large dormer window of Fontainebleau is subject to the hierarchy of the architectural system and seems, in fact, to have the right proportions to form a small temple.

Doric pilaster strips divide the area in which the cross-shaped window is set into compartments, the side spaces bearing niches that participate in the pyramidal shape. Above this is another pair of pilasters supporting a pediment and framed by volutes.

Giorgio Vasari, Uffizi
Palace, Florence,
begun 1560

The rows of windows make an
important contribution to the façade
and are a compositional motif
from Mannerist architecture.

The elegant windows of the Uffizi
change type floor by floor and are
visually divided by heavy belt
course cornices.

The windows of the second floor reflect
a simple series of deeply splayed square
openings in a sequence of strong
projecting cornices and paired brackets;
on the third floor elegant French windows are fronted by low balustrades
and crowned by alternatively triangular
and curvilinear pediments.

The alternation of three elements at
a time, separated by a pilaster strip,
creates a rhythmic and balanced
façade.

Andrea Palladio, façade
of the church of San
Francesco della Vigna,
Venice, 1568–72,
thermal window

Derived from classical motifs, the
thermal window—also known as the
Palladian or Diocletian window—is
named for its use in the Baths
(Thermae) of Diocletian, which is
probably where Palladio first saw it.
It is composed of a semicircular
opening divided into three compartments by two vertical mullions.

Repeated more or less accurately in
the Renaissance period, the thermal
window was later worked into highly
original and fanciful versions in
the Art Nouveau period.

Palladio's sharp lines are made even
more vigorous by the addition of a
dentiled cornice, by the molding of
the archivolt, and by the volute
atop the keystone.

Charles Rennie
Mackintosh,
School of Art, Glasgow,
c. 1899

The bay window is a closed body, usually glassed, that projects outward from the wall of a building and constitutes a functional extension with powerful architectural values. If it is semicircular it is called a bow window; if it extends from a floor above the ground floor it is an oriel window.

The bay window is typical of northern European architecture and has been widely applied in both modern and contemporary architecture. It provides illumination to interior spaces, which are often dark in northern European climates because of the latitude.

The treatment of natural light is one of the "modernisms" of this building, in which the space is brought to life through the dialectical tension between the exterior and the interior, in which light plays a decisive role.

Mackintosh uses the traditional English bay windows to spread light, arranging them in vertical lines, overturning them, and doubling them to obtain prismatic forms that generate luminous volumes.

Guglielmo Gerbella, plan for a structure called Sheds, from *Costruzioni Industriali I*, Milan Polytechnic, 1910

The shed has a north-light roof and rows of metal lattice girders with a series of windows at a single pitch, with transparent cladding filling the vertical sides.

A particular appeal of these skylights is that they can be opened even on rainy days. The regular rows of windows face north, so as to avoid direct sunlight and glare while offering uniform natural illumination.

Typical of industrial architecture, the shed is appropriate for those settings where illumination from side walls would prove insufficient.

The shed is made with special projecting elements in wood or metal alloys, worked to create the window frames, which can be fixed or openable. The open space is filled with a sheet of glass or polycarbonate.

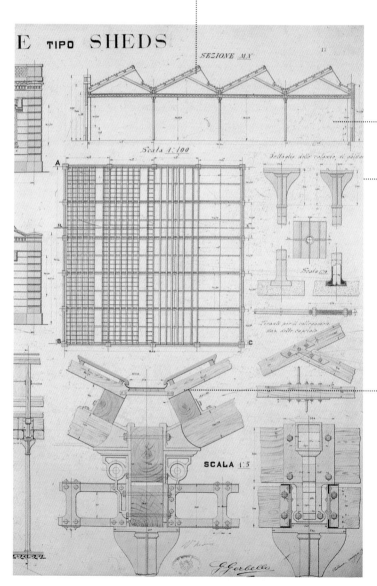

Pietro Fenoglio,
Villa Scott, Turin, Italy,
1902, windowed loggia

The sumptuous windowed loggia of
Villa Scott takes to an extreme the
exhibition of decorative motifs and
typological variations that do not
achieve a unitary composition.

The design of the
highly articulated
small villa is based
on the differences in
projection among
the building's
various parts.

The window is
divided in three by
heavy, tapering
columns with
swollen bases that
present a parody of
an architectural
order. The plant-like
decorations in
concrete, the
sinuous lines of
the wrought iron,
and the mixtilinear
outlines speak a
wearily Baroque
language, a sort
of Art Nouveau
applied exclusively
to the decorative
motifs.

Eladio Dieste, church
of San Pedro, Durazno,
Uruguay, 1967–71,
rose window

A window can assume
any form to meet the
intentions of the designer.

The highly original rose window
designed by Dieste presents an irregular
hexagon, composed of a series of thin
concentric walls in reinforced brick,
each 5 centimeters thick. Thanks to the
adoption of an innovative technology that
gives brick new lightness, the material
becomes a structural solution and not
merely an aesthetic choice.

Brick is thus being used as a structural material while at the same
time becoming a "fountainhead" of
reflected light, with great expressive
freedom. Its warm tonalities acquire
even more richness from the light.

Shigeru Ban Architects,
house at Shizuoka,
Japan, 2001, ribbon
window

The reduced depth of the building, combined with the 20-meter-long horizontal window of absolutely transparent glass, makes the house seem like a covered transitional space attached to the landscape. The window at Shizuoka is an extreme version of the modernist ribbon window—a longitudinal cut across the north façade of the house.

The design of the house, with its perfectly rectangular plan, involves materials and techniques that make the landscape enter the habitation. From inside, the view out the window is transformed into a panorama of exceptional beauty.

Le Corbusier said, "The window is one of the essential features of the house. Progress brings liberation. Reinforced concrete provides a revolution in the history of the window. Windows can run from one end of the façade to the other."

Jean Nouvel, Institut
du Monde Arabe, Paris,
1987, detail of
cladding panels with
photoelectric cells

Nouvel plays with
the geometry of
light, reviving the
principle of its
distillation, adapt-
ing it to the climate
and the variable
light of Paris.

The diaphragms of the windows,
like the diaphragm of a camera, open
and close automatically according to
the intensity of the daylight. They
represent a modern version of the
Arabic *mashrabiyya*, the wooden
screen with inclined or carved
rods that was used to enclose the
balconies of houses to provide
both intimacy and ventilation.

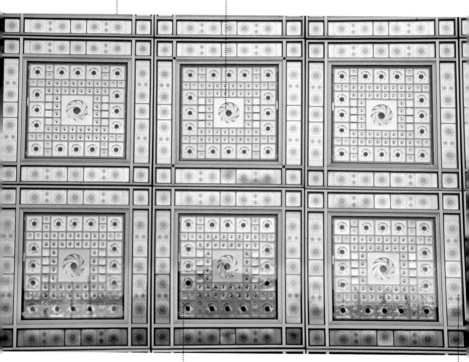

The "smart façade" consists of
panels with special sensors able to
regulate the flow of light and heat
with hexagonal photosensitive panels.
The panels are mounted on large
square sheets set between two
layers of glass, of which the
outer one is double.

With its clear reference to the
geometric designs of Islamic
tradition and its adherence to the
spirit of high-tech architecture, the
structure combines ancient art
and highly modern technology.

Lower City of Jaisalmer, India, nineteenth century, *jali* of a *haveli*

In Islamic societies great importance was given to family privacy, making it essential to prevent strangers from seeing into the home; it was also necessary to be able to see out without being seen. The solution was a kind of perforated grid that permits vision in a single direction, along with the passage of light and air: this is the Indian *jali*.

The *jali* is characteristic of Mogul architecture and also influenced Art Nouveau.

The *jali* is carved with great precision and has geometric and floral designs. In warm climates it offers the further advantage of letting in only reflected light, cutting off the direct sunlight that would overheat the interior.

Cut in stone or shaped in stucco, the grid features open spaces that can be filled with shaped pieces of colored glass to keep out air or rain or to create a decorative design with bright and translucent colors.

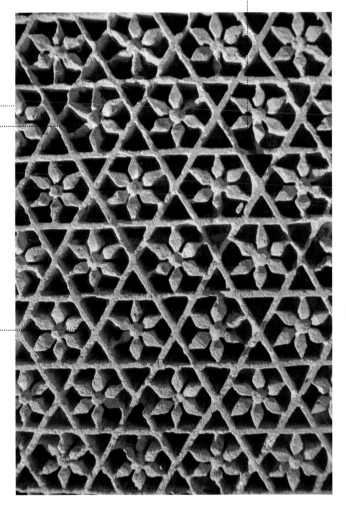

Stairs, Staircase, Ramp

Stairs are an architectural connecting element for overcoming, by a gradual progression, differences in height between the floors of a building, the internal parts of a building, or the building and the ground (in which case the stairs might become outdoor or open-air stairs). While serving an eminently practical purpose, stairs are also considered an element of spatial continuity; thus they are subject to all the problems related to the organization and design of space. For this reason all civilizations have paid special attention to the functionality and the creation of stairs.

There are also interpretations of stairs that, while meeting practical necessity, serve sacred and celebratory ends. Such is the case with the stairs in pre-Columbian civilizations or with the monumental versions of the Baroque and Neoclassical periods. All types of materials can be used in the construction of stairs, from brick to metal to reinforced concrete. The possible planimetric shapes have led to the establishment of different basic types: rectilinear ramps, wellhole, helicoidal, spiral, and so on. From the structural point of view a distinction is made between stairs with self-supporting steps and those with an independent structure.

Escalators are a modern type of stairs. In widespread use today in public buildings, the escalator consists of a conveyor belt inclined at a maximum of 35 degrees that presents steps, thus making possible the transportation only of people, in contrast to the elevator, which also enables the transportation of things. Recently, most of all in high-tech buildings, the escalator—along with the other elements of the engineering plant—has been moved outside, becoming an architectural element in itself.

In Depth
Because of their monumentality and the technical and formal possibilities they offer the architect, stairs have been used since earliest times. Beginning with the most ancient examples of stairways in front of religious or public structures, the history of stairs runs from the ramps of Roman amphitheaters to the unadorned severity of medieval stairs, to the sculptural richness and constructive audacity of Baroque spiraling stairs, to today's most daring architectural designs made possible by sophisticated techniques and materials.

Related Entry
Façade

Francesco de Sanctis,
Spanish Steps,
Rome, 1723–26

Treppenturm, Graz,
Austria, 1499,
double-spiral stairs

The most significant vestige of
the former residence of Frederick III
is a stair tower with a double
staircase that twists around
two axes.

This late Gothic stairway
is an architectural feat: the steps
extend directly from the walls while
the elegant balustrade in carved
stone follows and emphasizes
the double-helical route.

Michelangelo,
Laurentian Library,
Florence, begun 1524,
anteroom stairs

The diminution of the functional
elements and the enlargement of the
decorative elements create a dynamic
tension in the small space that finds
release in the triple staircase. Originally
designed by Michelangelo in walnut,
it was constructed of pietra serena in
1559 by Bartolommeo Ammannati
following Michelangelo's model.

Between the thoroughly
Renaissance straight lines, the
large central elliptical stairs
anticipate Baroque solutions.

The curving steps seem to flow
downward like a waterfall, barely held
in place by the lateral balustrades,
which in fact open outward at the
second section to permit the release
of two side ramps without balusters.

Francesco Primaticcio,
Château Fontainebleau,
France, begun 1528,
stairs of the Cour du
Cheval Blanc

The external stairs are a fundamental element in the appearance of the façade; they give a distinctive look to the elevation, connecting the courtyard level to the piano nobile.

Made of squared ashlars, the stairs present a balustrade regularly punctuated by upside-down brackets. They represent a laboratory of Renaissance and Mannerist shapes that rupture the rhythmic regularity and symmetry of the château's façade.

The planimetric irregularity of the stairs, a horseshoe shape with a broken concave and convex outline, matches the architecturally animated façade, distinguished by the vertical predominance of the central body.

Jacopo Barozzi da
Vignola, Palazzo Farnese,
Caprarola, Italy, 1550–59,
spiral stairway

The wellhole stairway is the
simplest type from a structural point
of view. It is supported by the outer
walls and open at the center
with an empty space.

The stairway at Caprarola is
helicoidal (spiral shaped): the
ascending ramp twists around
without a break or sudden
variation in perspective.

Originality, technical ability, and
virtuosic talent testify to the maturity
of Vignola's vocabulary as well as
the sources of his creativity and
their perfect assimilation.

Supported by paired columns and
embellished by splendid wall decorations, the stairway terminates in
the ingenious solution of an airy
space covered by a dome.

Balthasar Neumann,
Augustusburg, Brühl,
Germany, 1741–44,
interior stairs

Baroque stairways reached radiant heights because of the wealth of construction methods, the materials used, and the relationships established with the surrounding space (which is often affected by stairs' position and shape).

Many noble residences of eighteenth-century Germany were designed around central, elegantly dramatic stairways, the fruit of collaboration among architect, sculptor, and fresco painter. They were characterized by forceful dynamics and a sumptuous grandiosity, with a theatrical flair.

The initial single ramp leads to two side ramps supported by paired columns and impressive figural piers.

The stairway at Brühl represents the richest and most diversified kind of design: no spine wall interrupts the open vision of space, spreading out to offer a continuously varying view. The ramps extend upward, illuminated and airy, in a happy fusion of dynamic lines.

Perret's stairway clearly displays
the material from which it is
made. The stairway is shaped
from reinforced concrete, a
plastic-structural statement.

The stairs move away from their
purely functional role to become
an aesthetic event in themselves;
the curving ramps create an
exceptionally theatrical effect.

The double helicoidal stairs
extend across space not only as
a connecting element but also as
an architectural episode with its
own precise autonomy.

Pier Luigi Nervi,
Giovanni Berta Stadium,
Florence, 1930–32,
external ramp

The ramp is an architectural element that serves to connect two floors at different heights. It can be of two basic types: flat or helicoidal.

The external ramp of Florence's municipal stadium has a strong structuralist imprint: an acrobatic helicoidal stairway without weight, suspended in emptiness, in which the support elements narrow following its movement.

The structure was left in view as a statement—a demonstration of how, for Nervi, art was not conceivable purely in the aesthetic sense; it had to be a revelation of functionality and mechanics as well. It thus also contributes to the demystification of the Roman triumphalism of the period.

Thanks to the use of reinforced concrete, although the planimetric arrangement does not vary substantially, the stairs have been completely transformed in appearance, becoming elements of great constructive audacity as well as lightness.

Herman Hertzberger,
enlargement of the
Centraal Beheer,
Apeldoorn, Holland,
1995, exterior stairway

Applied to architecture, structuralism
creates an objective spatial stairway:
an external stairway with ramps and
landings, clearly defined inside a
cage composed of two curvilinear
metal-mesh screens.

Structuralist
architecture pays
special attention to
the basic elements
of architecture; stairs
are here conceived
as a unique, almost
sculptural, object.

I. M. Pei, enlargement of the Deutsches Historisches Museum, Berlin, 2003, helicoidal stairway

An architect of light, Pei designed a stupendous spiral stairway made of glass with a metal framework for the new wing of the Deutsches Historisches Museum.

The surprising combination of volumes—conoids and cylinders—is intensified by the curvature of the panes of glass, which leave the structural system and the central support pillar of concrete completely visible.

An admirable example of functional adaptation, the stairs make clear the new entrance to the museum.

Charles de Gaulle
Airport, Paris

In the terminal of Charles de Gaulle
Airport a complicated system of
intersecting escalators protected
by glass walls connects the various
levels to the central body, visually
dominating the great fountain beneath.
The construction reflects not only
functionality but also great attention
to aesthetic and formal concerns.

An escalator is a "conveyor belt
elevator" composed of articulated
mobile stairs that are mechanically
moved while remaining horizontal. The
concept was patented by its inventor,
the American Jesse W. Reno, in 1892.

Escalators are used
in public spaces
for the rapid
transportation
of large numbers
of people.

The invention of the elevator and its
widespread adoption—the first elevator
with an electric motor dates to 1880—
have made building types characterized by significant vertical development possible, such as skyscrapers.

One of the modern elements of
connection between one floor and
another is the elevator. Brought
outside high-tech buildings, along with
the other elements of the engineering
plant, it becomes an architectural
element with a powerful aesthetic
structure of its own.

The elevator is a transport device
with a fixed installation, designed to
move people and things, that serves
defined floors. Its cabin moves along
a rigid guide and its horizontal
inclination is over 15 degrees.

Materials
and Techniques

Wood / Stone / Adobe / Brick / Concrete / Reinforced Concrete / Iron and Metallic Alloys / Glass / Techno-polymers / Natural Elements

Santiago Calatrava,
Bodegas Ysios Winery,
Laguardia, Spain, 2001,
entrance

Wood

Wood has been the most widespread construction material since antiquity because of its availability and the fact that it can be used even without having to be worked. Constructions of a more enduring character can be fashioned from stone or brick, but until the nineteenth century—and, following its rediscovery, in recent times—wood has been the ideal material for certain parts of buildings, such as roofs, roof supports, and foundations, due to its ability to withstand water.

In countries rich in wood and poor in stone, wood is the basis for a variety of construction systems. These include balloon framing—a framework composed of standardized elements nailed together (used in residential construction in the United States, northern Europe, and Alpine areas because it is light, economical, and easy to assemble); the *blockbau* (log cabin) system, in which walls are composed of wood beams arranged one atop another in horizontal rows with ends overlaid at the corners; and *Fachwerk* (timber framing). The stave churches of Norway present a special type: timber churches with walls made of planks positioned upright between corner posts that reach up to the ceiling trusses.

In the twentieth century, with the availability of more convenient materials and the spread of new technologies, the use of wood in construction diminished. Aside from being highly flammable, wood presents a heterogeneous and discontinuous surface that alters over time. Even so, its diminished use in building structures has been paralleled by increases in temporary structures and carpentry. Wood derivatives—such as laminates that offer exceptional physical and mechanical performance and improved fire resistance, and the introduction of products that limit deterioration and damage from insects—have led to the rediscovery of wood for major constructions, so-called structural wood, especially in roofs and prefabricated systems.

In Depth
Recent developments in architectural design and new building techniques have made it possible for architects to exploit wood's many formal possibilities, from its extraordinary aesthetic qualities to its eco-sustainability.

Stavkirke, Borgund, Norway, c. 1150, interior

Aljafería Palace, Zaragossa, Spain, Throne Room, 1492, ceiling made with the artesonado technique

The splendid *artesonado* ceiling in gilt wood in the Throne Room, built for King Ferdinand and Queen Isabella, is a typical example of Mudéjar woodworking. The ceiling is supported by thick wooden rafters arranged to increase the strength and rigidity of the structure; these project below the level of the ceiling, thus dividing the space into regular panels. The three faces of the rafters are carved and painted.

The lower face of each rafter is made sumptuous with an abundance of gold and primary colors as well as decorations of intertwining geometric motifs that form eight-pointed stars at the cross points of the rafters.

The intricately joined wooden sections and the complex geometric design capture and reflect light: the ceiling is a masterpiece of carving composed of innumerable wooden polygons.

Inside each coffer is an octagonal motif bearing at its center a carved and gilt pine cone.

Giovanni Battista Aleotti,
Teatro Farnese, Parma,
Italy, 1618–19, cavea

The Teatro Farnese became a model
for other theaters and performance
structures because of the uniqueness
of some of its features, from the mobile
scenery platform, to the machinery for
moving actors to the stage, to the ingenious method used to flood the cavea
for the presentation of naval battles.

Given the complexity of the theatrical equipment and the high cost of performances, the theater was rarely used. After the last performance, in 1732, the building fell into decay; the wooden parts and the stucco statues were almost totally destroyed by a bombardment in 1944.

The theater was entirely rebuilt in 1956 following the original design. The wooden parts, all of which had originally been covered by decoration, were left plain to highlight the few remaining pieces of the original structure.

Located on the second floor of the Palazzo della Pilotta, the Teatro Farnese occupies a large hall 87.20 meters long, 32.15 meters wide, and 22.65 meters high.

The U-shaped cavea is composed of fourteen tiers able to seat more than 3,000 spectators. At the top are two rows of Palladian-style Serlian loggias, which are only partially functional.

The theater was built quickly using materials typical of ephemeral structures—wood, stucco, papier-mâché—in this case intended to simulate precious marbles and metals in a play of references and allusions completed by the painted decoration and the plastic ornamentation.

Church of the
Transfiguration,
Kizhi, Russia, 1714

The covering of the domes and
roofs is composed of split-wood
shingles, overlapped much like
tiles. This kind of roofing is typical
of snowy regions.

The building'
pyramidal structur
with overlappin
levels is visuall
emphasized by
forest of sma
onion domes set o
the ridges of th
roofs, with the
mixtilinear outlines

The Church of th
Transfiguration i
built entirely of woo
using the *blockba*
technique. The wall
are composed c
logs laid horizontall
one atop the ne
and overlappe
at the corners,
technique tha
required the use c
long, straight trees

Imre Makovecz,
Catholic Church,
Paks, Hungary, 1988

Makovecz uses materials like clay, bricks, and wood in his work—making strong references to nature—to create bizarre and ironic forms.

This design consists of a cone-shaped building over which an impressive tower rises, ending in three pinnacles about 25 meters high. The church's support structure is made entirely of pine, which is soft and highly malleable.

Makovecz sees the tower as a referent to both the history and the origins of a people. His work always includes emblematic and patriotic allusions, in this case the reference to the wooden bell towers of the Hungarian plain, which draw their inspiration from popular Transylvanian architecture.

The envelope of the covering, supported by "skeletons of trees"—almost ribs, which hold up the fabric of the protective shell—covers the spaces underneath and respects the organic nature of the whole by using real tree trunks: the interior of the structure is a sort of ribcage.

The wings of the complex come together to form an organic whole with a bearing structure using pillars that have a strong symbolic value.

Norman Foster, Chesa
Futura, Saint-Moritz,
Switzerland, 2000–4

The apartment building uses local
natural materials, with special attention paid to the environment. The
cement-and-steel structure is covered
by larchwood shingles, which over
the passage of time and in response
to atmospheric effects change color
from their original golden tonalities
to a more opaque gray.

The name Chesa Futura is emblematic
of Foster's desire to integrate the
building as much as possible into the
Alpine landscape and with traditional
Engadin architecture: in Romansch,
the local Ladin language, *chesa*
means "home."

Foster rounded off the building to
create an enigmatic object with
neither roof nor façade, conceived
using computer-aided design. The
prefabricated curved panels form,
from exterior to interior, a layer of
overlapping shingles and ledges with
a laminar structure and with an air
chamber for thermal insulation and
counter walls in plasterboard.

Chesa Futura is unrelated to the typical
Alpine chalet. It transmits instead a
futuristic image of the mountain—it is
a three-story balloon suspended off the
ground (if one overlooks the struts and
the glassed-in cylinders of the
entrance)—by means of its carefully
planned elevation.

To avoid the dis-
persion of heat,
the northern face
is practically
windowless; the
southern face
has large loggia-
terraces to opti-
mize exposure to
sunlight—which is
transformed into
heat—and to offer a
view of the valley.

Norman Foster was
assisted on the
project by Arup
Associates.

Karo Batak house, Tebingtinggi, Sumatra, Indonesia

A daring and complex architectural idea, the traditional Batak house is built entirely of wood and presents very particular formal aspects.

The home—called a *baga*—has a rectangular plan raised off the ground. It is a refined wooden structure, often richly decorated with sculptures and painted with geometric and floral motifs.

From the raised front entrance, accessible by stairs, one enters a central walkway, to either side of which are the apartments of the individual families.

The house has flared walls shaped like overturned truncated pyramids, and a gently curved straw-covered roof with a central saddle and triangular gables, cut obliquely at the short sides to protect the face of the building.

Stone

Stone is a natural rocky material that has been used since earliest times in the construction of buildings. Its resistance to wear over time and its special characteristics have made it the very symbol of monumentality.

Since antiquity, the difficulties of acquiring and working stone have tended to restrict its use to large-scale public works. With the passage of time and with the flowering of new technologies, stone lost its primacy, only to regain it in the contemporary age, offering as it does an architectural language that has been refreshed through new designs and new technologies. Stone is once again seen as a material—with a return to its essence, its colors and varieties, its true nature—that the architect can draw on freely.

Used both with and without a binder, in walls, in the creation of architectural elements, or as a material for dressing and for finishing in general, stone can be used in rough or polished blocks. Hewn into regularly shaped blocks, stone can be arranged with decorative effects; in slabs or in rough-hewn structural blocks it can be left visible on façades (as is the case with rusticated ashlars). Being heavy and difficult to manage, stone is often worked at the quarry or in the immediate area

and, as it is difficult to transport, its use is often limited to projects within the local region. Stone holds up well to compression, but poorly when subjected to traction: for this reason it is used most of all in supporting walls.

There are so many varieties of stone—differing according to country of origin, from highly prized marble to limestone to sandstone—that decisions regarding its use typically depend on its general characteristics, such as color, sheen, workability, and hardness. From the point of view of strength, durability, and overall quality, stone was long the best solution available, and as such it was used for the buildings of greatest prestige.

In Depth
The color and strength of stone differ according to its chemical and physical properties. For this reason, certain varieties are associated with particular geographic areas or with particular building techniques, from the widespread limestone of Roman and Gothic constructions to the highly prized marble of cathedrals, from the strength of granite to the easy workability of sandstone, widely used in Tuscan and Renaissance architecture in the variety called pietra serena.

Related Entry
Wall

Dar al-Hajar,
Wadi Dahr near San'ā',
Yemen, 1936

Treasury of the Pharaoh, Petra, Jordan, first century

The famous Nabatean monument is made of the stone of the cliff face into which it is carved—a wall of pinkish limestone that changes hue according to the angle of the sun and the time of day.

Petra means "rock" in Greek.

The carved-rock façade, nearly 40 meters high, is composed of two levels of relief decoration. The lower level is a hexastyle portico with a pediment; the upper bears a central tholos between two aedicules with a broken pediment.

Limestone, a sedimentary rock that occurs in many different colors, has always been used as a building stone and is by far the most widespread stone in constructions from Roman structures to Gothic cathedrals.

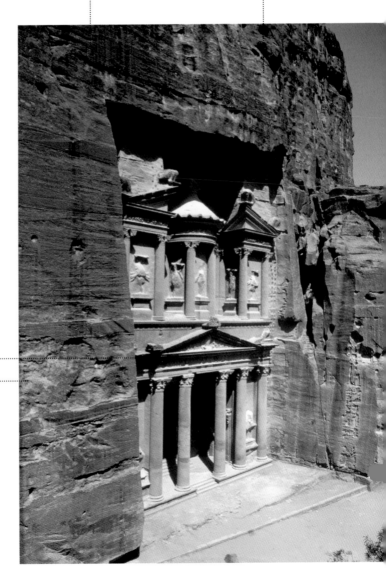

Mausoleum of Theodoric,
Ravenna, Italy, 520–26

The upper part is crowned by a
double circular strip, edged above
with an ornamental pincer motif.
It is topped by a dome composed of
a monolith with twelve handles along
its border that were used as anchors
for the hoisting ropes used during
the difficult operation of raising the
stone roof into position.

The mausoleum i
a centrally planne
structure with tw
superimpose
decagonal level
composed c
limestone blocks
perfectly square
and solidly con
nected without th
use of morta
The monolithi
dome is made c
the same Istria
stone, is 10 meter
in diameter, an
weighs 230 tons

On each side c
the lower level is a
niche with a barre
arch, the arche
being displayed b
wedge-shape
voussoirs; on th
western face this
niche become
the entryway to th
lower chambe

Cathedral of Milan,
founded 1386,
detail of the spires

The stylistic orientation, based on Gothic models from northern Europe, determined the selection of marble as the construction material for the cathedral of Milan—an unusual choice in a region where preference was usually given to brick.

The white and pink marble came from a quarry at Candoglia at the mouth of the Val d'Ossola, which was the principal supplier of construction materials for the cathedral—exerting a powerful effect on the building's architecture, execution, and mechanics.

The crystalline beauty of the Candoglia marble, combined with its chemical and physical properties, made an invaluable contribution to a work that was already splendid in its own right because of its sheer size and daring design. Marble was an excellent choice for a fine sculptural work, in terms of both robustness and resistance to compression (properties it shares with granite).

From the beginning a worksite was set up around the cathedral for the stone dressers and sculptors. Thus the transformation of marble blocks into decorations and statuary took place on site and on the basis of measurements and models made by the various artists, with precise reference to the structure being built.

Robert Smythson,
Longleat House,
Wiltshire, Great Britain,
1568

It owes the measured sobriety of its masses, its luminosity, and its refined use of details, such as the proportions between empty and full areas—all of which radically distance it from the typical feudal fortified home—to the use of juxtaposed limestone blocks.

Longleat House is one of the finest examples of Elizabethan architecture.

The typically English use of bow windows becomes a way to counterbalance the horizontal rhythm of the entablatures with vertical structures, resulting in networked surfaces.

Otto Wagner, Saint Leopold,
Steinhof, Vienna, 1906

A proponent of a spare architecture
that drew its raison d'être from the
principles of construction and from
the materials used, Wagner designed
the small church of the Steinhof
sanatorium, dressing it in marble
plates held in place by large bolts,
which were left visible.

Wagner's move-
ment away from the
decorative forms of
the Viennese
Secession in favor
of a more sober
and measured
approach is also
reflected in
the dressing,
which enhances
the building's
elegance.

Peter Zumthor, thermal baths, Vals, Switzerland, 1996

The thermal baths at Vals are composed of a large stone structure that is part of a mountain—an object that explains the relationship between primitive energy and the geology of the mountainous landscape.

Mountain, stone, water: to build with stone inside a mountain is what guided the project and, step by step, gave it form.

Although the dividing lines between the thermal baths and the setting are clear, the inside and the outside, the thermal baths and the nature that surrounds them blend together. This is the result of Zumthor's skilled technique and his choice of materials— most of all the locally quarried Valser quartzite, which is used everywhere and worked in a variety of ways: split, milled, smoothed, polished, fragmented. The visitor moves through a world of stone and water, interrupted only by brass rails and glass doors and windows.

Valser quartzite is a variant of green gneiss, a metamorphic rock distinguished by alternating bands of pale and dark minerals.

Much of the central-western Alps are composed of this rock. Zumthor thus drew on local materials, quarried no more than 2 kilometers from the town.

Alvaro Siza, Santa Maria, Marco de Canaveses, Portugal, 1999

Clarity and simplicity are the traits of the building designed by Siza. The white body of the church, with its mixtilinear outline, rises impressively over the darker enclosure wall.

The differing heights of the volumes are skillfully rendered through the use of different materials; the enclosure wall is gray granite.

Granite is an eruptive rock with a pale tonality overall that—because of its aesthetic qualities and physical and mechanical traits (most of all its notable resistance to atmospheric alterations)—is frequently used as a construction material for wall dressing, floors, and in the creation of monumental works.

Granite is here used for both its lightness and its aesthetic harmony with the enormous white volume. As Siza says, "According to the passage of the hours of the day the church dematerializes or stands out force-fully; this is another reason why it was necessary to use a basement that would anchor it to the ground, as can be seen in pre-Columbian constructions that I was able to see in Peru."

The perfectly assembled blocks of stone join the structure to the ground and give an unequivocal definition to the church's trilithic entrance.

Hans Hollein, Vulcania
Museum, Saint-Ours-les
Roches, France, 2002

The use of local volcanic stone and the red rock of the Jura accentuate the chameleon effect of the construction's "skin." The dialogue between nature and architecture is reinforced by the large-scale use of material quarried locally, such as the massive stone of the long ramp and the substances used to make the "*béton* Vulcania," an aggregate of basalt produced on the site.

One of Europe's most interesting designers, Hans Hollein makes significant use of natural stone in his buildings. In 2003 he received the Architettura di Pietra award at Verona, Italy.

Stone is used in a variety of ways at Vulcania. The great cyclopean wall that leads to the central space is made of unadorned and unworked basalt blocks. In the form of a volcano—a large cone 22 meters high reached by way of an elevated passageway and surrounded by a gilt-metal form that captures sunlight—that same stone has been cut and polished, worked by hand with refined and delicate results.

The deep exploration of a lava vein is a building theme drawn from Jules Verne's *Journey to the Center of the Earth* and from Dante's *Inferno*. The fundamental concept is that of establishing a close relationship with the site and with its natural materials, stone being the material best suited for that purpose.

Dark basalt is an effusive volcanic rock of great hardness and great strength, and thus not easy to work. In this case the material provides a visual sense of the meaning of the structure—a theme park based on volcanism and the forces within the earth.

Frank Gehry, American Center, Paris, 1988–94, detail of the limestone dressing

The fact that it is made of only a single material is one of the outstanding aspects of the American Center. The slabs of limestone that cover it are staggered 10 centimeters out of line, as though seeking to give the construction a superimposed rhythm to disorient the viewer. The absence of reference points—or of even a single perfectly horizontal or vertical line—sets off a swirling optical effect.

The exterior hides a steel framework. In terms of its materials, the American Center is in keeping with the tradition of Parisian architecture.

The American Center illustrates the sense of gravity generated by the monochromatic mass; the compactness of the walls expresses the work's sculptural reality.

The entrances materialize in the middle of the limestone masses like veins of pure crystal.

Adobe

Adobe is brick made of unbaked earth. It is produced by sun-drying a mixture of clayey soil or mud with sand and straw. It is used in place of stone. An ancient and widespread technique, adobe construction was used from the earliest times to make the first permanent constructions.

The first urban clusters were made with such unbaked bricks, including Jericho and Catal Hüyük in Anatolia. It was later used for the most important works of Mesopotamian architecture. It remained in use in Egypt until the period of Roman domination, at which time the use of bricks baked in furnaces was becoming widespread. Adobe was used in England until the eighteenth century, in the Middle East, and in pre-Columbian America; it is still used today in Africa, Asia, and Latin America. It is typical of the Spanish regions of Castile and Léon, while in Mexico the *casas de adobe* are a traditional patrimony handed down within families. Made of a mixture of dried grass and mud, they offer great resistance to severe weather.

Adobe is made of clayey soil, straw, and water put into a simple mold and left to dry in the sun. To keep the bricks from drying too much they are some-times wrapped in horsehair. The bricks are made into walls without the use of any kind of mortar. The raw earth used is not always simple mud; it is instead often composed of other compact sedimentary soils. An extremely friable material, adobe is not reliable over time and can dissolve in rain, thus requiring continuous maintenance. Adobe offers important thermal qualities, conserving heat during the winter and releasing it during the summer, and thus maintaining a fresh and constant interior temperature through all seasons.

The structures at Ur, including the famous ziggurat, were built of unbaked bricks using a bituminous binder that withstood poor weather and kept the walls from deteriorating rapidly.

In Depth
In Mesopotamia, polychrome wedges of terracotta were inserted into walls to strengthen them. These not only provided greater stability but also a pleasing visual effect. Adobe is still used today, from Africa to Central America, often in combination with concrete and with greater control over its composition (using 20 percent clay and the rest sand).

Related Entry
Wall

Ziggurat of Ur, Mesopotamia (modern Iraq), c. 2100 BCE

Citadel of Bam, Iran,
eleventh to twelfth
centuries

In the province of Kerman, on the
edge of the Dasht-e-Lut desert, stands
the citadel of Bam, built on a rocky
elevation over an area of about 6
square kilometers. It is composed
of a main fortress spread across
five levels and defended by three
separate rings of walls.

Because of the friability of the material,
the structure has been restored several
times over the course of the centuries,
always employing the same materials
and techniques used in the past so
as not to disfigure this exceptional
architectural and urban artifact. The
citadel was nearly completely destroyed
by the earthquake that struck Iran on
December 26, 2003, and today it is listed
among UNESCO's World Heritage sites.

Bam is a medieval frontier city constructed entirely of unbaked bricks
dried in the sun. These are made of
clay degreased with straw to avoid
cracks and breaks and further protected by the periodic application of
an additional layer of clay to maintain
the necessary impermeability.

Dogon village,
Kani-Kombole, Mali,
mosque

Adobe is a building technique well suited to large-scale buildings. The mosque of Kani-Kombole is based on a broken-pyramid module with a square tapering tower of a type common to the entire Sahara area, and probably originally derived from Yemen.

Dogon architecture has developed an original and highly expressive language thanks to the use of a pliable and refined technique in wood and clay that achieves "cultured" results in Islamic monuments.

An extremely economical material that is easily worked, unbaked brick is still used today in the semidesert regions of Africa.

Both the enclosure and the exterior walls of the mosque are the product of the serial multiplication of cone-like pillars of beaten earth over an interior wooden armature; the external surfaces are renewed annually and have a strong symbolic meaning. Mud pillars give the building its verticality; the horizontal connections are beams covered with mud.

The adobe technique remains tied to the environment and available resources.

William M. Rapp,
Museum of Fine Arts,
Santa Fe, New Mexico,
1917

By connecting itself to the ancient local building tradition of the pueblos, the Santa Fe Museum of Fine Arts presents a version of modern architecture especially attentive to the resources of its area.

The structure has its own aesthetic quality, a result of the smoothness of the external walls, with only the tips of the support beams projecting outward; the softness of the edges; and the window surrounds, which are cut directly into the thickness of the walls.

Given the scarcity of rain and the heat in the semidesert areas of Arizona and New Mexico, adobe construction is a good choice as a building technique, not only because of its ease of execution and the availability of its components but also for its thermal qualities—isolating inner rooms and protecting them from elevated external temperatures, maintaining a constant cool temperature.

Brick

A technical evolution of the working of raw earth, bricks are a kind of artificial stone manufactured by mixing clay with water to make it moldable and elastic and then baking the result in a kiln. Baking at high temperature hardens the clay, which thus acquires important properties: high mechanical resistance, lightness, elasticity, malleability, adaptability to stress, good aging qualities, good thermal-insulation qualities, and "natural" protection from environmental dampness.

Brick is used in construction in bearing walls or curtain walls, while in structures like attic stories and roofs it is associated with metal frameworks. The principal types are solid brick, hollow or perforated brick, and tiles. The size and weight of the bricks chosen will depend on the mason's requirements, since the mason must be able to easily and rapidly lay courses, or continuous layers of bricks along the same line.

Over the centuries bricks have been made in an enormous variety of sizes, derived from local building techniques, but over time economic considerations have led to the standardization of sizes. Brick was the most frequently used building material in Roman architecture, while in Byzantine building it was often employed for its figurative qualities. During the Middle Ages brick was widely adopted in regions without access to stone or where the working of stone presented difficulties. Various brick buildings provide examples of daring conceptions, such as the dome of Santa Maria del Fiore, with its courses of self-supporting brick in a herringbone pattern.

With the exception of certain works by Borromini and Guarini, brick was rarely left visible during the Baroque age, for it was looked upon as a humble material. Brick was rediscovered early in the twentieth century by such Dutch architects as Berlage and de Klerk. In contemporary architecture the use of brick as a dressing or building material is not widespread except to give a building a particular aesthetic value.

In Depth
Since antiquity brick has been the most widespread man-made material used as an architectural element. Employed in traditional techniques, brick is available at low cost, has the same structural qualities as stone, and offers great versatility and speed in building.

Related Entry
Wall

Michel de Klerk, elevation of a brick house near Weesp, Holland, 1904–5

Church of San Vitale,
Ravenna, Italy,
begun 532

The Byzantine region in the fifth and sixth centuries saw the codification of the use of wine amphorae as building elements in domes, perfected with the technique of clay tubes, which called for the use of empty cylindrical elements in terracotta, inserted one into another.

The dome of San Vitale, hidden by an octagonal lantern, is made of clay tubes about 14 centimeters in diameter and 60 centimeters long, arranged in concentric bands to lighten the weight and the lateral thrusts on the uprights.

San Vitale was inspired by imperial Byzantine models reworked according to local tradition. Its exterior presents a construction technique distinguished by smooth brick walls made of thin bricks separated by mortar, marked off by pilasters, and reinforced by corner buttresses.

Byzantine brickmakers perfected the chromatics of brick, varying the shades by changing the clay mixtures and the baking times.

The exterior of the church is the result of restorations carried out between 1899 and 1902 with the intention of making the original structure visible.

Marienkirche,
Prenzlau, Germany,
begun 1325

The use of brick in some areas
of northern Europe led to a distinct
style: the compact nature of
structures made of brick seemed
in stark contrast to the extreme
lightness that was the goal of
Gothic architecture.

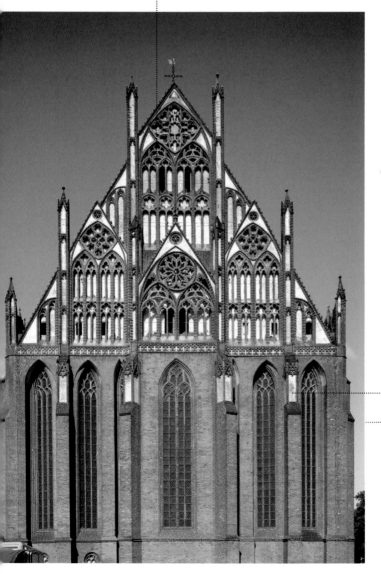

The structure of
these churches
clearly indicates the
desire for the kind
of simplicity seen
in the great Gothic
cathedrals. It is
dictated in part by
the materials,
which led to the
elevation of great
wall surfaces and
the tendency to
reject overly subtle
ornamentation. The
striking façade of
the church at
Prenzlau fully
reveals the formal
and pictorial
qualities made
possible through
the use of brick.

Toward the end
of the thirteenth
century German
architects
succeeded in
expressing the
Gothic through
the use of bricks,
leading to a style of
Gothic known to
art historians as
Backsteingotik.

Francesco Borromini,
San Andrea delle Fratte,
Rome, 1653–65,
detail of the lantern
and the bell tower

Looked upon as a humble material,
brick was rarely used for the creation
of exposed surfaces during the
Baroque age. Borromini, however,
made virtuosic use of brick, exalting
its potentials—not only structural
but also aesthetic.

Mindful of the
Lombard traditions
of his training,
Borromini intro-
duced the lantern to
the architectural
setting of Rome,
hiding the dome in
its body, with its
characteristic—
for Borromini—
mixtilinear outlines.

The unfinished
drum of San Andrea
delle Fratte reveals
the structural brick,
used for its great
resistance to com-
pression and for
its lightness.

Borromini's ingenious and
revolutionary exteriors ring out as
bold transgressions from the ordinary
Roman domes; the bell tower creates
an urban focal point that changes
appearance according to the
position of the viewer.

Fritz Höger, Chilehaus,
Hamburg, Germany,
1920–23

Nicknamed the "ship's prow,"
this building was designed as a
warehouse for merchandise
imported from Chile.

The early years
of the twentieth
century saw a
reevaluation of
exposed-façade
uses of brick. Here
the exterior is
dressed in dark red
clinker, a type of
brick obtained by
baking bricks at
temperatures high
enough to bring
them close to vitrifi-
cation, resulting in
a material particu-
larly well suited for
exterior dressing.
This treatment gives
the brick surface a
vitrified appearance
and makes the
material espe-
cially resistant to
mechanical stress.

Aside from recalling the shape of a
ship, the inspiration for the Chilehaus
came from the brick architecture of
churches in northern Germany.

Hans Kollhoff,
DaimlerChrysler offices,
Potsdamer Platz, Berlin,
1994–99

The dark red surfaces of this building result from the use of clinker. The surfaces are marked off by pilasters and cornices and proportioned windows in rhythmic arrangements. Kollhoff exploits all the potentials of clinker as a special architectural material, both precious and durable.

Rather than suggesting an archaic usage, the building exemplifies the modern method of hybridized building production combined with the use of traditional methods and materials.

The building sweeps upward by way of a series of steps, thus creating a volumetric dialogue with the lower buildings behind it. A panoramic terrace is located at a height of 88 meters.

The materials used, the stepped cubes, and the façade details recall North American architecture of the 1930s and 1940s. Kollhoff promotes a return to large-scale constructions that contrast with the reigning taste for transparent glass. He recognizes the settled nature of European cities and responds by rooting his buildings to the ground by way of vivid forms brought to life through materials.

Kollhoff's layered walls in clinker rework previous uses of that material as a dressing, in ways that are archetypical of historical Western architecture using brickwork.

Mario Botta, Museum
of Modern Art,
San Francisco, 1991–95

The Museum of Modern Art in San
Francisco, with its monumental
volume clad in brick, rises as
the dominant feature against the
profile of the surrounding buildings.

Botta explains: "Brick is one of the
tools that I use; its poverty fascinates
me—the fact that it is baked earth.
It is a prefabricated element that is very
flexible in terms of use while at the
same time being economical; it is an
essential material and for that reason,
perhaps, it is very expressive. . . .
Through my work I try to express as
best as possible even those materials
that might seem to be less interesting.
Then there is the aspect of endurance.
Brick is one of the materials that ages
best; in fact, it improves with time."

The project exalts a return to
monumentality—a quality totally
extraneous to contemporary
architecture—and does so through
architectural and functional expedients.
It is a building with simple and her-
metic volumes, illuminated by a large
central oculus and by fissures in the
walls. Botta's is an architecture
understood both as an art capable of
harmoniously blending with the nature,
culture, and history of a territory and
as a concrete testimony to historical
experience and human aspirations.
The material that interprets this
personal artistic vision is brick, an
element Botta prefers because of the
qualities of flexibility, solidity, and
expressivity it lends to buildings.

Recurrent themes in Botta's poetics are evident in this building, among them "the wall," "the opening," and "light." In this museum organism, natural light was treated as a building material equal in stature to the brick and granite that dress the building.

To meet the strict earthquake and fire codes of San Francisco, the classic brick surface is superimposed over prefabricated concrete panels—secured to the steel framework that forms the bearing structure of the building.

Surya Temple,
Modhera, India, 1026

A masterpiece of Gujarat
architecture, the temple at
Modhera, dedicated to the sun god,
is composed of two separate
structures erected on a
high podium.

The most spectacular construction is the *ramakund*, the magnificent rectangular basin in front of the temple, with ornamental stairs, enlivened by small aedicules for divinities along the sides and by *shikhara* in miniature on the corners. At the equinoxes the rising sun strikes the surface of the water, its rays progressively rising along the stairs to pass the *torana*, the triumphal entry arch to the *sabhamandapa*, the splendid pillars of which are still visible today. The light penetrates columned rooms until it reaches the cella and illuminates the statue of Surya; the radiant splendor of the sun transforms the water and the temple into an otherworldly setting.

This admirable structure is made of brick, and its outlines make abundantly clear the material's expressive and formal qualities, creating a delicately ornamental geometric design.

Concrete

Concrete is a conglomerate widely used in construction and in civil engineering, made by mixing a hydraulic binder—lime or cement—with inert materials like sand, gravel, brick fragments, additives, and if necessary additional minerals and water. This mixture can be poured into formworks. Because of the hydration, the binder hardens, giving the mixture a durability that makes it similar to stone.

Although the term *concrete* is usually associated with the modern building material, it actually embraces composite materials widely used in antiquity. The differences result from the diversity of binders used and from the range of particle sizes of the inert materials—an idea more or less absent in the ancient production of concrete.

The materials employed, their composition, and the ways of using concrete in Roman times are described in great detail by Vitruvius in his *De architectura*. The Roman wall technique—the so-called *opus caementicium*—involved making flat surfaces in brick or stone that acted as disposable molds; these were filled with mortar into which had been dumped fragments of stone and brick about 30 to 35 millimeters in size. This mixture was pounded down with an iron mallet. The binder was composed only of lime or lime mixed with pozzulana. The process of hardening was closely related to the amount of air penetration, and the more compact and impenetrable the barrier of stone and brick, the less air that could get through.

The discovery of hydraulic lime around 1750 accelerated the processes of hardening, eventually leading to the 1924 patent for Portland cement. The great prestige concrete has enjoyed since earliest times is a result of the opportunity it offers to create artificial stones of any shape.

In Depth
The Romans made wide use of concrete for the construction of foundations and walls, and, at least initially, it was the only material used for vaulted structures. Today concrete can be made in a variety of ways, including through the grinding of clinker.

Related Entry
Wall

Basilica of Maxentius, Rome, c. 308

Reinforced Concrete

Reinforced concrete is concrete into which steel meshwork or rods are embedded that are able to withstand the tensile stresses to which concrete alone offers only modest resistance. Its primary characteristic is mechanical resistance to the disintegration caused by the atmosphere, chemical agents, and ordinary wear.

A related material is prestressed concrete, which owes its properties to a state of preliminary stress created through the use of steel cables, anchored at one end of the element and subjected to stretching or tensioning before or after the concrete is cast.

The use of reinforced concrete has transformed the bearing structure of buildings into a continuous and elastic spatial system composed of support elements arranged with a freedom previously unknown. The material rose to greatness through the creations of the modern movement, thanks to which the structural use of reinforced concrete was formally integrated into the architectural design process. Reinforced concrete and prestressed concrete have facilitated the designing of plastic structures that follow the dynamic combination of lines of force.

The creations of Pier Luigi Nervi are exemplary for the complexity of their calculations and their spatial images. Nervi invented the building material known as ferroconcrete, in which the reinforcing component is various overlapping layers of metal mesh. The mesh is rotated and buried within the concrete to create structural elements that are light, strong, and very elastic, suitable for membranes and shells that do not require formworks for their creation.

In Depth

Many concretes have been produced as a result of technological developments; those created to serve specific construction needs have assumed special importance. Outstanding among these is pattern imprinted concrete (PIC), which is used primarily for paneling, dressing slabs, and similar applications.

Related Entry
Wall

Ignacio Vicens and José Antonio Ramos, journalism faculty of the University of Navarre, Pamplona, Spain, 1996, detail of the perforated concrete cladding

Max Berg,
Jahrhunderthalle,
Breslau, Poland,
1913, interior

In the Jahrhunderthalle, built for
the 1913 centennial exhibition in
Breslau, Berg took on the challenge
of creating a large covered space.
In the vast hall, the reinforced
concrete walls of the dome rise off
outer concentric ring beams and a
complex structure of thirty-two
radial ribs, supported in turn by four
enormous depressed arches.
This Herculean structure was
covered externally by concentric
rings of windows, with the dynamics
of the structure concealed by the
superimposition of neoclassical
elements.

The Jahrhunderthalle is considered
one of the key constructions in the
transition from historicism and
expressionism to a new rational and
functional architecture. Berg put
enormous faith in new materials
and new technologies, deliberately
choosing to build in concrete
because "it would give witness to
the culture of our time even after
the passage of history."

With its volume of 300,000 cubic
meters, diameter of 65 meters, and
height of 42 meters, the building
can seat 20,000 people. The gigantic
structure was one of the first in the
world to be built of reinforced
concrete.

The exposed reinforced concrete anticipates certain aesthetic trends that would be particularly widespread during the period after World War II.

François Hennebique,
Ponte del Risorgimento,
Rome, 1908–11

The bridge was built in 1911 to connect areas on opposite banks of the Tiber that were to be used for the headquarters of the International Exhibition of Art, which celebrated the fiftieth anniversary of Italian unification.

The bridge is made of Portland cement, so named because its strength seemed similar to that of the limestone quarried on the Isle of Portland. It was the first and most widely used of the modern hydraulic cements, whose industrial production found immediate applications in large structural undertakings.

The bridge was built using the so-called Hennebique system, a patented system based on a kind of concrete slab reinforced with evenly distributed steel bars.

A masterpiece for the audacity of its concept as well as for its formal result, the bridge is 159 meters long and 20 meters wide. The first bridge in Rome to be built of reinforced concrete, and using technical methods that were quite daring for the time, it has a single depressed span of 100 meters and a highly reduced thickness in its arch that gives it a thin, elegant line.

Frank Lloyd Wright,
Ennis House, Los Angeles,
1923–24

For this house Wright used the textile-block construction system, employing blocks of cement decorated with geometric motifs and connected with steel joints, similar to the warp of a fabric.

The textile-block system is economical despite a surface rich with "conventionalized" ornamental motifs, taking full advantage of the resources of modern technology.

The Ennis House, along with the other textile-block houses he designed in California during those years, offered Wright the opportunity to test the procedure of pouring the ornamental concrete elements on site. This was an efficient and convenient transfer of the fabrication process directly to the worksite, making it possible to create a different decorative motif for each situation.

In this way Wright proposed to blend the climate of the region with its typical materials: the geometric abstractions of the decorative motifs of the textile blocks express the essence of natural forms, making the architectural work conform to the "nature of the materials."

Auguste Perret,
Saint Joseph, Le Havre,
France, 1954, interior
with dome spire

Comparable to certain wooden structures, reinforced concrete—made by casting concrete in wooden formworks—facilitates a construction system centered on the relationship between the bearing elements and those being borne.

This technique speeds the creation of the bearing structure, while also disassembling it into individual elements—pillars, beams, and trusses—no longer bound by the planimetric distribution of the building.

Perret's works reveal his double role as both architect and part owner of a building and contracting company. His architectural work followed the ideals of classical formal harmony, but he combined this with use of the newest and most economical building methods, beginning with the adoption of reinforced concrete.

In Saint Joseph the framework of highly visible, prefabricated reinforced concrete panels serves both aesthetic and functional purposes; light enters the interior from the daring dome-spire following a regular system of openings that take the place of curtain walls.

Le Corbusier,
Unité d'Habitation,
Marseilles, France,
1947–52, detail of the roof

Beginning in the 1950s reinforced concrete, which previously had been concealed, covered with more valuable materials, or disguised under plaster, began to be appreciated for its material beauty and was left exposed—a usage in keeping with the figurative style of the period.

On the roof of the building rise the large volumes of the high chimneys and the various structures for community life, supported on pilotis that are also made of reinforced concrete.

The Unité d'Habitation is both an expression of Le Corbusier's theories of new ways of building cities and a fundamental embodiment of the architectural revolution in city planning that was initiated by the modernist movement.

The enormous structure of the Unité, 140 meters long, 24 meters wide, and about 60 meters high, has 23 floors of uniquely arranged living spaces.

Amid all the reinforced concrete only the *brise-soleils* (sun shades) add notes of color—painted red, blue, green, and yellow.

Reinforced Concrete 251

Kenzo Tange,
Yamanashi Press
Broadcasting Center,
Kofu, Japan, 1961–66

A student of Le Corbusier, Tange designed a building of united parts that houses a radio-television center, a news agency, and a telecommunications firm. The building's structural system is designed to simplify future enlargements: the technical services and elevators are all located in the sixteen external towers, so its size can be increased simply by adding new floors among the towers.

The sixteen towers are the principal structural supports on which the floors rest. Like the remainder of the structure, they are made of exposed concrete, free from intermediate structural supports, and completely self-sufficient in terms of plant engineering. The structure of the administration building is steel, and the floors of the offices all project out from the central support pylon on two sides.

The phrase "exposed concrete" refers to a type of architectural finish in which the surface is left free of plaster or cladding. Concrete that has been left exposed is characteristic of the works of many modern and contemporary architects, from Le Corbusier to Kenzo Tange to the architects of the so-called Brutalist style. The bare concrete exalts the expressive potentialities of the medium.

Tadao Ando,
4 × 4 House,
Kobe, Japan, 2001

The 4 × 4 House derives its name from its dimensions and its vertical extension: it measures 4 × 4 meters and is four stories high. The dislocation of the cube of the top floor, off center and shifted outward from the three lower floors, creates a formal solution of great breadth and gives the final composition a dynamic sensibility.

The house is made entirely of concrete—reinforced with steel—cast on site. It stands like a refuge amid the desolation left by the terrible earthquake that devastated the coast in 1995.

Ando's buildings are characterized by complex three-dimensional lines that cross one another in the interior and on the exterior; these are generated by large geometric shapes and by the spaces that separate them.

The house overlooks the sea and contains large glass surfaces that contrast with the areas of exposed concrete. Mold lines were left visible in the concrete in a typically Japanese way of evoking material reality.

In contemporary architecture this material, with the signs and traces of molds still visible, can achieve unexpected formal and aesthetic results. The concrete no longer seems heavy and blocky but instead presents balanced solids, while open spaces dematerialize the structural work.

Iron and Metallic Alloys

The perfecting of innovative building materials and techniques—such as the production of iron and steel alloys, introduced on an industrial scale in England between the end of the eighteenth century and the early nineteenth century—made it possible for engineers and architects to experiment with new forms that accentuated a sense of flexibility.

The history of the development of iron is divided into three periods, based on the three principal types of iron: cast iron, wrought iron, and steel. Cast iron was developed in England for functional building elements and was initially used in industrial buildings to reduce the space lost to support elements. By the middle of the nineteenth century it was being replaced by malleable (or annealed) cast iron—originally used in a complementary way, most of all for trusses, and then as a material in its own right for entire structures. Certain architectural structures leant themselves to the use of new materials: greenhouses, exhibition pavilions, large commercial centers that exalted the ductility of metallic structures and permitted the creation of expansive glass surfaces in place of traditional walls.

The age of steel began only after 1850; before then, given its high cost and the limitations imposed by production methods, steel had been reserved for the fabrication of small objects. Between the end of the nineteenth century and the opening years of the twentieth, it became the ideal material for experiments in new formal styles. With the increase in the production of steel and its technological perfection, the material entered widespread use and affected the entire field of construction—becoming, along with reinforced concrete, one of the basic materials of the period.

Metallic alloys offer buildings good resistance both to tension and to compression; they also offer considerable plastic adaptability. They make it possible for building elements to be made and preassembled in the workshop. Other advantages include rapidity of construction, a high strength-weight ratio, simplicity of calculation, precision of execution, and efficiency in connection. On the other hand, alloys require maximum design precision, are vulnerable to fire and corrosion, and readily transmit noise and vibrations.

Alloy components are joined by means of heated rivets driven by pneumatic hammers, by bolts, or by electrosoldering. Today steel is often flanked by other materials, such as reinforced concrete, and is widely used in architecture. The types most commonly used include high-tensile steel, which has a high percentage of carbon and can thus be more fragile; stainless steel, which is particularly resistant to corrosion; and prestressed steel, which is used to make the cables for prestressed reinforced concrete.

In Depth
Although metals like bronze and iron were used in buildings from earliest times, they usually played only a complementary role until the eighteenth century. Their systematic use dates to the nineteenth century, when engineers and architects began to see their great constructive possibilities, most importantly for the resolution of static problems and the unloading of inertial forces.

Related Entry
Wall

Decimus Burton, Temperate House, Kew Gardens, London, 1859–99, interior

Abraham Darby,
Coalbrookdale Bridge
over the Severn River,
Great Britain, 1776–79

The discovery of metallic alloys at the
end of the eighteenth century led to the
construction of large infrastructural works.
The Coalbrookdale Bridge, made entirely
of cast iron, was the first of a family of
bridges that revolutionized both the
landscape and modes of transportation
while showcasing the level of complexity
attainable through civil engineering.

The structure is
based on a net-
work of elements
resistant to traction
and compression,
combined with
junction elements
that made possible
the spanning of
large areas. The
continuous reticular
parabolic trusses,
called Vierendeel
trusses, are
assembled with fixed
joints and without
diagonal bracing.

The structure of the arches, which
make use of centering, is innovative;
they are composed of iron pieces
bolted into shapes not unlike those
of wooden structures. The metal
arches and the railroad bed are
joined by horizontal rings,
also of iron.

Henry Labrouste, Bibliothèque Nationale de France, Paris, 1858–68, column of cast iron in the reading room

This remarkable roof—nine small eggshell-shaped domes supported by sixteen thin columns 10 meters high—marked an early synthesis between engineering and architecture that demonstrates the aesthetic possibilities of metal structures.

In the reading room of the Bibliothèque Nationale, Labrouste created functional and nontraditional forms whose late Gothic heritage proved conducive to the use of innovative materials: the columns and arches are of cast iron, as are the perforated floor slabs.

During this period Eugène-Emmanuel Viollet-le-Duc—architect, restorer, and scholar of medieval art—hypothesized a connection between the skeletal structure of Gothic architecture and the metal frameworks and reinforced concrete that engineers were beginning to use. This notion of Gothic structures created in innovative materials and techniques found felicitous expression in the reading room designed by Labrouste.

Gustave Eiffel, Eiffel Tower,
Paris, 1899, detail of the
metallic frame

For the Paris Exposition Universelle of
1889, French engineer Eiffel designed
a tower symbolic of the modern age,
made of an iron framework left completely visible, to demonstrate the
expressive potentials of the new material.

Graceful and spare, with its
unforgettable profile, the iron
structure's efficiency legitimized the
abandonment of traditional figurative
schemes and facilitated a drastic
increase in the height of buildings.

The Eiffel Tower is 304 meters high
(including the antenna) and uses
7,300 tons of wrought iron in the form
of a network of riveted beams joined
by thermally assembled rivets that
contracted during cooling. The
choice of material offers the greatest
measure of strength and flexibility
with minimum weight and wind
resistance.

Because of exposure to corrosion,
the tower's metal structures must be
repainted every seven years using fifty
tons of dark brown paint. Depending
on the ambient temperature, the
height of the tower can vary by
several centimeters, a result of
the metal expanding; on windy days,
given the elasticity of the material,
the top can oscillate by up to
12 centimeters.

Hendrik Petrus Berlage, Commodities Exchange, Amsterdam, 1898–1903, detail of iron trusses

The central vault of the Amsterdam stock exchange is made of malleable or soft iron, a material initially used for complementary parts of constructions, most of all trusses.

The hall is in a neo-Romanesque style, symbolic of the most modern mercantilism.

The rooms are delimited by bare brick walls. The large hall, a kind of critical rereading of the Roman model of the basilica, presents a large urban square covered by a network of trusses in iron that support a roof of glass and wrought iron.

William Van Alen,
Chrysler Building,
New York, 1930, spire

Completed in 1930, the Chrysler Building, with its Art Deco styling, is one of the best-known symbols of New York City. It is 319 meters high with 77 floors.

What makes the Chrysler Building so unique is the terminal part of the structure: the famous terraced crown, with its profile of overlapping semicircles topped by triangular windows and by the spire, which stands out unmistakably against the city's skyline.

The 56-meter-high crown is clad entirely in Nirosta steel, a combination of chrome-nickel and steel with an extraordinary sheen, creating magnificent reflections according to the angle of the sun while requiring almost no maintenance. Since the year the building was completed the crown has required maintenance only once: in 1995, as part of a large-scale cleaning of the façade.

The Chrysler Building is a celebration of the age of the automobile. Van Alen used construction details that refer to the shape of tires, fenders, hood ornaments, and hubcaps.

There are also decorations inspired by the winged hat of Mercury, and near the top are enormous stainless steel gargoyles in the shape of American eagles, emphasizing the power of the building.

Renzo Piano and Richard Rogers, Centre Pompidou, Paris, 1971–78, detail of the structure

The architects of the Centre Pompidou, better known as Beaubourg, created a work emblematic of technological experimentation applied to structural elements, as well as of the poetic ideal of the building as machine.

This artisan-made product was constructed piece by piece. The custom-built elements of the load-bearing structure in steel and cast iron were made by hand, and each one is unique. The single-cast Gerber girders that support the main structure are strong enough to span 50 meters without intermediate supports.

The high-tech architecture externalizes the physical plant. Each color corresponds to a function: white is used for the bearing structure and the air intakes; red for the platforms and elevator shafts; blue for the air conditioning system; yellow for the electrical system; and green for the water pipes.

Designed in collaboration with Ove Arup, the building is a steel-and-glass parallelepiped about 140 meters long, 50 meters wide, and 50 meters high. The structural system allows for open space on each floor without internal bearing walls or partitions, permitting the space to be transformed as needed.

The support structure of the Pompidou is composed of tubes and reticular steel beams attached to the façade by means of special joints called gerberettes.

Frank Gehry,
Walt Disney Concert Hall,
Los Angeles, 1989–2003

The Walt Disney
Concert Hall is the
mature archi-
tectural expression
of an investigation
of architectural
forms strongly
oriented toward the
plastic and the
sculptural that here
adopt a syntax
similar to a work of
collage: it is a
curving building
made of stainless
stell and limestone
blocks.

The dressing in
stainless steel
reflects changing
light.

At first glance,
Gehry's graceful
steel panels, which
he referred to as
"wing on wing,"
seem to suggest
a large sailboat.

Daniel Libeskind,
Jewish Museum,
Berlin, 1989–98,
plan and detail of
cladding

The layout of the museum disguises a complex symbolic system, including distortions of the Star of David, the hexagon of which is deconstructed in the irregular forms of broken and twisting lines. It is like a gigantic lightning burst, whose irrational zigzag is multiplied in the shiny silver cladding.

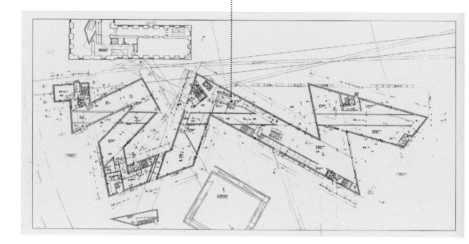

The metallic skin that covers the entire building—the patented brand Rheinzink—is a zinc-copper-titanium alloy of great flexibility. The material offers good resistance to atmospheric agents. In fact, a protective patina forms on the exposed surface that does not require constant maintenance and guarantees durability. The Rheinzink has a gray-zinc color, and its aesthetic value is heightened by the color change it undergoes over time.

The 12,500 square meters of façade have been dressed with vertical panels with oblique cut ends applied over a ventilated support. The numerous oblique slashes required special solutions, in particular the flashing to accommodate water runoff.

Derived from the theoretical postulates of fractal geometry, according to which the shape of the cosmos itself cannot be reduced to the primary forms of Euclidean geometry, the Jewish Museum presents nonlinear dynamics generated by the encounter between the forces and resistances within the material and the exterior flow of climatic and ecological forces.

The tortuous sculptural volume is dressed entirely in modular zinc panels and presents no visible entrances or other means of communication with the exterior except the cuts and slits in the metal skin of the covering. These set off an infinite series of fissures of different sizes that multiply the dynamic and aggressive effect.

Herzog & de Meuron,
National Stadium,
Beijing, 2004–8, view of
the worksite

Known as the Bird's Nest, the
Beijing National Stadium is a forest
of steel trees: the external framework
consists of a grid of girders, beams,
and arms that interweave and support
one another, forming both the façade
and the support structure for the
immense roof.

The architectural firm of Herzog &
de Meuron, attentive to materials and
to innovative building methods, saw
this project as an opportunity for
experimentation and research both
during the planning phase and
directly at the worksite.

Built for the 2008 Summer Olympics, the central arena is wrapped in concrete. The retractable roof is an integral part of the structure, a transparent shell that permits the outward reflection of beams of light.

Seemingly accidental, the arrangement and direction of the "branches" are actually the result of precise structural calculations.

The majestic yet light construction recalls a nest. In the finished structure the empty spaces between the interwoven branches are covered externally with panels of ETFE, a translucent and impermeable fluoropolymer, and internally with sound-absorbent materials.

Glass

Glass is a highly transparent manufactured product made of silicates, combined with oxides and other substances to add color or opacity, and then fused at high temperature. During this phase of the work glass has a viscous consistency and can be made to assume a desired shape, which is later fixed by cooling.

Given its low elasticity, glass is extremely fragile. However, it possesses excellent transparency and good resistance to chemical and atmospheric agents as well as to high temperatures. It has low thermal conductivity and very low electric conductivity. Because of these qualities—in addition to its lightness, impermeability, ease of cleaning, and malleability—glass has enjoyed great popularity since 3000 BCE.

Glass has been used in architecture since the twelfth century, in particular in the stained glass windows in large Gothic cathedrals, reaching its most felicitous results in the following two centuries. The first examples of the large-scale use of glass in buildings are the nineteenth-century pavilions with metal structures and the skyscrapers of the Chicago School. These mark the first use of a structural framework supporting lightweight curtain elements, creating walls composed more or less entirely of glass. The evolution of the basic technologies of modern architecture, such as the curtain wall and the structural facade, has been made possible in part by the creation of glass panels of increasingly large size with notable physical and mechanical qualities.

Certain kinds of glass are of particular importance. These include reflective or spandrel glass, which owes its qualities to the use of oxides on its external surface and metallic mesh on the inside, thus creating a visual barrier to hide interiors from view. So-called selective glass serves the same function and is in addition colored with special pigments.

Today glass often serves a structural function, for example in concrete-framed glass panels and U-glass (structural colored glass manufactured in bars with a U-shaped cross section that is so strong that it does not require a support framework). The most widespread system in use is structural silicon glazing, which confers very high resistance on the glass, allowing it to act as both fixative and decoration. Another technique involves the use of tubes and exterior steel cables or metal clamps on which glass panels are literally hung; in this case it is called a suspended façade.

Origins

Although used for windows in the Roman age as well as in the Middle Ages, glass came into use as a building material only in the early nineteenth century.

Related Entry
Wall

Herzog & de Meuron, Library, Cottbus, Germany, 2004, detail of the system for anchoring the glass façade

Joseph Paxton, Crystal Palace, London, 1851 (destroyed in the 1930s), lithograph

Built following a competition held in 1850, the Crystal Palace—the centerpiece of London's Great Exhibition of 1851—inaugurated a new architectural typology. Taken apart and rebuilt in 1854, it was completely destroyed in the 1930s.

Six hundred meters long, the palace was the first and most important architectural structure to adopt modern systems of prefabrication. The possibility of potentially unlimited space and the reduction of surfaces to transparent diaphragms were further developed in twentieth-century architecture.

Based on a square unit about 7.3 meters on a side, the building called for 77 × 17 of those units, reaching a total surface area of 84,000 square meters; the division of the various exhibition spaces followed this modular scheme. The use of iron supports allowed for the total elimination of support walls, so that nearly the entire exterior perimeter, as well as the stunning barrel vault, could be made of glass. This structural system facilitated the building's later reconstruction, even in an enlarged version.

The characteristics of the building, so well suited to an exhibition space, called for the use of prefabricated elements in wrought iron and cast iron with glass surfaces—easy to assemble and reusable. Various technical details, such as the support system's design for the runoff of rainwater, contributed to the successful implementation of these new architectural methods.

Bruno Taut, Glashaus (Glass Pavilion), Cologne, Germany, 1914, destroyed

The dome represents an enormous crystal composed of large glass panes connected by thin ribs of reinforced cement. The internal surfaces were woven with small glass tiles (Luxfer prisms), soldered to a very fine grid framework that blocked all views of the exterior, creating a suffused light without shadows.

Color was by no means a secondary element of the pavilion's spatial definition. A chromatic symphony ranged from the night blue of the lower part of the dome to a moss green, rising through golden yellow to culminate at the top in a radiant pale yellow.

Influenced by the technical writings and drawings of Paul Scheerbart's proposals for a *Glassarchitektur* (glass architecture), Taut created several structures in iron and glass, including this Glass Pavilion, designed for the Deutscher Werkbund exposition in Cologne in 1914.

The pavilion is a pioneering undertaking in reinforced concrete and glass constructions. Raised on a circular concrete base, expanding at its lower part in the shape of a bell, and decorated with large spheres of colored glass, it consisted of a polygonal (14-sided) drum with thin columns of reinforced concrete, supporting a Gothic-style ellipsoid dome.

Glass stairs between walls of reinforced vetroconcrete lead the visitor to the kaleidoscopic dome, articulating the space and giving it consistency and orientation. From Taut onward, glass architecture became a key symbol of the architectural avant-garde.

Philip Johnson, Glass
House, New Canaan,
Connecticut, 1949

At one time the private home of
the architect, the Glass House is a
simple glass prism resting on a brick
base, measuring 9.75 × 17.96 meters,
set atop a hill with panoramic views.
The floor is made of dark brown
herringbone brick.

The finite space of the Glass House
is a result of the elimination of the
structural system; Johnson ended the
plane of the roof at the corner columns,
making the house into a closed box
with splendid details. To amplify the
effect he tinted black the support
structures along the edges of
the glass walls.

Inside the 167-square-meter glass
box Johnson placed furnishings,
accessories, and works of art to
turn the open space into an
orderly structure with
specific purposes.

The absolute transparency of the
volume, obtained by using glass
panes framed on all four sides by
a thin steel frame, contrasts with
the cylindrical masonry mass that
houses the bathroom.

Making walls entirely out of glass
poses concerns about materials,
architecture, and form and raises
questions about vulnerability and
the total absence of privacy.

Part of the ingenuity of the Glass
House is derived from the fact that,
although based on the architecture
of the modern movement, it is
intrinsically classical: a symmetrical
space, clear and orderly.

Emilio Ambasz, Lucille
Halsell Conservatory,
Botanical Garden,
San Antonio, Texas, 1987

This conservatory is composed of various circular buildings, partially blended into the surrounding landscape, on which spectacular cylindrical or pyramidal glass structures rest. The interior spaces are flooded with sunlight that takes on pyramidal and semispherical forms and permits the cultivation of a wide variety of plants.

Ambasz's architecture overcomes the dichotomy between environment and landscape. Here, humans give technology the role of life support, adding it to the circle of the elements. Hence the archetypical images of the crystal pyramids, the cones that rise from rock or from the ground; trees, water, and earth are used as compositional and constructive biomaterials.

The glass panes of the roof are connected to a mesh of thin metallic ribs that are hinged and can thus be opened. The arrangement of the glass panes was carefully determined based on an analysis of the angle of incident solar rays.

The Lucille Halsell Conservatory is a group of greenhouses built on land with an irregular surface. The location is unusual, since glass greenhouses are usually used in cold climates to exploit solar rays.

Nicholas Grimshaw,
International Terminal,
Waterloo Station,
London, 1993

Waterloo Station came into being as a monument to the new railway age that began with the tunnel dug beneath the English Channel. In terms of both its technology and its spectacular visual impact, the focal point of the architecture is the roof: a large covering, 440 meters long and from 35 to 50 meters wide, on a thin, curving structure.

The system of windows is entirely adjustable between the trusses and is fixed to the structure with special stainless steel gaskets. The shape of the roof, based on wind tunnel tests, was designed to withstand significant levels of damage without collapsing.

The roof is entirely covered in glass with the support structure on the exterior, thus creating a sort of picture window, putting on display both the high-speed trains within and Westminster and the Thames without. The structure consists of thirty-six asymmetrically paired trusses, constructed following the geometry of a three-centered arch raised westward to make room for the tracks; these are located in an off-center position, while the angle of the trusses is less sharp above the platform.

Because of the twisting course of the roof, it is composed of glass panels cut in different sizes, each supported by its own frame. These are arranged so as to overlap one another and connected by concertina-shaped neoprene gaskets that can flex and expand to accommodate the dual curve of the roof arch and the track.

Ranked among the most important exponents of high-tech architecture, Grimshaw likes to keep the structural aspects and physical plants of his buildings visible, revealing the flexibility of the layout and the transparency of its functions.

Renzo Piano,
Kansai International Airport,
Osaka, 1994

The roof is composed of 82,000 identical stainless steel panels, whose shape was based on aerodynamic studies of the air currents that flow around the building. In this way the structure is able to withstand earthquakes.

The Kansai International Airport is located in Osaka Bay on an artificial island 1.7 kilometers long.

Despite their formal immensity, the buildings have a sense of structural lightness due to their absolute transparency.

The entirely glass façade integrates advanced technology—including a high-resistance metallic mesh—with a close analysis of natural phenomena. The need for illumination is translated into a search for lightness and an exploration of the technical and expressive potentials of materials and metallic tensile structures. The design of the structure paid close attention to particular details of the location; the airport is located far from densely populated areas in order to minimize noise pollution.

Rafael Viñoly, Tokyo
International Forum,
1997, glass atrium

The large glass atrium in the shape
of a ship's hull was the result of a
collaboration with the structural
engineer Kunio Watanabe. The entire
124-meter-long structure is supported
by only two pillars, with a maximum
diameter of 4.5 meters, located at
the ends.

The use of glass
in a region of high
seismic activity
presented a
technical challenge:
resistance to earth-
quakes and wind
was achieved by
joining the block
with the conference
rooms to the pillars.

Made of modular
panels of lami-
nated glass with
a thickness of 16
millimeters and a
height of 57 meters,
the wall was
stabilized by an
auxiliary structure
independent from
that of the roof.

To stabilize the façades and
give them greater rigidity, a large
ramp was built on the western
façade; pedestrian passageways
high up on the structure
transfer lateral thrusts.

The design of the Tokyo International
Forum allows various divisions of the
interior spaces. The structure is designed
to include four halls for concerts, exhibits,
and conferences, in different volumes
but with a shared façade.

Jean Nouvel, Agbar
Tower, Barcelona, 2005

The Agbar Tower is a steel-and-glass skyscraper that stands out on the city's skyline with its height of more than 142 meters divided into 32 floors.

Designed for Aigües de Barcelona, the city's water company, the tower seems to burst from the ground like a geyser. The continuous, smooth, and vibrant surface becomes as transparent as the colored glass it is made of, and evokes water in a play of lights and shadows.

The building is composed of two nonconcentric oval cylinders, one inside the other. Beginning at the 26th floor the structure curves inward in a cone-shaped form; between the two interior cylinders is open space without pillars that can be organized as desired. At the top is a steel dome with glass set between the structural members.

The façade serves a structural role and is dressed in a double skin designed according to bioclimatic criteria, creating a thermal shield that insulates the building from cold and heat. It has 4,400 panes of transparent glass arranged following a fractal composition based on careful studies of solar exposure and structural calculations, while still keeping in mind the different views.

The orientation of the glass panels, which oscillate between 20 and 76 degrees, is based on a close study of the building's exposure to sunlight.

The project combines the two opposing concepts of lightness and solidity; the first results from the generous use of glass, the second from the presence of the reinforced concrete that forms the core of the building.

Around the concrete core of the building is a layer of multicolored corrugated aluminum sheets; this is covered in turn by a layer of tinted glass louvers that blur the tones of the aluminum sheets.

The louvers are inclined at different angles according to their location on the building, and some, located to the south, are fitted with photovoltaic panels to generate electricity.

Technopolymers

The term technopolymers refers to those synthetic or artificial polymers that are used to create, through shaping while in the plastic state, solid products. The plastic materials, which can be classified into thermoplastics and thermohardeners, have numerous applications in architecture because of their insulating and nonconducting properties, often accompanied by high strength and transparency.

Thermoplastic materials preserve their plasticity when hot and harden on cooling. Among the principal ones used in building are PVC, polyethylene, Plexiglas (which because of its great mechanical strength and transparency can be used in place of glass), polystyrene, and polycarbonate. The thermo-hardening resins harden through heat, assuming a permanently rigid consistency. Among the most frequently used are the phenolic resins and the ureic resins, used as finishing material in the fabrication of laminated panels; polyurethane, with its great insulating power; the polyester resins made with reinforced fibers, such as glass fabric; and the epoxy resins.

The primary use of techno-polymers is in the creation of tensile or membrane structures, which came into being in the twentieth century but have illustrious progenitors not only in the tents of prehistoric peoples but also in the velariums of Roman amphitheaters. Today they are used most often to cover large sporting complexes, outdoor performance sites, and airport terminals, which are typically designed with membranes held in tension by a system of cables and support elements. Their use makes it possible to cover large open spaces without intermediate supports. They are also extremely light, quick and easy to install, and offer excellent control of structural efficiency with great versatility and formal freedom.

The roof of the Olympiapark stadium in Munich is a sort of tent composed of a web of Plexiglas plates supported by inclined steel pylons.

Origins
Created in the twentieth century, technopolymers are widely used in architecture for their ductility. Light and easy to assemble and disassemble, they are extremely versatile from a formal point of view. They are the ideal material for covering extremely large spaces.

Günter Behnisch and Frei Otto, Olympiapark, Munich, 1968–72, construction of the Plexiglas roof

Herzog & de Meuron,
Allianz Arena, Munich,
2006

The shape of the Allianz Arena marks it as the natural heir to the stadium designed by Behnisch and Otto. As in the 1972 project (see facing), the roof is made of a light plastic material, in this case using foil panels inflated with air at a controlled humidity.

The foil panels of the covering are kept inflated to a pressure that varies from 200 to 1,000 pascals. Despite its soft appearance, the covering is supported by a complex metallic frame. Thanks to the neon tubes installed on its internal face (red, white, and blue, the colors of the various home teams), the building can be transformed into a reactive agent that becomes the perfect symbiosis between container, event, and spectator. Such sophisticated allusions do not, however, rule out the simplest and most immediate reference: the big inflated shape echoes the dimpled surface of a soccer ball, and the lighting effects speak the language of opposing groups of fans.

Each of the 2,816 panels is made of two sheets of EFTE, an entirely recyclable material, nondeformable and durable, of varying sizes. The different combinations of the two sheets are the only distinction between façade and covering; white or transparent sheets are used for the vertical skin, transparent ones for the horizontal. Thus all distinction between elevation and roof is discarded as the membrane wraps the entire building without interruption: the stadium becomes a work of architecture without faces.

Samyn and Partners,
M&G Research, Venafro,
Italy, 1992

The research center is composed of a series of buildings and installations designed for industrial experiments, enclosed beneath a pretensioned tensile structure with an ellipsoidal shape. The center is surrounded by an artificial lake in open countryside.

This revolutionary use of innovative architecture presents a distinctly technological image perfectly inserted into the natural environment. The lake, oval like the buildings, is part of the landscape but also serves to control the environmental conditions within the chemical laboratories.

The tensile structure is composed of a membrane of polyester fiber coated with PVC and protected on the surface by a layer of Tedlar (a trademarked film of polyvinylfluoride with excellent chemical, electrical, and stress-resistant properties). It is divided into independent sections suspended from six transverse reticular steel arches, and connected to the ground by longitudinal cables that maintain tension. It measures 85 × 32 meters and is 15 meters high.

Aside from covering the structures and forming their external wall, the tensile membrane performs a secondary role as structural member. The transparent PVC is located above the arches, which remain visible from the exterior while still beneath the layer of the roof. The same material is used to enclose the spaces between the outer edges of the membrane and the glass perimeter walls.

The interior receives light filtered through the tensile structure; direct sunlight enters through the arches, which act as windows.

Vito Acconci, Murinsel, Graz, Austria, 2003, detail of the roof in glass and polycarbonate

Constructed in 2003 for Graz's year as European Capital of Culture, the Murinsel (Mur island) is a sort of seashell floating on the Mur River, made of glass and polycarbonate and connected to the riverbanks by two footbridges. It features a café, open-air theater, and playground.

The idea of an artificial island was intended to fulfill the request of the Graz authorities to connect the two banks of the river; it also sprang from a vision of the river as part of the urban context. The connection was made by way of an articulated, organic organism composed of cloud-volumes that meet and combine.

The absolute transparency of the materials creates a dialogue between interior and exterior, continually offering new views and new ways of looking at reality.

Santiago Calatrava, roof
of the Olympic Stadium,
Athens, 2004, detail of
the paraboloid

The roof of the Olympic Stadium
in Athens was made to cover a
preexisting structure and is
completely unattached to the
original construction.

As in the other works by Calatrava,
every element of the project is
conceived with specific structural,
figurative, and expressive qualities
that recall organic forms. The project
required the roof to be capable of
withstanding winds of up to 120
kilometers an hour.

An inclined paraboloid steel arch
and tensioned cables hold the roof,
which is made of polycarbonate,
a technopolymer offering high
resistance both to mechanical forces
and to damage from atmospheric
agents. Because of its workability,
polycarbonate can replace glass
in the creation of surfaces with
special curvatures.

The Water Cube was designed to hold the 2008 Summer Olympic pool. Designed by the Australian studio PTW with the collaboration of Ove Arup, the building features an external covering that recalls a mass of water bubbles—irregular, weightless, luminous.

The project was baptized the Water Cube because of its strange geometry—a disorderly mass of water bubbles crystallized to form an enormous rectangular shape, which is based on a study of the natural formation of soap bubbles.

The building, designed according to principles of ecology and sustainability, uses ecologically friendly materials and technologies as sources for renewable energy. The unusual geometry of the framework responds to the antiseismic demands imposed by the location.

The covering—made with a double membrane of ETFE, an innovative, light, and transparent covering—was designed to create special plays and projections of light. It offers an extraordinary vision and is a vivid sensory experience even for television viewers.

ETFE is a special kind of Teflon that reacts to the color of the sky, creating fantastic visual effects. It also captures 20 percent of the solar energy that hits the building, using it to heat the water in the swimming pools as well as the interior areas.

Natural Elements

In addition to the traditional materials that have been used in architecture since its beginnings, other elements make equally important contributions to the definition of an architectural object and thus never escape the attention of the designer. These are the natural elements that interact with the building, often amplifying its technical and formal qualities.

Light and water, for example, are understood as actual materials, not merely as atmospheric agents. Architecture becomes a mimesis of the creative processes of nature and a transposition of the natural into the realm of the artificial. Light is not only electromagnetic radiation; it also plays an extremely important role in design, from the cosmic symbolism of the oculi opened at the apex of domes to the multicolor deity depictions of medieval stained-glass windows, from the use of mirrors and chandeliers to the arrangement of windows, right up to the most modern lighting techniques, which are the result of the scientific study of artificial illumination.

Much the same is true of water, a precious, flowing material. One must only think of the extraordinary ceremonial basins in medieval monasteries, magical sites of ablution and purification, or of Islamic gardens, metaphors for paradise, never without splendid fountains, or Baroque fountains, in which water itself becomes the protagonist in a piece of urban theater.

Then there are plants, which in their natural or artificial growth at times hide elements—as in the recent Musée du Quai Branly in Paris, designed by Jean Nouvel, in which the façade becomes a vertical garden—and at times constitute architecture itself—as in the highly original Tree Cathedral by Giuliano Mauri. Japanese architecture has always presented a perfect synthesis of tradition and technology, natural and artificial materials.

In Depth
Light, water, plants: nature and the human hand can together create an ecologically sustainable architecture. This is not at all an invention of our own time, for architecture has always reasoned in terms of nature and artifice.

Jean Nouvel, Musée du Quai Branly, Paris, 2006, detail of the façade

Pierre de Montreuil,
Saint-Chapelle, Paris,
1241–48

Light became a fundamental element
in Gothic figurative theories, and it was
used physically and metaphorically to
reveal the logical and constructive
procedures that supported the
construction of the church.

"God is light," affirmed the abbot Suger; so the walls are transformed into a diaphanous and radiant surface, always changing at every hour of the day as a result of atmospheric events. The evocative rays of colored light penetrate the interior, transfiguring the space and making manifest the immaterial substance of the creator, as reflected in the harmony of the proportions and luminosity of the building.

The extraordinary airiness of the upper area is created by both the solidity of the external buttresses and the use of ingenious technical artifices, such as metallic chains sunk into the walls, tie beams above the vaults, and iron clamps. These carry the skeletal structure of Gothic architecture to extremes: the walls disappear, replaced by a nearly continuous expanse of stained glass.

The refined quality of the architecture
is matched by the rich and fanciful
naturalistic decorations of the cornices
and the capitals, the use of color, and the
marvelous polyphony of the sparkling multicolored light that enters through the tracery
of the enormous stained glass windows.

François de Cuvilliés,
Amalienburg Pavilion,
Schloss Nymphenburg,
Munich, 1734–39,
circular hall

The interior of the pleasure villa of
Amalienburg—a simple rectangle
with a central rotunda projecting
outward—hides a splendid Rococo
jewel: in the circular mirrored hall
Cuvilliés dissolves the architectural
structure in a play of ornamentation,
with mother-of-pearl, mirrors, and
delicate pastel tonalities.

At night candlelight from the
chandelier, reflected and multiplied in
the mirrors and the silver decorations,
transforms the hall into a jewelcase
of sparkling light.

Mirrors were given particular importance in the design of the room. They
occupy an entire wall, producing
spectacular effects by reflecting
and multiplying light.

Tadao Ando, Church of Light, Osaka, 1987–89, interior

The building is intersected by a diaphragm wall that, breaking into the central volume at a 15-degree angle, separates the entry area from the space used for religious rites.

Light needs darkness in order to shine and demonstrate its power; the interior of the church rests in profound darkness, within which an isolated cross made of light floats.

Promoting a harmonic fusion of artifice and nature, Ando uses the techniques and components of modernism to give identity to architecture: the Church of Light is conceived as a simple space surrounded by solid concrete panels, thus isolated from the external world.

As Tadao Ando has said, "Light brings life to objects and unites space and form. . . . The appearance of things changes with changes in the intensity of light and with variations of time and season. . . . I give natural changes the role of producing a multiple array of complex visions inside simplified forms."

External light, having been architecturally manipulated and rendered abstract by the opening in the wall, generates a sort of sacred tension in the interior space of the building.

Toyo Ito & Associates,
Wind Tower, Yokohama,
Japan, 1986

Wrapped in an elliptical cylinder of perforated aluminum and surrounded by twelve neon rings dressed in plates of reflective acrylic, the tower continuously changes appearance.

This change occurs thanks to 1,280 small bulbs that respond to variations in wind intensity, light, temperature, and the number of decibels produced by the surrounding urban traffic.

In darkness the surface dematerializes, reducing itself to a framework that captures and filters the changeable conditions of the surrounding environment: the direction and speed of the wind and the sound of traffic are transformed into electrical impulses and an aerial architecture of light.

Ito has said, "The urban space is composed of static architectural structures that are however struck by a heterogeneous flow of information, like people, objects, or natural elements like water and wind that create a hybrid and immaterial space."

The tower is an immaterial mirror of the surrounding space, an ephemeral construction forever in transformation.

It is a sort of marvelous kaleidoscope, designed by Ito in collaboration with the TL Yamagiwa Laboratory and controlled by two computers.

Kengo Kuma,
Water/Glass House,
Shizuoka, Japan, 1995,
detail of the dining room

Located on the edge of a reef, this house seems to be suspended between the sea and the sky. The design theme was the relationship between architecture and landscape, and thus Kuma used light and natural materials such as glass, steel, and wood. The house explores the ambiguity of visual perception, acting on the sensory dimension of the materials.

Water and glass are not only construction materials but also incarnations of the generative principle; they give material form to the idea of transparency and continuity in space.

The roof, screened by grids of sun blocks, is composed of stainless steel louvers. Light, filtered through the louvers above, is reflected in the water below, creating a changeable perception of space accentuated by the ambiguous relationship between what is near and what is far. Making use of limited elements, Kuma constructs a deceptive perspective view, generating an artificial continuity between the surface of the water in the basin, the ocean, and the sky in the background.

A passageway connects the main structure to this pavilion, its floor level with the surface of an artificial body of water 15 centimeters deep and faced in black granite. The pavilion is composed of panes of laminated glass from 15 to 25 millimeters thick. The body of water that surrounds the room was designed as an integral part of the architecture and seems almost to dissolve into the ocean; the pavilion's floor, made of backlit glass, has a sense of depth similar to that of the water outside the structure.

Tadao Ando, Modern Art
Museum, Fort Worth,
Texas, 2002

The buildings have a double covering
that creates a play between the
qualities of the materials: they are
cement boxes inside cases of transparent glass—lightness contrasting
with solidity, transparency with
opacity.

Water and light are potent aspects
of this architectural design, with
mutations and reflections on the
surface of the water, on the glass,
on the surrounding environment. And
then there is the action of the wind,
which ripples and animates surfaces.

The six rectangular volumes, aligned
on the banks of a lake, reflect in the
water, creating a changing and
mutable vision according to the time
of day and the weather conditions.

The design called for a large artificial lake—to establish a harmonic
relationship with the adjacent Kimbell
Art Museum by Louis I. Kahn—and is
distinguished by its simple yet striking
spaces, in which all separation between
internal and external is nullified.

Herbert Dreiseitl, Tanner
Springs Park, Portland,
Oregon, 2005

The Portland project reworks the
urban model on the basis of new
aesthetics and functionalities, with
the intent of improving the living
conditions of citizens by reducing
traffic. The nucleus is an aquatic
park that celebrates the values of
happiness, environmental respect,
sustainability, and energy savings.

Herbert Dreiseitl here works with
what is perhaps the most fluid of
natural elements—water, a source
of endless fascination for him that
contributes to the invention of a
surprising landscape. The waterscape
is a specialty of his studio, which
creates projects that combine avant-
garde technology, environmental
sensitivity, and aesthetics.

The result is a concentration of technology and beauty in which water
becomes the key to understanding a new
way of living in the city. Creator of the
famous Water System of the Potsdamer
Platz in Berlin, Dreiseitl emphasizes the
symbolic aspects of water. Since the park
has a pattern, it presupposes the idea of
relationships between the city planner,
the engineer, and the landscape artist,
and draws upon different kinds of
knowledge from them all.

Giuliano Mauri, Tree Cathedral, Malga Costa, Italy, 2001, view and project sketches

The Tree Cathedral looks like a true Gothic cathedral, composed of a nave and two aisles with eight columns of interwoven branches, 12 meters high and 1 meter in diameter; planted inside each of these columns is a hornbeam (beech family).

Growing about 50 centimeters a year, the trees, having been trimmed and pruned, will over time form a true "tree cathedral." The structure is a rectangle of 82 × 15 meters, with a projected height of about 12 meters, enough to cover an area of 1,230 square meters.

Within about twenty years nature will win out: the artificial structures constructed to facilitate the growth of the trees will rot, making more room for the hornbeams. It is thus an entirely ecological architecture in which what is no longer necessary will disintegrate, resolving the problem of the elimination of waste.

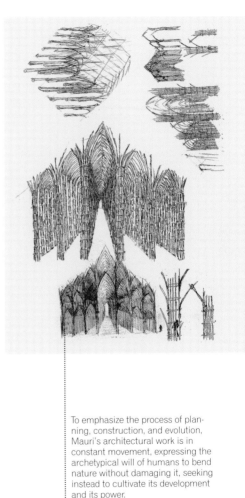

To emphasize the process of planning, construction, and evolution, Mauri's architectural work is in constant movement, expressing the archetypical will of humans to bend nature without damaging it, seeking instead to cultivate its development and its power.

Architecture and Decoration

Architectural Gilding / Polychromy / Murals / Sculpture / Mosaic / Ceramics / The Art of Wood / The Art of Metal

Antoni Gaudí, Casa Battló, Barcelona, 1904–6, detail of the façade

Architectural Gilding

"Architectural gilding" refers to an ornamental language that finishes off an architectural object and that can be expressed through the addition or super-imposition of various elements to the building structure—whether three-dimensional, chromatic, or material—or through the exploitation of the surface itself, whether in terms of its physical components or through the compositional potentials of the basic material.

Serving to both protect and decorate the building, orna-mentation can employ any of several basic methods: finishing the building material itself, which can be sculpted or carved; fashioning architectural ele-ments to make them more ornamental; using differing colors or the patterned arrange-ment of building stones.

Common in Far Eastern and Latin American architecture, architectural gilding finds full expression in decorative brick-work, reaching its apex in Roman and Byzantine architecture. Bricks can be made in different colors or can be specially shaped, and brickwork can take the form of patterns incor-porating lengthwise, herring-bone, or head-on patterns. Bricks can also be used in other decorative motifs, such as the Christological symbolism set into the church of the monastery of Kato Panagia at Arta.

Architectural gilding has assumed different forms and meanings over the decades: the profusion of galleries and arcades of Romanesque churches, the tracery façades of Gothic cathedrals, the proportional and chromatic relationships of cornices and rusticated stones on Renaissance façades, the ambiguity of Baroque façades, the integration of architecture and the visual arts promoted by Art Nouveau.

Although the modern move-ment and much of contemporary architecture have eliminated architectural decorations in the classical sense from buildings, the category of architectural gilding still includes the rela-tionships established among the materials that compose the covering of a building, the level of finishing applied to surfaces and their plastic possibilities, as well as the suggestions evoked by lighting.

Related Entries
Wall; Façade

Kato Panagia, Arta, Greece, 1231–71, decorative brickwork

Cathedral of Pisa,
consecrated 1118

Romanesque architecture exploits
and amplifies architectural gilding
through a profusion of elements—
galleries, pilasters, blind arcades,
lozenges—that articulate building masses.

The play of color effects and the
articulation of surfaces reached their
culmination in the splendid façade
of the cathedral of Pisa, made of
a delicately hued sandstone and
decorated by layers of glass and
majolica and marble finials, flowers,
and animals.

The upper part
of the façade is
one of the most
beautiful creations
of Romanesque
architecture: the
flat wall disappears
behind the tracery
of four levels of
functional galleries
filled with color
and light.

The pattern
maintains the
geometric
unity of aligned
surfaces on the
façade while at
the same time
creating a
diaphanous
exterior.

The harmonious articulation of the
exterior volumes includes an uninter-
rupted series of blind arcades that
encircles the lower part of the outer
walls—embellished by marble mosaics
with refined color effects and by the
motif (of Armenian origin) of the
lozenge inserted into the
curve of each arch.

Donato Bramante,
tribune of the church
of Santa Maria delle
Grazie, Milan, 1492–97,
detail of an apse

During the Renaissance, the idea
of directly integrating the various arts
into a single decorative display seems
to have diminished. Decoration was
then expressed exclusively through the
architectural forms and materials—
pilaster strips and cornices in
terracotta or stone—that stand out
against plastered surfaces, revealing
proportional and chromatic
relationships.

The decorative forms represent an
inseparable complement to the
architectural forms; terracotta is here
used mostly to emphasize pilaster strips
and cornices, which are given special
prominence through the chromatic
contrast between the red of the
terracotta and the white of the plaster.

Terracotta pieces cast in molds are
one of the characteristic decorative
elements of fifteenth-century
Lombard buildings.

The façade of Palazzo Medici Riccardi is distinguished by broad extensions of rusticated surfaces, their typological differences indicating the succession of floors.

The building passes from the rustic appearance of the ground floor, with its projecting rough-hewn ashlars, to the smoother rustication of the second floor, to the smooth surfaces of the top floor, where the stones are merely drawn in the plaster.

Rustication is a kind of masonry decoration, known since antiquity, that makes use of blocks or ashlars that project from the surface in a uniform and continuous way. Rustication is achieved in a variety of forms, including smooth, that is, showing only light relief; cyclopean (rock-faced), with rough-hewn blocks; and diamond-point, in which the projections have a pyramidal form.

The use of rustication—reappraised in all its forms in the Renaissance, and later to become a recurrent motif in nineteenth-century neoclassical and eclectic architecture—gives a tremendous pictorial quality to the square volumetric solids of this building, which was typical of an urban aristocratic residence in Renaissance Florence.

Casa dos Bicos, Lisbon, sixteenth century

Diamond-point rustication, a refined treatment for exterior surfaces, uses squared stones whose visible faces are worked into the shape of a low pyramid, similar to the facets of a diamond.

In use in the Italian Renaissance—an emblematic example is the Palazzo dei Diamanti in Ferrara—and repeated in northern European countries, most often in the decoration of ground floors, this decoration was also widespread in Spain and Portugal.

In the Casa dos Bicos, the diamond-point working of the stones gives the external elevation great dynamism and pictorial vividness through the differing chiaroscuro effects created by the changing angle of the light striking the prisms of the stones.

In the compact mass of the palace, its four floors indicated by heavy belt courses, the windows are arranged in an irregular way and are of different styles, from the three-light mullion window with round arches to two-light windows with complex cornices to simple square or single-opening many-lobed windows that defy any geometry

Auguste Perret, house in
Rue Franklin, Paris,
1903–4, detail of the
façade decoration

As a result of the expressive
possibilities offered by new, highly
malleable construction materials,
the Art Nouveau movement returned
to decoration based on the integration
of architecture with the visual arts.

In the house in
Rue Franklin,
Perret, a pioneer
in the use of rein-
forced concrete,
capitalized on the
expressive values
of a material
previously con-
sidered rough and
bereft of aesthetic
qualities.

The house is
dressed in an
extremely lively
ornamental
display. Even so,
the structural
system is revealed
with surprising
clarity by stylistic
alterations in the
decorative order:
smooth ceramic
for the beams
and pillars, and
recessed ceramic
panels with floral
motifs for the
curtain walls.

Second, or western, tomb tower, Kharragan, near Qazvin, Iran, 1093

Seriously damaged by an earthquake in 2002, the second tomb tower has an octagonal base with corner buttresses and a double-shell dome. The brick structure and wall texture echo Sassanid (third Iranian dynasty) prototypes.

A decorative motif common to all the elevations—reiterated and varied—the hexagon generates a series of lines composing other geometric figures, whose irregularity gives the panels a special dynamic sense.

The tomb tower is outstanding for the exceptional variety and originality of its decorative motifs, including the fine texture of the material, the subtle play of entrances and projections, the apparent symbolism of the decorative motifs, and finally the variable arrangement of the bricks, sometimes on end, sometimes lengthwise.

The presence of such architectural elements as cornices and ogee blind arcades also creates a surface made vibrant by sunlight because of its strong chiaroscuro and pictorial qualities, while the buttresses and external ribs of the dome give upward thrust to the structure.

Temple of Teli ka Mandir, Gwalior, India, ninth century

The many wall surfaces of Indian architecture make it possible to maximize the decorative possibilities of the building material. The temple of the Fort of Gwalior, dedicated to Vishnu, is made entirely of yellow sandstone and has richly decorated faces.

The decorative potential of the construction material is fully exploited: it is cut, modeled, and positioned in unusual forms.

A decorative display, of unequaled richness, covers more or less every available surface.

Set on a stepped base, the temple has façades cut directly into the stone, with a non-representational decorative repertoire composed of small-scale repetitions of the same structural elements that compose the building.

Polychromy

The use of polychromy (a variety of colors) to decorate the exterior faces or internal walls of buildings has been known since ancient times in the Far East. Achieved with pictorial techniques and a variety of materials or even merely different colors of plaster, polychromy can be used to highlight architectural elements, for symbolic purposes (even in the earliest times precise values were attributed to colors), or to create illusions.

Little is known about the use of polychromy in archaic architecture, but the use of different materials in Greek architecture must have conferred an intense polychromatic richness on those works. Perhaps less prevalent in the Roman age, thanks to the influence of Far Eastern art, polychromy reappeared during the Middle Ages in splendid multicolored façades of materials such as stone and brick. In the fifteenth century the range of polychrome wall decoration was amplified through the use of monumental marbles, and polychromy was used to complement architecture in wall coverings.

Polychromy is common in Islamic art, which attributes symbolic meaning to colors, and also in Indian art, where the statues of the Hindu pantheon are covered in brilliant colors. The modern movement eschewed color in favor of simple, neutral walls, either plastered or with materials left visible. Contemporary architecture has rediscovered polychromy, thanks to materials that interact with sunlight, reevaluating the autonomous creative power of color.

Related Entries
Wall; Façade

Temple of Madurai, India, seventeenth century, detail of the external decoration

Romanesque architecture presents a singular type of ornamentation, covering wall surfaces with polychrome marbles and interpreting structural elements, spatial dialectics, and plastic values in terms of clearly defined spaces and the rational harmony of geometric relationships.

The highly refined dressing in geometric motifs that covers the walls further emphasizes the architectural elements. The use of white and gray, with the addition of a pale sand color for the horizontal lines, creates a sacred setting with a triumphal character to which the small, round-arched windows contribute a sweet light, uniformly diffused by slabs of selenite (a variety of gypsum).

The structure of San Miniato makes its statement in the volumetric synthesis of the interior space, conceived as a spatial solid. The chromatics of the inlays give linear definition to the planes, transforming the thick Romanesque walls into pure architectural lines.

Church of San Miniato al Monte, Florence, c. 1150, interior

Postnik Yakovlev,
Saint Basil's Cathedral,
Moscow, 1555–60

The cathedral stands out in the urban setting of Moscow due to its vertical structure and for the lively polychromy of its surfaces.

The building combines northern European architectural forms, especially Karelian (Russian region near Finland), with decorative styles from more southerly countries into an eclectic monument that presents Romanesque arches, Gothic spires, Renaissance motifs, and Islamic roofs.

Built entirely of red brick, Saint Basil's Cathedral is an architectural work unique in its genre, arranged symmetrically on a single white stone podium with eight radiating chapels around a larger central space covered by a tent roof. The chapels, each of which is dedicated to a military victory, are remarkable for their singular onion domes of different colors.

Each of the brightly colored onion domes, with their clear Islamic derivation, has a different decorative motif that transfigures the architecture beneath these decorative coverings: red and green with a diamond-point pattern, spiraling motifs in green and yellow, red and white frets. They were all originally painted white and were given these vivacious colors in the seventeenth century.

Friedensreich
Hundertwasser,
Hundertwasserhaus,
Vienna, 1983–85

More painter than architect, Hundertwasser chose to decorate the exterior faces of his own home using a style based on polychrome surfaces with irregular shapes.

Far from ordinary, the Hundertwasser-haus is a worker's condominium famous for its bizarre and colorful architecture, which contrasts with the classical buildings around it. Hundertwasser chose to break with what he saw as the banal style of modern architecture.

The building is distinguished by its lively poly-chromy, created by apparently accidental but highly original contrasts among elements made of different materials, such as glass, metal, brick, and ceramic tiles, not to mention the irregular stripes of colored plaster and the golden domes.

The colors of its external walls are not the only source of the building's unique sensibility; there are also the undulating surfaces and the hanging gardens. When construction was finished, Hundertwasser considered letting the tenants paint the walls— but only the areas they could reach from outside their windows.

Murals

The painted decoration of buildings has always been a part of human life, beginning with the rock paintings of Lescaux and Altamira, dating to the Paleolithic era, which decorated the interiors of caves with depictions of animals and hunting scenes.

Wall painting, used most often in interior settings because they are sheltered from the damaging effects of atmospheric agents, can serve didactic purposes. Such is the case with the so-called *Biblia pauperum*, manuscript pages, and prints that presented a visual translation of Holy Scripture and were often arranged along the walls of medieval churches.

Sometimes the intention of a wall painting is to alter the visual perception of the box of walls or to deform it through the introduction of false perspectives. Already known to Pompeian art, this effect took the form of trompe l'oeil and images with realized perspectives in the Baroque period and later centuries. While the intention is often to imitate visible reality, there are also instances of the transposition of signs and abstractions more or less tied to the figural element.

Many techniques can be employed in murals. The most widespread is fresco, used to decorate large surfaces. Particularly well developed in Mediterranean countries, it was used only rarely in northern Europe because of the damp atmosphere. Mural painting is quite popular among young artists today. It includes not only the traditional fresco or encaustic techniques but also newer methods that make use of industrial tools, such as spray guns loaded with automobile paints or quick-drying synthetic resins, which are resistant to atmospheric agents and thus ideal for exterior works.

Related Entries
Wall; Façade

Decorated house, Ardez, Switzerland, seventeenth century

Church of the monastery of Voronet, Romania, 1488–1547

Designated a UNESCO World Heritage site, the monastery of Voronet was built to commemorate the victory over the Turks in 1475; its construction began in 1488. With its reduced size, the church—measuring about 25 × 11 meters—is all that remains of the original complex, and it is covered by decorations, both internally and externally.

In 1547 the exterior of the church was painted in fresco with subjects drawn from Holy Scriptures; on the western façade, a magnificent Last Judgment stands out against a background in a very particular shade of blue that has come to be known as Voronet blue.

The arrangement here seems to reverse the usual relationship of architecture and decoration, for the building becomes the handmaid to the painting, with the entire church, both inside and outside, merely a frame within which to exhibit numerous icons.

Tradition has handed down the name of the presumed artist, the hieromonk Gaurila. The building was dedicated to the Virgin Mary, and the iconography of the Virgin recurs many times on its walls, most often at important or symbolic structural points. Even so, the exterior decoration presents an entire catechistic cycle, both from the biblical point of view and from the devotional and historical. Along with the traditional iconography of saints and stories drawn from Holy Scriptures, episodes related to the struggle against the Turks are also presented.

Baldassarre Peruzzi,
Villa Farnesina, Rome,
1509–11, Sala delle
Prospettive

Trompe l'oeil decoration is emblematic of the period's widespread interest in perspective effects. The false loggia on paired columns looks out over 360 degrees on an extraordinary and equally false landscape: hilltop towns, views of the countryside, and in the background, set off against the sky, the city of Rome. Running along above this false opening is a frieze presenting stories drawn from Ovid's *Metamorphoses*; various depictions of divinities are located below the frieze and in direct conceptual relationship to it.

The Sala delle Prospettive of the Farnesina is a perfect example of "represented" architecture, meaning architecture that has been painted on a wall with an exclusively aesthetic purpose and that expands the physical space through illusion.

The room, designed for banquets, audiences, ceremonies, and theatrical presentations, is based on an analysis drawn from ancient Roman villas.

The hall presents a method of depiction—taken to the limits of virtuosic skill—that uses perspective to simulate the ideal continuation of the villa's ground-floor loggias. The artist's fiction goes so far as to depict the marble of the shafts of the Doric columns and the corner pilaster strips, the molding of the cornices, the niches, and the balusters.

Perspective tricks reached their height during the Baroque and Rococo periods—a time when the building, both real and illusory, was seen as a spectacular "representation of space" and architecture was conceived in terms of "theater."

Friedrich Sustris,
Antiquarium of the
Residenz, Munich,
1569–71

The large barrel vault with its
decorated lunettes is an exquisitely
classical architectural type;
its grotesque decorations are in
perfect harmony with the style,
which owed its origin to archaeological discoveries in Rome early
in the sixteenth century. The
allegorical depictions in the dome
are the work of Peter Candid.

The Antiquarium is considered one of
the greatest secular buildings of the
Renaissance. Displayed along the
frescoed walls of the hall are busts
and statues from antiquity.

With his perfect coordination of
architecture, decoration, and exposition, Friedrich Sustris made the
Antiquarium the first museum in
Germany suitable for displaying
classical-style statuary.

Grotesques are a type of pictorial
decoration that was very popular in
sixteenth-century art. The name is
taken from the chambers known as
grotte, found on the Oppian Hill, that
were in fact the remains of Nero's
Golden House. The style is characterized by fanciful twisting figures
blending with geometric and naturalistic decoration, all expressed in an
almost calligraphic manner against
a usually blank background.

Rodolfo Fantuzzi,
hall of the *boschereccia*
in Palazzo Hercolani,
Bologna, c. 1810

The oval continuum of the walls of the ground-floor hall in Palazzo Hercolani presents extraordinary painted decorations: an idyllic landscape with plane trees, willows, oaks, and pines reflected in the waters of a small lake. This sort of diorama creates a perfect illusion, a confusion of interior and exterior that is further expressed in the shadows and stones painted on the floor in imitation of a path in the country.

The hall, which leads to an English romantic landscape garden and plays an integral part in the perspective, is the most successful and evocative example of a pictorial genre called *boschereccia* (sylvan, rustic) or *stanza paese* (country room), a thoroughly Bolognese artistic specialty that flourished from the end of the eighteenth century until the middle of the nineteenth, with artists amusing themselves painting woodlands and gardens on the walls of aristocratic homes.

Thanks to this pictorial fiction, the walls open onto nature, capturing its more picturesque aspects in keeping with the style of the British romantic landscape garden. The walls present a rustic setting no less true than the actual garden, such that in 1821 Astorre Hercolani had a copy of Antonio Canova's *Cupid and Psyche* placed in the middle of the room, in imitation of the statues in the painted park.

Sculpture

Used for decorative, symbolic, and edifying purposes, architectural sculpture should be seen as complementary to the building; even when it possesses an artistic value of its own, it cannot be disassociated from the architectural work to which it belongs. Sculpture can be directly inserted into the architectural system (as, for example, with a classical metope); it can extend it (as with the gargoyles used as waterspouts on Gothic cathedrals); or it can cover a structural element or membrane (as with a capital). At times it can be formally separate from the building while making subtle symbolic references to it.

Usually made of stone, architectural sculpture has been in use since antiquity, in Egypt and Mesopotamia, and flourished in the tympanums and friezes of Greek temples decorated in relief or sculpture in the round. In Roman and Byzantine architecture it did not have particular importance, but during the Middle Ages it was used on an increasingly large scale to decorate capitals, portals, and entire façades. During the Renaissance it achieved autonomy—although it was limited to the replication of forms like telamons and caryatids—before returning to its exclusively decorative function in the Baroque age. In that period interior rooms were often decorated in stucco, an ideal material for the modeling of such decorative elements as cornices, friezes, and moldings as well as for the creation of more complex figurations in high relief or even fully round.

Architectural sculpture is also recurrent in Far Eastern cultures, and many of the decorative forms devised by Islamic art were later repeated and further elaborated in Western architecture. There are, for example, the *muqarnas*, the tiers of small three-dimensional stalactites that make possible the creation of richly modeled and carved repetitive schemes. The form was used early in the twentieth century by Hans Poelzig in the Schauspielhaus (now destroyed) in Berlin.

Related Entries
Wall; Façade

Cathedral of Chartres, France, 1194–1221, detail of a gargoyle

Notre-Dame-la-Grande,
Poitiers, France,
1130–50

The façade at Poitiers—vertically tripartite in the sequence porch, window, mandorla, and horizontally divided by belt course cornices—is one of the outstanding examples of a modeled and carved church building from the Romanesque period.

The front wall is enlivened by double rows of arches containing statues, by blind arcades to the sides of the porch, and by a triangular gable decorated with circular motifs.

The iconography is based on stories from the Old and New Testaments; on the ground floor the sacred narration is depicted in bas-reliefs on the surfaces between the tops of the arches and the cornice, while the archivolts are animated by plant volutes and the obsessive reiteration of the zoomorphic motifs typical of medieval bestiaries.

In the central row, the twelve Apostles along with two bishops are presented seated or standing within small arches; the relief-carved mandorla on the triangular gable bears a standing Christ surrounded by the tetramorph.

In the Romanesque architecture of southwestern France the sculptural decoration of façades involved a network of small motifs that does not spare any surface.

Bernardo Buontalenti,
façade of the Great
Grotto of Boboli Gardens,
Florence, 1583–88

The artificial grotto is a bizarre
invention, its façade based on a
rigorous trilithic structure, adorned
with statues and reliefs. The sharply
defined volumetric layout is contradicted by its applied decoration,
as is also true of the three interior
rooms with their limestone masses,
stalactites, and shells.

This masterpiece of Mannerism,
distinguished by its original mixture
of architecture and decorations, is in
keeping with the sixteenth-century
taste for fantastic complex recon-
structions of natural grottoes decorated with sculptures, paintings,
and fountains.

The Great Grotto
is one of the
outstanding works in
the Boboli Gardens,
conceived as a
setting dedicated to
courtly love.

Matthaus Daniel Pöppelmann and Balthasar Permoser, Zwinger Pavilion, Dresden, 1709–32

Built as a site for festivities at the request of Augustus II, king of Saxony, the Zwinger presents a highly original architecture of pavilions, porticoed wings, and stairways.

Pöppelmann created a dynamic complex that exploits the chiaroscuro effects of the full and empty spaces, in which sculpture and architecture work together to create an indivisible whole designed to celebrate power.

The plastic structures are perfectly integrated in delimiting the space by means of continuous horizontal lines.

The façade of the Zwinger achieves perfect equilibrium between architecture and sculpture, setting off a fully theatrical display typical of the Baroque: it is a sort of oversize molding.

The mixtilinear structure is made extremely dynamic through the play of pilasters that transform into tela-mons, in the balusters and pediments that lose their architectural charac-teristics as they are transfigured by statues, masks, heraldic emblems, and volutes.

Giacomo Serpotta, Oratory of the Rosary in the church of Santa Cita, Palermo, 1717, detail of the stucco decoration

The stucco decoration is presented in high relief with such projection that it almost seems a sculpted form not attached to a background, separated from the wall. In this way the ornamentation acquires a more distinct autonomy, resulting in an especially animated architectural form.

Asked to decorate the entire oratory with subjects drawn from the Glorious Fifteen Mysteries of the Rosary along with the history of the battle of Lepanto, Serpotta presented an extraordinary carved story on the walls with a highly articulated and complex lexicon.

Stucco is here used as a replacement for white and colored marble, reducing both the time and the cost of the work.

The entire decorative repertoire is made of stucco, a malleable plaster not strong enough to hold up to atmospheric agents because it is composed of gypsum, lime, sand, and water. For this reason it is reserved for the decoration of interiors. Already used in Roman architecture, stucco achieved its highest splendor in the Baroque and Rococo periods as an element suitable for the blending of architectural structure and plastic decoration.

The entrance wall presents the battle of Lepanto, allegorically illustrated by the two boys "naturally" seated on a molded cornice: the one on the left, victorious and serene, represents Christianity; that on the right, unhappily threatened by the muskets, represents the defeated Muslims.

In Sicily Giacomo Serpotta took an age-old tradition kept alive by numerous local schools and made it into an art of the highest level. Thanks to the special technique called *allustratura* he refined the work through the addition of wax and marble dust to the stucco mixture, which gave the result a shiny softness.

Forbidden City, Beijing,
eighteenth century,
detail of the roof
decoration of a pavilion

The carved and painted decorations
located along the ridge pole of the roof
of a pavilion are particularly appealing.
A building's importance is indicated by
the sumptuousness of its architectural
decoration, and here acroterions in
the shape of dragons and fantastic
animals seem to form a long and slow
procession that follows the sloping
shape of the roof.

Like an ideal continuation of the
bracket system that supports the roofs
of Chinese architecture, a protome
with the face of a dragon is located
below the eaves and serves
as a waterspout.

The hierarchy of Chinese architecture is reflected in the many rules
concerning three-dimensional decoration, establishing colors, materials,
and placement. The yellow-gold
ceramics, in a color reserved for
the emperor, display a particular
chromatic richness of chiaroscuro.
The greater the importance of a
pavilion, the more numerous—and
the more highly placed—are the
statuettes that decorate the ridges
of its roof.

With the clay tube decoration of the
beam ends, the use of tiles on the
roof assumes both technical and
aesthetic value.

Ismail Khan, Taj Mahal,
Agra, India, 1632–54,
detail of bas-relief floral
decoration

Extremely smooth and shiny, the
marble reliefs of the Taj Mahal exalt
the beauty of this precious material,
through which the Mogul sculptors
showed off their skills and artistic
talents.

A flower just
beginning to fade
is symbolic of
the transience of
earthly life. Thus the
panel immortalizes
in marble—emblem
of eternity—an
image of mortality.

The ivory white
marble presents
an elegant floral
decoration in
bas-relief of
extraordinary
naturalness.

Thanks to its
delicate dressing
and to the coloristic
qualities of the
material used, the
Taj Mahal varies
in appearance
throughout the
day, according to
changes in sunlight
and the various
optical effects
caused by shadows
on the marble.

Mosaic

Mosaic is a decoration that covers walls and floors. It is composed of small, colored tesserae of different shapes and materials—pebbles, precious stones, vitreous paste, terracotta, ceramic, marble, shells, enamels, and so on—arranged with a binder of mortar. Time consuming and costly to create, mosaic is suitable for a great variety of highly original decorative applications primarily because of its pictorial adaptability—it is perfectly applicable to both abstract and figural designs. The shape of the image is defined through the arrangement of the different colored tesserae. When observed from close up these reveal strong contrasts, but from a distance they blend to form a coherent image.

The oldest examples of mosaic work date to ancient art and are floor decorations that, evolving from the simplest geometrics, reached complex compositions in imitation of carpets. These include mythological or religious depictions, hunting scenes, animals both real and fantastic, geographical maps, and personifications of the zodiac, the months, and the phases of the moon. In Byzantine architecture mosaic decoration seems designed to intervene in the perception of space, with cavity-wall mosaics with a unifying gold background. Primarily for economic reasons, preference was given to frescoes during the medieval period, but as late as the twelfth century immense masterpieces of floor mosaics were being created. The later profusion of ceramic tiles led to the gradual decline of the medium. The nineteenth and twentieth centuries saw the rebirth of the mosaic, thanks to the color divisions of impressionist and pointillist painters. Art Deco and Art Nouveau made the mosaic a primary art form once again, as one can see in the figures of Klimt in painting and Gaudí in architecture.

Origin of the Term
The origin of the term *mosaic* is uncertain. Some trace it back to the Greek *musaikón*, meaning "patient work worthy of the Muses," rendered in Latin as *opus musivium*. Others see it instead as from the Arabic *muzauwq*, "decoration."

Related Entries
Wall; Façade

Basilica of Aquileia, fourth century, floor mosaic of the crypt with depiction of a lobster

Basilica of Saint Mark's,
Venice, 1063–94, detail
of the mosaic decoration
of the domes

The sense of space inside the basilica results from the interpenetration of five hemispherical domes bearing a complex mosaic cycle with a gold background that completely covers all the walls, hiding their material and structural reality. The building's covering seems to dematerialize, deprived of its structural components and its physical walls.

The basilica's architectural concept is essentially Byzantine, so mosaic was a natural choice as an integrating element. The play of light on the mosaic covering transfigures the walls and the surfaces, giving them pictorial values and negating any sense of spatial depth.

The iconography is based on stories from the Old and New Testaments, allegorical figures, and episodes from the lives of Christ, the Virgin, Saint Mark, and other saints. Warm tones predominate, particularly that of gold tesserae, which, set at an angle, reflect light. The space is enveloped in a veiled light that constantly varies throughout the day, with evocative effects of great intensity.

Study of the laws of optics led to the use in some mosaics of "inverse perspective," the deliberate reversal of the point of convergence of lines on the same vanishing point on the horizon. This expedient was used to eliminate all sense of the reproduction of reality and to diminish the status of the viewer, who faced a perspective view based on another realm.

Juan O'Gorman,
UNAM library,
Mexico City, 1956

The mosaic decoration of the façade of the central library of the Universidad Nacional Autónoma de México evokes the history of the country, with Aztec motifs and mythological creatures joined to contemporary images and subjects.

A fortunate rediscovery of the twentieth century, the art of mosaic was embraced in Mexico as an extension of the typology of the mural.

O'Gorman planned the library, which is twelve stories high and without windows, as a giant matrix on which to present brightly colored mosaics depicting aspects of pre-Columbian history, not leaving even a square centimeter of the exterior of the book repository open.

Moving against the trends of contemporary architecture—which he considered lacking in decoration and historical and symbolic values—and thanks to adroit use of materials and light, O'Gorman united volumes and shapes with a clear functionalist matrix in a decoration that produces magical effects.

Santiago Calatrava,
City of Arts and Sciences,
Valencia, Spain, 2005,
detail of the mosaic-
decorated air intakes.

The strong point of modern
ceramic tesserae, used on exteriors,
is their union of important aesthetic
qualities with high levels of resistance
to a variety of stresses, whether
mechanical, chemical,
or atmospheric.

The rediscovery
of an ancient deco-
rative technique
at the onset of the
twenty-first century
is owed to an
architect who is
extremely attentive
not only to forms
but also to the
qualities of materials
and their expressive
and technical
possibilities.

As Calatrava has
said, "To tie this
palau (palace)
to Valencia even
more deeply I used
the ceramics of
our age-old tradi-
tion, even those
broken in pieces
called *trencadis*."

The special air
intakes, positioned
in a row, have a
mosaic decoration
based on blue and
white, the colors
of the city and the
sea of Valencia.

Ceramics

Ceramics—a technique with deep roots in Mediterranean and Far Eastern cultures—plays a primary role in architectural decoration. A material with an ancient tradition that is fundamental to many other construction materials, ceramics are the result of a mixture of purified clay and other earths with water; the mixture is shaped and dried at room temperature, then baked in a kiln.

The characteristics of the resulting substance vary according to the temperature at which the piece is fired, from porous and not overly resistant terracotta to compact and vitrified wares covered in a transparent glassy layer, such as glazed grès, which is used for an exterior dressing because of its impermeability. Some types of glaze and decoration (slip and graffito) are added before the first firing; others are added later.

Some qualities of ceramics, such as durability, have gradually improved over time, and they are suitable for a great number of decorative and artistic uses— in internal settings, on exteriors, and in urban settings. Ceramics offer a great many aesthetic qualities, the evolution of which has paralleled the development of production systems and technologies.

Glazed bricks and colored ceramic tiles were being used for decorative purposes in ancient Egypt, but it was with the gates of Babylon and the decorations of Islamic art that ceramics reached their highest aesthetic and formal expression, leading in the Iberian area to the *azulejos* tradition. Elsewhere in Europe, the brick architecture of northern Germany often made use of glazed bricks. Southern Italy in the seventeenth century became the site of polychrome tiles on domes and bell towers, as well as home furnishings made of ceramics and porcelain. Ceramics returned to significant use as a decorative architectural material only in the nineteenth and twentieth centuries, in works of historicist and Art Nouveau architecture.

Origins

As early as the second century BCE, glazed ceramic objects were being used for construction in Mesopotamia, while porcelain, with its characteristic white color (a result of the kaolin that is its principal clay), was invented in China around the eighth century.

Related Entries
Wall; Façade

Temple of Wat Pho, Bangkok, seventeenth century, detail of the floral decoration of the *stupa* made of polychrome porcelain

Estoi palace, near Faro, Portugal, nineteenth century

The former residence of the Estoi counts is a fascinating palace richly decorated with *azulejos* and gardens in the English romantic style.

The impressive double-ramp stairway has lively decorations based on vegetal motifs and landscape scenes.

The *azulejo* is a tile covered with majolica or lacquer, usually painted in bright colors and decorated with ornamental motifs, used for interior and exterior decoration in Portuguese, Spanish, and Latin American architecture. It is often based on blue and white tints.

Domenico Antonio
Vaccaro, cloister of the
monastery of Santa
Chiara, Naples, 1742

In 1742 Domenico Antonio Vaccaro
transformed the great cloister of
Santa Chiara, originally of Gothic
style, by covering the old structure
and its seventy-two octagonal pillars
with astonishing polychrome majolica
tiles in a Rococo style. These were
designed by Vaccaro himself and
manufactured by the Neapolitan
riggiolari (tile makers) Donato
and Giuseppe Masa.

The pillars, separated by benches, are
decorated with motifs of vines and
wisteria that wrap around them up to
the level of the capitals that support
the pergola. The backs of the benches
are covered in majolica tiles, with
decorative motifs of rustic settings,
seascapes, masks, triumphs, and
mythological scenes. The garden's two
fountains are also decorated with
majolica, their bases bearing
depictions of fish.

The cloister is divided by two large
internal pathways that cross at the
center, marking off large garden areas
used primarily for citrus trees. As can
be deduced from the themes of the
decorations, when it was built the
cloister was more a garden of delights
than a site designed purely
for meditation and prayer.

Villa di Sammezzano,
Reggello, Florence,
Peacock Room,
c. 1853

Historicist architecture used the
ancient art of ceramic decoration
to give sumptuous ornamentation
to the interiors of villas and
residences.

The Peacock Room of the villa of
Sammezzano presents a hybrid style
derived from the Moresque tradition
and from the rich version of Spanish
Gothic known as plateresque.
The peacock tail is reproduced in
elaborate stuccos on the ceiling in
the form of fans, while the base band
is decorated with polychrome tiles
forming extremely dynamic
geometric motifs.

Ödön Lechner, Institute
of Geology, Budapest,
1898–99, detail of the roof
decoration

The fanciful roof of the Institute of
Geology dominates Pest, with its blue
ceramic tiles and its spires inspired
by the shapes of Indian temples.

On the elevations and the pediments,
the pale yellow of the walls, decorated
with traditional blue Zsolnay ceramics,
contrasts with the toothing of the
bricks and the cornices of the windows.

The harmony of the
chromatics and the
use of light cele-
brate the splendor
of the Hungarian
Secession style.
Bricks, concrete,
iron, ceramics,
glass—Lechner saw
no limits to his
choice of materials.
His imagination has
left its imprint on
many buildings
in the capital.

Antoni Gaudí,
Casa Vicens,
Barcelona, 1883

The colored surface of Casa Vicens is dressed in irregular fragments of majolica tiles, whose sumptuous use created geometric designs in sharp contrast with the raw brick and stone.

Built for a manufacturer of bricks and ceramics, Casa Vicens shows an absolutely original use of decorative motifs, drawn from the Spanish Moresque and Mudéjar traditions, and represents an extraordinary showcase for the products of the building's patron.

The colors and designs on the façade are particularly spectacular, even bizarre—and become even more so moving up toward the top of the building, which culminates in numerous Moresque-inspired towers. On the corners of the upper floors are balconies with intricate ceramic decorations.

The generous use of colored majolica, in alternating combinations of vertical lines connecting checkerboard motifs, gives the palace great visual appeal.

The Art of Wood

Although perishable by nature, wood has been carved, curved, and assembled to produce a vast number of decorations for architectural constructions. Such decoration is the result of a creative process based on precise knowledge of the material. The choice of suitable wood is fundamental and depends not only on availability but also cost. The expense associated with particular kinds of wood restricts their use to creations of a certain prestige.

The skill of carpenters, joiners, and cabinetmakers is clearly displayed in the geometrics of inlaid ceilings and floors, made using strips of wood in different colors—which can at times achieve three-dimensional effects—or of pierced panels of complementary elements, such as doors and window shutters. Wood is also important in the field of furnishings.

Woodworking in the orna-mental sense assumes a special meaning in Islamic architecture, in the creation of the so-called *mashrabiyya* screens, used to close off balconies and control the flow of sunlight, generating an effect of variable chiaro-scuro; the *muqarnas*; and the *artesonado* ceilings. The use of wood in ceiling decoration is also found in Western architecture, in wooden trusses or in the ornamentation of vaults that makes them resemble upside-down ship hulls. There is the singular example of the octagon of the cathedral of Ely, which supports a wooden lantern—made of oak timbers supported on cantilevered hammerbeams—dressed to make it look like a vault of ribbed stone.

In Depth

Cabinetmaking, a branch of wood-working, includes the art of making decorations, mosaics, and designs in wood, primarily in the making of furniture. The figure of the cabinetmaker came into being during the Renaissance with the transformation of the carpenter from artisan to artist.

Cathedral of Ely, Great Britain, octagon and lantern, 1322–42

Alhambra, Granada,
Spain, wooden ceiling

The splendid inlaid wooden ceiling
is a typical product of Mudéjar
woodworking. It presents a refined
geometric design in which plant
motifs of leaves and fruits take shape.

Interwoven geometric forms are the
characteristic element of Islamic art;
Islamic buildings are famous for their
abundance of delicate decoration
based on the serial repetition of forms
that adorn every surface.

The ceiling is decorated with
different kinds of wood inlays whose
patterns and complex decoration
catch and reflect light.

The Art of Metal

The art of working metals to decorate and complement architecture has ancient origins. The techniques of iron founding were known in China by the sixth century, and iron was used to make the bases of pagodas.

Iron's strength, functionality, and versatility would make it a material highly suitable for functional applications, but beginning in the twelfth and thirteenth centuries blacksmiths also began using it for ornamental purposes through the technique of wrought iron. This method, which calls for hammering the metal into the desired shape, was used from the beginning to make splendid gates, handles, door knockers, and decorations for doorways and balconies.

During the Renaissance balustrades and gates were integrated with architecture as shapes were simplified, while the Baroque and French Rococo periods reached levels of unusual splendor. The use of wrought iron declined during the period of neoclassicism, only to rebound in nineteenth-century England with the Gothic revival and the affirmation of the Arts and Crafts movement. Wrought iron then rose to new heights with the various forms of European Art Nouveau. Giving preference to natural forms as the source of its inspiration, and thus preferring plant and floral forms along with curving lines (all stemming from a rejection of classical architectural orders and any rigidly codified stylistic elements), Art Nouveau made wrought iron the material of the age, capable of meeting every formal and construction need.

Related Entry
Façade

Henri Gutton,
CCF Bank, Nancy,
France, 1900–1, detail of
a wrought-iron balcony

Joseph Maria Olbrich, Secessionhaus, Vienna, 1898, detail of the gilt-bronze dome

The Secession Pavilion—dubbed "the golden cabbage" by contemporary critics—was based on a square module with an atrium topped by a hemispherical dome of gilt bronze laurel leaves.

The pavilion is notable for its basic forms and balanced distribution, embellished by shiny decorations that turn it into a work of "architecture-painting" as well as one of the most important steps in the passage from late nineteenth-century sensibilities to the modern movement.

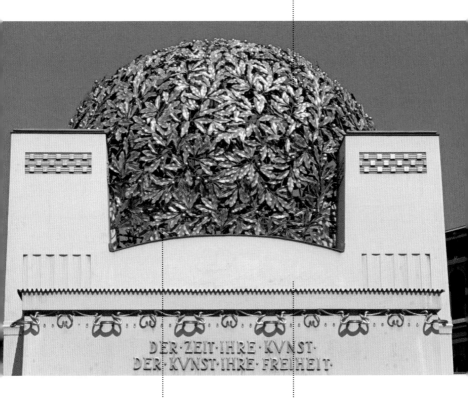

DER·ZEIT·IHRE·KVNST·
DER·KVNST·IHRE·FREI·HEIT·

The dome presents its metallic structure beneath typically Art Nouveau vegetal decoration. The metallic sphere filters light into the vestibule beneath it through a dense web of gilt laurel leaves, in allusion to the creative power of nature.

The palace is directly connected to the climate of the Viennese Secession and its debate over the supremacy of abstract ornamentation and the ongoing use of floral ornamentation. The building seems to take a third route, based on the values of mass and proportion, according to which the decoration can only reveal the underlying guiding principles of the construction.

Masterpieces

Parthenon / Hadrian's Villa / Hagia Sofia / Notre-Dame / Palazzo Te / Saint Peter's / Upper Belvedere / Cumberland Terrace / Grand Palais / Bauhaus / Centre Pompidou / Guggenheim Museum / Temple of Amun / Shah Mosque / Angkor Wat / Forbidden City / Katsura Detached Palace

Shreve, Lamb
& Harmon Associates,
Empire State Building,
New York, 1931

Parthenon, Athens,
447–38 BCE

The temple represents the essence of Greek architecture, based on the balance and harmony of proportions. It was subject to a series of refinements designed to improve its appearance, such as the curving of the stylobate, the narrowing of the walls of the naos, and the entasis of the columns. The outline of the architraves and cornices of the crowning part is slightly convex at the center, while the columns and walls incline inward to correct the visual impression of foreshortening.

The interior of the temple has both Doric and Ionic elements. The naos has the traditional two-tier Doric colonnade, while the opisthodomos has four full-length columns of the Ionic order.

Dedicated to Athena Parthenos (Maiden), the Parthenon was built on the Acropolis of Athens during the rule of Pericles. The construction was entrusted to the architects Ictinus and Callicrates, with the collaboration of Phidias, who supervised the rich sculptural decorations. An octastyle peripteral temple with seventeen Doric columns on the long sides and eight on the short sides, the Parthenon is made of white Pentelic marble; the sculptures bear traces of polychromy. The temple uses the trilithic system: architraves support a roof, and the various elements are joined with iron clamps.

The diameter of the end columns is greater than that of the others to compensate for the visual impression of outward inclination caused by the luminosity of the sky against which they are projected. The intercolumn spacing of the end columns is less than that of the central columns for the same reason.

The exterior decoration is in keeping with the Doric order; the west pediment bore carved reliefs—today in the British Museum in London—depicting the contest between Athena and Poseidon for possession of Attica, mythical local heroes, and personifications of rivers.

The ninety-two metopes of the entablature, separated by triglyphs, depict myths and legends: the Centaurs, the Amazons, the Giants. The cella is decorated with a continuous frieze of the Ionic order depicting the Panathenaea. The colossal chryselephantine cult statue of *Athena Parthenos* by Phidias was destroyed in antiquity.

The planimetric outline provided for a rectangular plan of 31 × 69 meters oriented along the east-west axis. The module used is based on the inferior diameter of the column, 1.905 meters, and the ratio among the various elements (height to width and width to length) is 4:9.

Hadrian's Villa,
Tivoli, 118–38 CE,
the Island Villa

Hadrian himself designed the
large complex of buildings known as
Hadrian's Villa. The arrangement did not
reflect any necessities of use, for the villa
was a pretext for the architect-emperor to
work out innovative ideas—a true
architectural laboratory, destined to be
closely studied many centuries later
by Baroque architects.

The Island Villa,
or Maritime
Theater, has a
circular outline
inside of which is a
structure designed
for the emperor's
amusements,
with a complex
arrangement of
apses, exedras,
and curving rooms
arranged sym-
metrically around
a central axis. The
main axis is rotated
slightly to the west,
toward the main
entrance. A module
of five Roman feet
was used for the
overall design.

The number of
manufacturers
of bricks bearing
identifying seals
multiplied in
Hadrian's time,
and the large-scale
presence of such
bricks in the walls
of the villa makes it
possible to date it
to around 123.

The forms evoke monuments Hadrian had admired during his long travels throughout the empire's provinces; the Island Villa closely recalls the Herodion in Jerusalem.

The use of brick translated the emperor's fervid imagination into Roman forms. He preferred mixtilinear plans, curving lines, round rooms, and vaults of different types, in an attempt to achieve a synthesis between amateurish eclecticism and an architecture with an innovative conception of space.

The ringed portico, originally covered by a barrel vault, rests on the perimeter wall and on forty smooth Ionic columns spaced at regular intervals one from the next; the Ionic columns of the Island Villa are fluted. The trabeation of the curving colonnade bore friezes of winged putti (cupids) leading chariots, ranks of marine animals, tritons, and mythological figures.

The structure has been stripped bare of its external dressing and its decoration, both internal and external: stuccoes, painted vaults, and mosaic floors. The internal surface of the enclosure was originally painted red over the bands of brick and yellow over the stone network; this was later replaced by decoration in red and black stucco with a marble molding at the base.

The Island Villa, which is about 2.5 meters lower than the courtyard of the residence, is surrounded by a high wall made of bricks with stones set in the diamond *opus reticulatum* pattern.

Arranged in concentric rings in an annular space is an artificial pond, 1.5 meters deep, used as a swimming pool. It features a true island reached by two bridges.

Hagia Sofia, Istanbul,
532–37, interior

Dedicated to Holy Wisdom, Hagia Sofia represents the greatest construction undertaking of the emperor Justinian, who wanted a religious building of unsurpassed plan, size, and decorative richness. The exceptionally well-organized worksite employed thousands of laborers, with on-site brickworks and its own stone quarries. It was built on an extremely tight schedule—all of five years, excluding the decorations.

The choice of architects seems of singular relevance: Anthemius of Tralles and Isidorus of Miletus— two mathematicians, experts in statics, stereometry, and geometric projection: two theoretical scientists, rather than engineers or building experts.

The bearing structures are distinguished by multicolored marbles, from the red Egyptian porphyry of the columns of the exedra to those in *verde antico* from Thessaly for the nave.

The great central space has a two-tier gallery supported by smooth columns with elaborate Byzantine capitals worked in tracery motifs that include Justinian's armorial bearings.

In its original form, the magnificence of the interior— polychrome marbles, mosaics with gold backgrounds, precious furnishings, stuccoes, purple drapery— seemed to make the walls vanish, rendered immaterial by the splendor of light and color. The half-light that reigns today is a result of the loss of many of the decorations along with the closing of numerous windows because of structural problems.

Hagia Sofia presents a mixed planimetric arrangement in which a central plan converges with a longitudinal plan, resulting in a vast domed space of a size and structure that were at the limits of the technical and constructive possibilities of the times. The entire church measures 77 × 71 meters, with an interior square space, 32.5 meters on a side, covered by a dome resting on four spherical pendentives flanked by two half domes that extend over angular exedrae.

Following the Turkish conquest of Constantinople in 1453, Hagia Sofia was transformed into a mosque; in 1934 it was made into a museum. The four enormous medallions in waxed canvas bear the names of Allah and Muhammad in Arabic writing.

The half domes are dressed in mosaics with gold backgrounds. The decoration, initially aniconic with floral and geometric motifs of Persian derivation, was integrated with cycles from the Gospels and scenes from the Dodecaorto, the calendar of twelve Byzantine feasts.

Given the size of the dome, most of the thrusts are absorbed by the four main piers, made strong by the use of stone, and only a small portion by the half domes of the exedrae. The stone used was a local limestone, somewhat soft but certainly less subject to compression than brick.

Cathedral of
Notre-Dame, Paris,
c. 1163–1250

The vast choir, internally a double ambulatory with radiating chapels opened by Pierre de Chelles between 1296 and 1302, is externally consolidated by the system of aerial double rampant arches with intermediate pilasters that stand on massive buttresses.

In the upper part are elegant twin lancet windows topped by oculi with historiated stained glass; on the ground floor are large mullioned windows with foils and geometrical tracery. The head of the transept bears a large rose window with tracery, created c. 1268, featuring stories from the Old Testament.

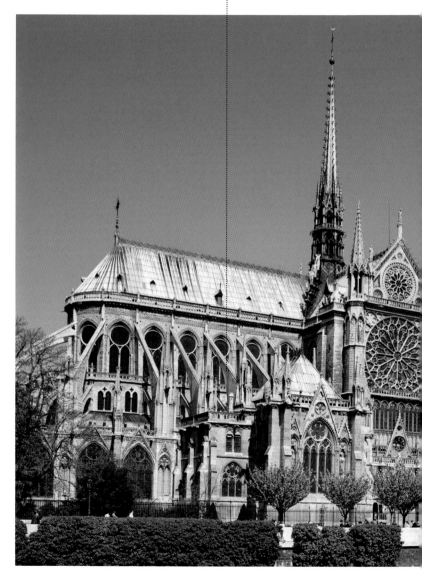

Work on the cathedral began in 1163, and it was consecrated in 1182 after completion of the choir. Work began on the façade in 1204; in 1250 Jean de Chelles built the façade of the north wing of the transept, and in 1258 he began the south wing, which was completed by Pierre de Montreuil.

Made entirely of stone and covered by a roof of lead shingles, Notre-Dame presents the last great example of the early Gothic. The entire building is decorated with the usual ornamental motifs, which animate the Gothic surfaces: spires, pinnacles, niches, and surprising gargoyles carved in the fantastic forms of medieval bestiaries. All of these were restored in the nineteenth century under the supervision of Eugène-Emmanuel Viollet-le-Duc. Notre-Dame's romantic image was amplified when it was used as the setting for Victor Hugo's *Hunchback of Notre-Dame* (1831).

The cathedral has a longitudinal Latin-cross plan with a short non-projecting transept and a very deep choir. The harmonious façade is framed by two square towers, 69 meters high, completed in 1245, each of which aligns with the width of two side aisles.

Notre-Dame has a nave with four aisles and a short transept, all of which are externally reflected in the stepped shape of the sides. The height of the nave and aisles and the thinness of the walls—about 1 meter—required external buttressing to balance the side thrusts of the vaults, at the same time enabling the use of large windows.

Giulio Romano,
Palazzo Te, Mantua, Italy,
c. 1524–35, west façade

The rusticated triple arch of the entry is the natural point of departure in the longitudinal design of the palace, arranged along a west-east axis, around which the architectural components of the building are arranged: the courtyard, garden, and path from the exedra toward an invisible vanishing point.

The composite order of the strongly horizontal exterior faces of Palazzo Te springs from the reiteration of a module composed of smooth Ionic pilasters around a central niche. Set within the wall spaces are eight large windows, each with a smaller window set beneath the frieze of the trabeation. The tri-partition of the entryway reflects the architectural layout of the atrium.

Vasari relates that, because of the lack of local stone quarries, Giulio Romano "made use of bricks and baked stone, which he afterward worked over with stucco."

Palazzo Te, the suburban residence of the Gonzaga court, is the architectural masterpiece of Giulio Romano, a student and collaborator of Raphael who received his training at the height of the Roman Renaissance. He went to Mantua, thanks to assistance from Baldassare Castiglione, where he was named "superior general" of the Gonzaga buildings and undertook an active campaign of architectural design and urban planning that changed the city's appearance.

The palace is distinguished by its balance between classical motifs—pilasters that mark off the walls and connect the perimeter walls, friezes, loggias on arcades, and columns—and others that are purely mannerist, such as the rustication with its strong plastic flavor and the series of niches and windows. The low, elongated shape is likely based on models codified by Sebastiano Serlio.

The architectural design of the façade appears to be a result of the juxtaposition of full and empty spaces, continually on the point of transforming themselves in an ornamental motif based on chiaroscuro.

Such is the theme of Giulio Romano's ornamental architecture: the façade is composed of a lower, rusticated part and a smoother upper part, divided by a cornice decorated with a classical frieze showing a Greek key pattern.

Basilica of Saint Peter's,
Rome, 1504–1657

It fell to Michelangelo, between 1546
and 1564, to undertake the design of
the dome, supported on a high drum
with windows that served both static
and formal needs thanks to pairs
of columns similar to buttresses.
Consisting of a double shell, the dome
has a hemispherical outline on the
interior and a raised outline on the
exterior. Its vertical thrust is emphasized
by sixteen ribs that culminate in the
lantern, which repeats the rhythm of
the paired columns of the drum and
the façade. As many as ten iron chains
have been installed over the years
to contain the lateral thrusts at
the base of the perimeter.

Carlo Maderno designed the façade,
with its 51-meter-high horizontal profile
(the only solution that made it possible
to see the dome) marked off by a giant
order of Corinthian columns and
pilasters 27.5 meters high. The project
also called for two twin bell towers at
the ends, but these were not built
because of the instability of the
foundations.

The elliptical colonnaded space,
designed by Bernini in 1657, connects
to the façade by way of a smaller
square created by the convergent
wings and is emphasized by the
obelisk erected by Domenico
Fontana. The colonnade runs on an
imperceptibly inclined plane, and
circular stone marks the center of the
ellipse, from which the colonnade
seems to be composed of a single
row of columns instead of four.

The history of the construction of Saint Peter's revolves around the debate between a central-plan layout and a basilican layout. Bramante's original Greek cross was reworked into a longitudinal layout by Raphael in 1514, and this was continued by Antonio da Sangallo the Younger in 1520.

In 1547 Michelangelo reaffirmed the validity of the central plan, returning to a Greek cross accentuated spatially by the dome, which was built after his death by Giacomo della Porta (1568–88). The design debate ended with the creation of a longitudinal naved body by Carlo Maderno, c. 1607.

Johann Lukas von Hildebrandt,
Upper Belvedere, Vienna,
1721–22

The ascending and descending progress of the roofs, as well as the advance and retreat of the bodies, is made dynamic and given unity by the decorative system—the heart of which is the entire lower floor, emphasized by a plastic cornice that also embraces the side pavilions.

Built as the summer residence for Prince Eugene of Savoy, the complex is composed of two separate buildings, the Lower Belvedere (1714–16) and the larger Upper Belvedere (1721–22); the two are connected by a French-style garden.

While presenting aspects of Austrian state art, the Upper Belvedere reveals the refinements and sensibilities of Rococo and is considered one of the most successful works of secular architecture of the late Baroque.

Hildebrandt united all the leading trends of the period in a highly original synthesis: the volumetric integration and the external walls create a vibrant surface on which forms appear, disappear, and are transformed.

The Upper Belvedere has an elongated central plan, based around the courtyard, and is distinguished by the unusual and unexpected arrangement of a monumental series of components of different heights. The central pavilion rises to crown the entire building; in front of it are a staircase and a vestibule with an animated segmented cornice.

Each of the wings ends in a domed octagonal pavilion that continues and concludes the rhythm set by the varying heights of the structures.

The Upper Belvedere is a highly original structure in which the boundless vistas of the Baroque garden have been reduced to a closed space: the elevated position of the palace dominates the surrounding space.

This artifice leads to two ways of seeing this great work of integration between architecture and nature. The first is from a distance. The second would be from a middle distance, but because of the large body of water in front of the building, the only other way to view the complexity of the volumes is from near the entrance.

John Nash, Cumberland
Terrace, Regent's Park,
London, 1827

As part of an elaborate urban plan—
a work by John Nash destined to
change the face of the center of
London and distinguished by an
outline that exploited, rather than
disguised, the irregularities of the
terrain—Cumberland Terrace is
one of the monumental elevations
that faces Regent's Park.

The building presents a clear
neoclassical front with a giant
order of Ionic columns atop a high
rusticated base. The way in which the
short wings are slightly pulled back
makes the front colonnade look like a
portico set in front of the building.

The neoclassical volumes, the sharp
division of the planes, and the overall
symmetry are amplified by the clarity
of the pale plastered surfaces.

Situated amid the neoclassical
remodeling of an entire residential
zone of London, and following a
scheme that involved the harmonious
combination of streets and gardens,
the regularity and uniformity of this
structure make it an outstanding
example of early nineteenth-century
city planning.

The building is crowned by a balustraded terrace and an impressive triangular pediment with a tympanum bearing carvings against a blue background.

Grand Palais, Paris,
1897–1900

The roof is made of iron and glass
to provide interior illumination; set on
reticulated beams, the large depressed
vaults cross at the center with a dome,
also depressed, that culminates
in a lofty lantern.

Built for the
Exposition
Universelle held
in Paris in 1900,
the Grand Palais—
designed to house
the exhibitions
of fine arts and
decorative arts—
was the product
of three different
architects: Henri
Deglane, author
of the main body;
Louis Louvent,
who designed the
central part; and
Albert Thomas,
responsible for
the rear wing.

The principal aisle
has a monumental
façade in stone
with a gigantic
Ionic colonnade,
240 meters long
and 20 meters high,
and is decorated
with a mosaic frieze
with scenes
illustrating great
moments in the
history of art. The
entrance is
emphasized by a
large portico on
paired columns.
At the corners of
the building are
curved façades
with secondary
entrances topped
by embossed-
copper sculptures.

The building, which can be seen as a showcase for the new techniques and materials of the late nineteenth century, has an irregular H-shaped layout with the short rear arm slightly open with respect to the main body.

The eclectic building was put up by three different teams of workers. The construction of the Grand Palais was an enormous undertaking, to which about 1,500 workers contributed. It involved both traditional work methods and innovative techniques, including the utilization of diamond-pointed saws to cut stone and the use of reinforced concrete.

Walter Gropius,
Bauhaus, Dessau,
Germany, 1925–26

A material expression of rationalist ideals, the building is an articulated structure without a main front and façade. It includes one body for classrooms and one for laboratories; the two are connected by a body suspended over the street, and by a third, five-story body that serves as the students' dormitory.

The scholastic complex is composed of a rectangular body on the ground floor to house classrooms and laboratories, and a second L-shaped body for an auditorium and services.

Although free of decoration, the Bauhaus has a highly original appearance thanks to the varying treatments of the façades: the white of the concrete areas, the profiles in black metal, and the transparency of the glass.

Designed by Walter Gropius, the Bauhaus has an open plan that owes its marked dynamism to the arrangement of the several buildings.

In this combination of volumes, the materials of construction are those typical of 1930s European rationalism: concrete plastered white, metal, and glass. Using glass and steel—materials he considered "without essence"— to create curtain walls, Gropius gave the building a form at once compact and transparent.

The concrete support structure is separated from the face of the building, which, freed of any structural function, can form continuous surfaces of glass.

Renzo Piano and
Richard Rogers,
Centre Pompidou,
Paris, 1971–78

Located in the heart of Paris, the Centre Pompidou was designed by Renzo Piano and Richard Rogers with the collaboration of the engineering studio of Ove Arup.

The use of an open plan, repeated on all five floors above ground, gives the building exceptional flexibility. The structural arrangement—without bearing walls or partitions—enables the continuous transformation of the interior spaces.

The structure and the materials used make clear the building's industrial aesthetic. At the same time, different colors identify different functions, from the white of the bearing structure and air intakes to the red of the platforms and elevator cages. The air conditioning system is blue, the electrical system is yellow, and the water pipes are green.

The uneven line of the escalator is emblematic of the building and at the same time offers an understanding of its structure— not a random heap of tubes but a care- fully arranged system of modules that repeat according to a particular rhythm.

The technical aspect of the building, with its physical plant and support structure outside, is an integral part of the design solution: a technological way of understanding the architecture of façades.

By overturning the usual construction approach and putting its physical plant, technical services, and support structures in full view, the Centre Pompidou becomes an enormous empty container, about 60 × 170 meters, ready to host museum activities, exhibitions, and games.

The Pompidou is a true triumph of modernism, the product of a new architectural language. The bearing structure in cast iron and steel includes reticular tubes and beams—made artisanally and thus different one from the next—jointed by rocker beams called gerberettes. Diagonal tie rods embrace the entire structural framework and are positioned slightly back from the perimeter of the façade to minimize the visual impact.

Frank Gehry,
Guggenheim Museum,
Bilbao, Spain,
1990–97

Frank Gehry's preliminary studies for the museum were translated into the fluid, informal shapes that distinguish its outline by a complex computer program.

The forms Gehry produced were geometrically defined in three-dimensional digital models via computer. These were then tested through both graphic and scale models, with every step of the project subject to detailed cost controls, so that in the end the building was completed on a financially competitive basis.

With its layout composed of twenty-seven petals wrapped around the central nucleus of the entrance, the museum is an exemplary model of the so-called open plan so essential to contemporary architecture. The large central atrium, 50 meters high, crowned by a metallic flower, connects three wings facing east, south, and west. To the north the museum faces a river in which it is reflected; this fourth truncated wing bears an enormous glass door.

The wonderful fluidity of the building is given further dynamism on days of strong wind, when the thin (0.38 mm) titanium plates of the cladding vibrate, expanding in surface area.

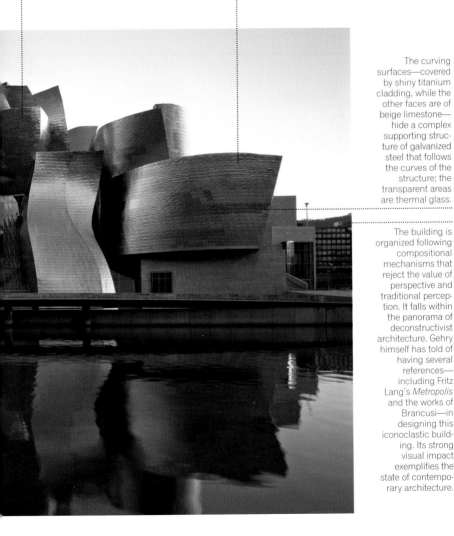

The curving surfaces—covered by shiny titanium cladding, while the other faces are of beige limestone—hide a complex supporting structure of galvanized steel that follows the curves of the structure; the transparent areas are thermal glass.

The building is organized following compositional mechanisms that reject the value of perspective and traditional perception. It falls within the panorama of deconstructivist architecture. Gehry himself has told of having several references—including Fritz Lang's *Metropolis* and the works of Brancusi—in designing this iconoclastic building. Its strong visual impact exemplifies the state of contemporary architecture.

Temple of Amun, Karnak, Thebes, Egypt, 1530–323 BCE, exterior of the hypostyle hall

The only permanent constructions handed down to us by the ancient Egyptians are for the most part religious buildings that reflect the basic values of Egyptian civilization: the cult of the dead and idolatry of the pharaohs. For this reason the buildings used by the pharaoh— and in fact designed by the pharaoh—assume a position of absolute preeminence.

The design procedure called for the pharaoh to illustrate the project for the priests, defining on his authority the site and the orientation of the temple as well as its typology and the constructive and decorative details. Then the architects and builders drew up the plans for the actual construction and set to work.

Located on the edge of the fertile Nile Valley, the temple was built using blocks of limestone transported on the river and brought to Karnak along a navigable canal. Given the abundance of clay at the site, the powerful trapezoidal outer wall (about 8 meters thick) was made entirely of raw brick; it extended about 400 × 600 meters.

The monumentality of the temple complex at Karnak reflects the desire for control of the new capital, center of worship of the god Amun. The temple is composed of three distinct areas, one dedicated to the god himself, one to his wife Mut, and one to the falcon god Mont. The temple saw its greatest activity under Thutmose I (1505–1493 BCE) and Ramses II (1304–1237 BCE), who created the grand hypostyle hall.

The sanctuary was under construction for so long—with a consequent layering of the work of several periods—that it constitutes a summary view of ancient Egyptian history. It preserves all the typical types of Egyptian temples. The temple is a series of areas and courtyards, introduced by large pylons and marked off by statues and obelisks, arranged along a rectilinear axis aligned with the route of the sun, along which ritual processions took place.

The great hypostyle hall has a basilican shape and was covered by a flat roof of stone arranged over the central, raised aisle, supported on columns and illuminated by windows with stone grilles. The complex was built using the trilithic construction system.

The exterior enclosure is carved with reliefs depicting the triumphant military campaigns of the pharaohs Seti I and Ramses II, scenes of ceremonies and of daily life, and hieroglyphic writing.

Shah Mosque
(Masjed-e Shah),
Isfahan, Iran,
c. 1612–38

Construction of the mosque began under Shah Abbas I, but it was completed by his successor, Safi. The building represents the summation of nearly a millennium of Islamic architectural experience and is distinguished by its unique majesty and splendor.

The large building, measuring about 100 × 130 meters, presents the typical layout of an Iranian mosque: a large rectangle oriented toward Mecca, with a symmetrical axial arrangement.

Over a continuous band of alabaster, the entire building is covered in polychrome enamel tiles—partially restored in the 1930s—that decorate all the surfaces. Their dominant color is blue, and they were made by an enameling technique called "seven colors," in which the tile is painted with different colors separated by a contour of a black oily substance that disappears during the firing. Less expensive than those used in mosaics, these tiles made it possible to cover enormous surfaces in a short period of time, giving preference to the overall effect rather than to the intrinsic beauty of the materials. The rest is left to the effects of light, skillfully exploited by the architects.

The widespread distribution of color assumes a unifying function; the walls blend in with the successive layers of floral ornamentation, forming a decorative carpet, abstract and fantastic, that expresses Persian lyricism and refers to the flowers of paradise.

By the end of the seventh century the principal functions and the typology of the mosque had been rigidly codified; designed to welcome large multitudes of the faithful, the space was composed of a large central inner courtyard with four rooms—the *iwans*—on all four sides.

Pairs of minarets, from which the muezzin calls the faithful to prayer, rose over the entryway and *iwan* leading toward the *qibla* (prayer direction). The dominant element of the mosque is the large onion dome, 52 meters in diameter, that crowns the prayer hall.

The inner court is about 70 meters on a side and is surrounded by a two-tiered arcade.

The majesty of the space is reinforced by the rhythmic repetition of the structural elements, the symmetrical arches, the facing *iwan*, and the motionless serenity of the ablution pool.

Angkor Wat, Angkor,
Cambodia, c. 1113–50

Built at the decree of King
Suryavarman II and completed in less
than forty years, the temple covers a
rectangular area of about 1,500 ×
1,300 meters, delimited by an artificial
moat; it is reached from the west by
way of a stone causeway. The east-
west axis is taken to indicate a
funerary use for the palace.

The five central towers represent
the five peaks of the sacred
mountain, while the walls and
moat symbolize the mountains
and the ocean that surround it;
each gallery has a *gopura* located
at the first cardinal points.

Protected by the
moat from the
advance of the
jungle, the temple,
restored during
the past century,
preserves more
or less entirely
the structure of
sandstone and
laterite (surface in
hot, wet tropical
areas; used to
make the outer
wall and more
hidden parts),
while all those
more perishable
materials, such as
the gilt stucco of
the towers and the
wooden panels of
the ceilings, have
been lost.

A masterpiece of
classic Khmer art—
both for its
architectural
rhythm and for the
fineness of its
execution—Angkor
Wat is a "temple-
mountain." It
symbolizes the
sacred Mount
Meru, which in
Indian mythology
is located at the
center of the
universe and is
home to the gods.

Angkor Wat has a checkerboard layout composed of three rectilinear vaulted galleries in concentric rings at different levels. The lower level is supported on quadrangular pilasters. The inner one is supported by four corner towers shaped like lotus flowers, and these are connected by colonnades to the central tower, which is about 65 meters high. The towers have roofs composed of tiered stone blocks; the roof of the galleries is of stone blocks carved to imitate overlapping courses of roof tiles.

The entire structure is covered in richly carved decoration, although the polychrome decoration that once enlivened the bas-reliefs, depicting *devatas* (guardian spirits), scenes drawn from Indian mythology and from epics, as well as the floral ornamentation of the pediments, has been lost. The counterclockwise direction of some of the bas-reliefs reinforces the hypothesis that Suryavarman conceived the building as a mausoleum, since Brahmic funeral rites take place in that order.

Forbidden City,
Beijing, seventeenth to
eighteenth centuries

The construction follows geomantic
(method of divination using tosses of
earth), ritual, and sumptuary rules.
Monumentality is conceived only in
the horizontal sense, meaning with low
and wide buildings, orderly arranged
following a rule of correlation according to which no element can exist
alone but must be complemented
by a similar or opposite one.

The building has a roof with curving
gables in yellow-gold ceramic, the color
reserved for the emperor; the building's
importance is also indicated by its elevated position and by the number of
small statues along its roof ridges.

The Forbidden City
extends along three
parallel axes that
run from south to
north, along which
are arranged the
principal buildings.
The ceremonial
halls are aligned
along the giant
central courtyard,
standing on high
podiums and
enclosed by
delicate balusters
in white marble and
enlivened by stairs.
Confucian
pragmatism is
responsible for the
rigid rules of axiality
and symmetry that
make the royal
palace the center of
the urban system.

The building type of the pavilion, or *tien*, has been codified since ancient times. Its tripartite structure is composed of the base (*chieh-chi*), columns (*chu*) that support the bracket system (*tou-kung*), and the roof, which is of primary importance in the structural harmony of the entire building.

Wood was the primary building material in constructions made following an age-old technique, but because of fires it was replaced by stone. The original stone came from quarries near Beijing, but the columns, beams, and trusses were made from enormous trunks of laurels and related species from the forests of Yunnan and Sichuan.

Katsura Detached
Palace, Kyoto, Japan,
seventeenth century,
Old Shoin

Many parts of the structure are wood,
from the bamboo of the terrace to the
long planks of cryptomeria (cypress
family) in the floor of the Large Veranda,
from the cypress-bark shingles to the
platform set on large, regularly spaced
stones, from the thin quadrangular pillars
to the parapets and the grating of the
windows that give the interior light.

The lack of a precise date makes it
difficult to reach a certain attribution
for the Katsura palace; the Old Shoin,
the first building in the complex to
be built, is referred to in ancient
documents as the "teahouse in the
melon patch" that had been requested
by Prince Toshihito around 1615.

The palace is arranged according
to an open plan that relies on the
interpenetration of square and
rectangular geometric modules that
follow the shape of the landscape—
the so-called "flock of geese in flight"
arrangement. According to this
pattern the buildings are distributed
around a central axis, progressively
set back one from another to give the
front parts the same orientation to the
southeast, so as to optimize the
illumination of the main rooms.

Unaltered despite its fragility, the
palace is an exceptional example of
classical Japanese architecture
that has survived the adversities
of time thanks to periodic
and careful restorations.

The classical *shoin* style—typical
of the residences of the samurai—
is here blended with the so-called
sukiya style, more open and
whimsical, and better suited
to country homes.

A path of random stepping-stones leads from the small dock at the edge of the lake to the so-called Moon Viewing Platform; the lake was the scene of boating parties to view the rising moon.

Set amid the thick garden vegetation and facing the still waters of the lake, the Old Shoin—the heart of the residence—has a typical sloping roof. Visible on the tympanum is a chrysanthemum-shaped symbol covered by six layers of gold leaf.

The terrace is closed externally by a series of white shoji (paper partition) screen shutters that accentuate the sharp clarity of the white walls, interrupted only by the dark edges of the windowsills, lintels, and pillars.

References

Glossary of Terms / Photographic Sources / Index of Topics / Index of Names and Places

I, M. Pei, Grand Louvre, Paris, 1983–93, stairway of the entrance pyramid.

Glossary of Terms

abacus: a flat slab forming the uppermost part of the capital of a column

acroterion: a pedestal placed on the pediment of a Greek temple to hold a statue; has come to be used to refer to the statue itself, and more generally to the uppermost element on a facade

aedicule: little building; a window, door, or shrine that is decorated as a building itself, with columns, an entablature, and often a pediment

ambulatory: aisle surrounding the end of a choir or chancel of a church; covered walk of a cloister

aniconic: describes a belief system or tradition characterized by the absence of representations of a particular kind; also used to refer to a building or master plan that was constructed without drawings

annulets: rings around the shaft of a column

apse: a semicircular extension to a room roofed by a half-vault

apsidal: used to describe an architectural feature that resembles an apse

architrave: main beam; the lowest part of the entablature that rests directly on the capitals of the columns and is topped by the frieze and cornice

archivolt: an ornamental molding following the curve of the underside of an arch

ashlar: stonework composed of large rectangular blocks over a foot long and usually much larger, sculpted to have square edges and regular faces

astragal: a molding profile composed of a half-round surface with two flat planes on either side

attic base: base of an Ionic column with two large rings of convex moldings joined by a spreading concave molding

baluster: a molded shaft, square or circular, that is used to support the handrail or the coping of a parapet, collectively forming a balustrade

belt course: a very deep molding, continued across a whole facade, a deeper version of a string course

caisson: box; refers to a sunken panel in a ceiling formed by beams and cross-bracing or ribs

cavea: subterranean cells in a Roman amphitheater

cavetto vault: a concave molding in the shape of a quarter-circle

cella: also naos, the inner chamber of a temple

chryselephantine: describes a Greek cult statue made using a wooden frame with thin plates of ivory to represent the flesh and gold leaf to represent the garments

cincture: a small convex molding around the shaft of a column

clerestory: feature providing natural lighting to a space by means of windowed walls that rise higher than the surrounding rooflines

clinker: the solid material that comes out of cement kilns and is then ground to become cement

Composite capital: late Roman combination of elements from Ionic and Corinthian orders

corbel: a projecting block, usually of stone, supporting a beam or other horizontal member

cyclopean walls: type of stonework found in Mycenaean architecture; built with huge limestone boulders, roughly fitted together with minimal clearance between adjacent stones and no use of mortar

cyma: S-shaped molding profile that blends from a concave surface into a convex one

cymatium: a cyma topping an entablature

dentils: projecting rectangular blocks tightly spaced in a row like teeth, usually placed below the cornice

diaphragm wall: underground structural elements, used for water retention or as permanent foundations

directrix: the curve that bounds the base of a cone or cylinder

dolmen: a single-chamber megalithic tomb

echinus: a convex molding forming part of the capital in the Doric and Ionic orders

encaustic: used to describe a painting technique using hot wax infused with pigment

entablature: a structure supported by columns and composed of the architrave, frieze, and cornice

entasis: the sculpting of columns with a larger radius in the middle than on either end, making them seem to flex like a muscle under the weight of the entablature

exedra: a semicircular recess with a semicircular vault, often set into a building's façade or into an interior wall

extrados: outer curve of the voussoirs of an arch

fillet: a thin, flat molding between larger moldings

gopura: tower entrance to a temple

groin vault: the intersection of two barrel vaults at right angles

guttae: small projections under the triglyphs in a Doric frieze; may represent pegs in the original timber construction

hammerbeam: a horizontal head beam projecting at wall head level toward the center of a roof space, supported on corbels

helicoidal: spiral

hexastyle: of a portico with six frontal columns

historiated: adorned with the figures of humans, animals, or birds in the form of a narrative; can apply to decoration of capitals of columns in architecture

historicist architecture: style from between the end of classicism to the beginning of Art Nouveau; adopted forms from a variety of past styles

hypostyle: describes a space with a flat ceiling supported by columns

impost: a wall member on which the end of an arch rests

impost line: the line from which an arch springs

intarsia: form of inlaying in wood or polished stone

intrados: inner face of the voussoirs of an arch

kaolin: type of clay

lancet (windows): a tall vertical window with an arch at the top, resembling a lance

lantern: small circular turret with windows all around, crowning a roof or dome

lavabo: sink, or small device to provide water for washing hands

lesene: pilaster without a base or capital; also called a pilaster-strip

listel: narrow band separating moldings

loggia: gallery or porch open to the air on one or more sides

lunette: semicircular opening (also tympanum) or flat surface

mandorla: almond-shaped aureola formed by interactive circles that symbolize the tension of complementary opposites

martyrium: church or other edifice built at a site, especially a tomb, associated with a Christian martyr or saint

metope: space between two triglyphs on a Doric frieze

mixtilinear: geometry that includes lines of different types, such as curved and straight

mullion: vertical upright that divides a window or other opening

mutule: rectangular block under the soffit of the cornice of the Greek Doric temple, which is studded with guttae

naos: cella, the inner chamber of a temple

narthex/exonarthex/esonarthex: entrance or lobby of a church at the end of the nave, composed of two parts, the exonarthex, which is outside the main façade of the building, and the esonarthex, which is inside but is divided from the nave and side aisles with columns or a wall

nuraghe: a monolithic megalithic edifice in the shape of a truncated cone found on Sardinia and dating from the pre-Roman era

ogee: double-curved line made up of a convex and concave part

ogival: having the form of an ogee; one of the diagonal arches or ribs across a Gothic vault

opisthodomos: space or open porch at the back of a Greek temple, sometimes used as a treasury

opus caementicium: Roman construction of structures using concrete

opus reticulatum: a form of brickwork used in ancient Roman architecture consisting of diamond-shaped bricks of tuff placed around a core of opus caementicium

orthogonal: right angles (orthographic projection: projection of a single view of an object onto a drawing surface in which the lines of projection are perpendicular to the drawing surface)

ovolo: rounded convex molding, sometimes carved with an egg and dart ornament

paraboloid: quadric surface of a special kind, either shaped like a saddle or an oval cup

parallelepiped: three-dimensional figure defined by six parallelograms, somewhat like a cube, but without the requirement that all angles be right angles

pediment: triangular element supported by the horizontal entablature of a Greek temple

pelta: crescent-shaped wicker shield commonly used in the ancient world before the 3rd century BCE

pendentive: a sort of curved triangle, which is the solution to the problem of placing a dome on top of a square

Pentelic marble: marble of which the Parthenon is built, from a mountain range northeast of Athens

pergula: "pergola," a structure usually consisting of parallel colonnades supporting an open roof

peripteral: having a single row of columns on all sides

peristyle: a row of columns surrounding a temple or courtyard

phytomorphic: in the form of a plant

piano nobile: main floor of a house, which contains the principal rooms, and which is given added emphasis by having a ground floor or basement, and minor floors above

pietra serena: a grey sandstone from Italy

pilaster: a partial column that projects from the wall

piloti: a column of iron, steel, or reinforced concrete supporting a building above an open ground level

planimetry: measurement of surfaces indicating only the horizontal positions of features, without regard to elevation

polylobate: having more than one lobe

porphyry: a very hard rock, quarried in ancient Egypt, having a dark, purplish-red groundmass

containing small crystals of feldspar

portico: a porch in the form of a classical colonnade

pozzulana: a volcanic ash originally found in Pozzuoli near Naples and used as an additive in mortars to achieve an hydraulic set

pronaos: inner area of the portico of a Greek or Roman temple

protome: adornment on works of art in the form of a frontal view of an animal head or bust of a human

pulvin: a block above the capital supporting the arch above

punctiform: very small but not microscopic, as in a point

pylon: Egyptian gateway building in a truncated pyramidal form

Rayonnant architecture: French Gothic architectural style in which multiple design components radiate from a center

reticulated: to construct as to form a network

rupestrian: describes something that is painted on rock

rustication: masonry cut in massive blocks separated from each other by deep joints

scansion: rhythm established by repetitive systems in a building

scenographic: decorative effects; theatrical perspective space

scotia: hollow concave molding at or near the base of a column

serried: pressed together or compacted

spandrel: the space between two arches or between an arch and a rectangular enclosure

spandrel glass: glass that is translucent or opaque applied to the space between the windows or floors to maintain the continuity of glass on a façade

squinch: an arch that spans the angle formed by two walls meeting

stereometric: solid, dealing with the geometry of solids

stupa: mound-like structure containing Buddhist relics

stylobate: the top step of the base on which a classical temple sits

telamon: a sculpted support or column in the form of a man; the male equivalent of a carytid

telluric: of or relating to the earth

tenia: a band in the Doric order that separates the frieze from the architrave

tesserae: decorative treatment of walls or floors composed of small stones, or glass

tetramorph: a symbolic arrangement of four differing elements, often related to the division of space or the horizon into four zones

tetrastyle: having four columns

tholos: a circular building with a conical or vaulted roof, with or without a peristyle

torus: the lowest molding at the base of a column

trabeation: having horizontal beams or lintels rather than arches

travertine: a form of limestone deposited by springs, especially hot springs

trefoil: an ornament composed of three lobes, divided by cusps, radiating from a common center

tribune: a raised part or gallery with seats, as in a church

triforium: a shallow gallery of arches within the thickness of inner wall, which stands above the nave in a church or cathedral

triglyph: the vertically channeled tablets found in the Doric frieze

trilithic system: a series of structures consisting of two upright stones supporting a horizontal stone

trulli: dwellings of the Apulia region of Italy, roofed with conical constructions of corbeled dry masonry

truss girder: a large structural member that spans horizontally

tufa: a very light sponge-like limestone formed in aerated springs, and used decoratively in grottos or where lightness is important, for example at the top of domes

two-light window: a window divided into two parts, usually by a column in the center

tympanum: the semicircular or triangular decorative wall surface over an entrance bounded by a lintel and arch, often containing sculptures or other ornaments

unitary involucrum: surrounding envelope or sheath

velarium: awning over an ancient Roman theater or amphitheater

volutes: spiral scroll-shaped ornaments forming the chief feature of the Ionic capital

voussoir: wedge-shaped stone or brick forming one of the units of an arch

zophorus: any decorative band at the top of or beneath the cornice of a wall having representations of people or animals

Photographic sources

AKG-images, Berlin, 148, 225, 258, 332 / Bildarchiv Monheim, 12, 75 left, 81, 87, 89, 91, 101, 107, 111, 115, 122, 124, 127, 146, 149, 154, 157, 163, 186, 203, 236, 250, 317, 352–53, 356–57, 360–61 / Richard Booth, 162 / Herve Champollion, 66, 78, 190 / Mark de Fraeye, 219 / Gérard Degeorge, 77 left / Stefan Drechsel, 153 / Werner Forman, 85 / Rainer Hackenberg, 177 / Hilbich, 110, 118 / Dieter E. Hoppe, 151 / Jànos Kalmàr, 183, 336 / Tristan Lanfranchis, 244 / Joseph Martin, 67 right, 126, 372 / Jean-Louis Nou, 221 / Robert O'Dea, 255 / Pirozzi, 65 / Profitlich, 239 / Jurgen Raible, 261
Archivi Alinari, Florence, 198
Archivio Fuksas, 175
Archivio Mondadori Electa, Milan, 8, 11, 16–17, 19, 21, 22, 24–25, 41, 43, 90, 143, 147, 155, 167, 204, 223, 287, 310 / Graziano Arici, 323 / Fabrizio Carraro, 88, 120, 156 / Maurizio di Puolo, 76 right / Gorge Fessy, 187 / Andrea Jemolo, 202 / Alejandro Leveratto, 132 / Marco Ravenna, 222, 235, 318–19 / Giovanni Ricci Novara, 42 / SPADEM, Paris, 77 right / Arnaldo Vescovo, 188–89, 297, 299, 316
Archivio Richard Rogers, 46
Archivio Zaha Hadid, 47
© Artur / Zooey Braun, 228 / Dennis Gilbert/VIEW, 274 / Gerard Hagen, 282 / Roland Halbe, 277 / Jochen Helle, 218, 268 / Christian Michel/VIEW, 226 / Monika Nikolic, 161 / Dirk Robbers, 229 / Grant Smith/VIEW, 358–59 / Barbara Staubach, 207
Achim Bednorz, Cologne, 212, 315
Biblioteca Apostolica Vaticana, 30
Fabrizio Carraro, Turin, 119, 193
Giovanni Chiaromonte, Milan, 18
© CORBIS, 33, 168–69, 266–67 /

Paul Almasy, 109, 114, 201 / Archivo Iconografico, SA, 70, 213/ ART on FILE, 129, 273, 291 / Yann Arthus-Bertrand, 354–55 / Atlantide Phototravel, 214–15, 240–41, 242–43, 303, 342–43 / Tiziana and Gianni Baldizzone, 309 / Jonathan Blair, 278 / Chris Bland/Eye Ubiquitous, 196, 274 / Christophe Boisvieux, 82 / Richard Bryant/ Arcaid, 60 / Inigo Bujedo Aguirre/ Arcaid, 176 / Demetrio Carrasco/ JAI, 172 / Elio Ciol, 322 / Dean Conger, 108 / Richard A. Cooke, 160 / Pablo Corral Vega, 56 / Marco Cristofori, 112, 130–31, 294 / Barry Cronin/ZUMA, 276 / CSPA/NewSport, 283 / Gianni Dagli Orti, 179 / Edifice, 334 / Abbie Enock/Travel Ink., 220 / Rufus F. Folkks, 262–63 / Werner Forman, 340–41 / Franz-Marc Frei, 279 / Michael Freeman, 289 / Todd Gipstein, 61 / Lindsay Hebberd, 164–65 / John Heseltine, 137 bottom / Historical Picture Archive, 270 / Angelo Hornak, 59, 185, 265, 336 / Ladislav Janicek/zefa, 54 / Andrea Jemolo, 80 above, 138, 180, 182, 260, 306 / Mimmo Jodice, 74 / Thom Lang, 304 / John Edward Linden/Arcaid, 96, 290 / Xiaoyang Liu, 320 / Massimo Listri, 84, 141, 166, 311, 314, 333 / Ramon Manent, 73, 113 / James Marshall, 326 / Kevin R. Morris, 366–67 / Michael Nicholson, 191 / Richard T. Nowitz, 83, 209 / Clay Perry, 224 / José F. Poblete, 199 / Carmen Redondo, 362–63 / Hans Georg Roth, 300 / Gregor M. Schmid, 216 / Richard Schulman, 272 / Paul Seheult/Eye Ubiquitous, 233 / Grant Smith, 97 / Lee Snider/ Photo Images, 150 / Paul A. Souders, 49, 75 right / Tim Street-Porter/Beateworks, 249 / Rudy

Sulgan, 350–51 / Murat Taner/zefa, 98, 121 / Arthur Thévenart, 63, 364–65 / Paul Thompson, 256 / Vanni Archive, 137 above, 140, 296 / Sandro Vannini, 181, 232, 298 / Francesco Venturi, 327 / Brian A. Vikander, 136, 368–69 / Patrick Ward, 103 / Nik Wheeler, 58 / Roger Wood, 135 / Adam Woolfitt, 117, 208, 333 / Michael S, Yamashita, 230
Roland Halbe, Stuttgart, 92, 95, 133, 210, 246–47, 284, 325
© Erich Lessing / Contrasto, 100, 238, 257, 285, 307
Yoshiharu Matsumura, 370–71
Luca Mozzati, Milan, 57, 71, 134, 144, 170, 197, 231, 302, 321
Luciano Pedicini, Naples, 328
Courtesy of the Fabbrica di San Pietro in Vaticano, 44–45, 67 left
Matteo Piazza, Milan, 280
Francesca Prina, Milan, 308
Rabatti & Domingie, Florence, 99, 106, 116, 200, 205, 305
Mauro Ranzani, Milan, 171
Marco Ravenna, Bologna, 128, 312–13
© Scala Group, Florence, 123, 346–47
© Sime / Giovanni Simeone, 348–49
© The Bridgeman Art Library, 158–59 / Paul Maeyaert, 286 / Ian Pearson/Mexicolore, 324
© Tips / Sunset, 344–45
Arnaldo Vescovo, Rome, 173, 237, 248

The illustrations on the following pages are from Electa books: 13, 14, 15, 20, 23, 26, 27, 28, 29, 31, 35, 36, 37, 39, 40, 48, 51, 52, 64, 76 left, 80 below, 139, 142, 184, 192, 234, 264, 293.

Index of Topics

Index of Names and Places